ABOUT the AUTHOR

John Purner is an avid pilot, golfer, publisher, website developer and writer. For more than two decades, his **$100 Hamburger** *(www.100dollarhamburger.com)* website has been the world's most popular information source for recreational flyers. John's first work of fiction, **02 Golf** has been an aviation category **Best Seller** since publication, over two years ago.

The following is a list of other John Purner books you may enjoy. They are available at Amazon.com and pilot shops across the world.

1. **The $100 Hamburger Guide to Buying & Selling Aircraft**

2. **02 GOLF**

3. **6 Weeks to Winning Weekend Golf**

4. **BUYcycle: The Best Kept Secrets of Amazingly Successful Salespeople**

5. **15 BEST Airport Restaurants plus 2,347 Runner-Ups!**

6. **The $100 Hamburger – A Guide to Pilots' favorite FlyIn Restaurants 3rd Edition**

7. **101 Best Aviation Attractions**

8. **The $100 Hamburger – A Guide to Pilots' favorite FlyIn Restaurants 2nd Edition**

9. **The $500 Round of Golf : A Guide to Pilot-Friendly Golf Courses**

10. **The $100 Hamburger – A Guide to Pilots' favorite FlyIn Restaurants**

www.100dollarhamburger.com

The $100 Hamburger

A FlyIn Restaurant and Recreation Guide

2014/15

by
John Purner
$100 Hamburger Publishing

ISBN-13: 978-0615961675 ($100 Hamburger Publishing)
ISBN-10: 0615961673
For quantity discounts on volume orders please contact

$100 Hamburger Publishing
PO Box 915441
Longwood, FL 32791-5441

Internet: www.100dollarhamburger.com
Email: pirep@100dollarhamburger.com

First Printing: March 2014

Foreword

Thank you for purchasing this copy of the **$100 Hamburger**. The journey that resulted in this book began two decades ago with the creation of the $100 Hamburger website – **www.100dollarhamburger.com**. In 1998 I wrote the **$100 Hamburger – A Guide to Pilots' Favorite FlyIn Restaurants.** It was published by McGraw-Hill and was an instant hit with the pilot community. A second and third Edition followed. They are the ancestors of this book. Along the way, I have had the privilege of meeting many readers of those three books. They have been generous with their praise and helpful with their suggestions.

The most important thing on their "want" list was maps. Next, they asked that I cut out the fluff, which they defined as the restaurants that weren't **ON** an airport. Message received! Maps are included and every restaurant in this book is on an airport. You won't have to worry about ground transportation ever again.

I have added a few of my favorite flyin museums, golf courses, camp grounds, resorts and hotels. Future editions will have many, many more as I attempt to change **The $100 Hamburger** from a flyin restaurant guide to an all-encompassing guide to all of the interesting venues located on the many airports that serve general aviation.

The years of the economic downturn have been very hard on the folks who operate airport restaurants. Many did not survive. In most cases they have been replaced by new operators with new dreams. It is interesting to point out that not a single restaurant that made our annual **Best of the Best** list during the last decade failed, not one. They are all still in business. In the case of the **Southern Flyer Diner** in Brenham, Texas business is so good that they are forced to post advice on their website for tour bus operators to call before coming to make certain that their passengers can be accommodated. It is a very popular place with the entire community not just pilots.

The biggest change in this book is the reviews. All of the earlier content was crowd sourced, which meant that the reviews were drawn from the PIREPs (*Pilot Reports*) posted on the $100 Hamburger website by its subscribers. This time all but three of the reviews come directly from me and are based on my personal experiences.

I am often asked about our star rating system. It is based on six factors: ambiance, cleanliness, service, food, price and attitude. The first five are easy to quantify. The last one, attitude, is summed up with the answer to a simple question. Do I feel welcome? By the way, I go to each restaurant as you do – privately. No one at the restaurant knows who I am, even the ones that I frequent. I sit at the same table you will, am served by the same wait staff, eat the same food and pay the same price.

Let's start at the top. What's it take to get five stars? Two words apply – something special. This can point to a restaurant that rivals New York and San Francisco's finest. It doesn't mean that the restaurant is necessarily upscale and pricey rather that it is off the charts in each of the six measurement areas I value. I know that each of you will have a wonderful experience at any of the restaurants that has earned five stars.

Four stars are given to really good restaurants that are a little off base in one of the six areas but that can't be attitude. You must feel welcome. Maybe the ambiance isn't all that it could be or maybe the food is just a cut below best in class.

Three stars is our average. A seriously good place that measures up to all of the other good places that you expect to find at an airport but there is nothing about it that hits the outstanding button. It is good in all six areas and neither excellent or awful in any of them.

Two stars restaurants are troubled but adequate. You can get a meal that you'll be OK with and service that isn't offensive though it may be slow and sometimes really slow. The lower quality is ALWAYS reflected in attitude. You may feel welcome or you may feel that you are a bother but you'll never feel special.

One star is my way of saying – **AVOID**. It is on an airport so we include it but I certainly don't support it and neither should you unless you're really in a pinch.

One final thought. Please use this book as an information resource only and not as your be all and end all. I have included email addresses and website URLs and phone numbers where ever possible. Check out the place you're about to visit before you launch. Flying has never been more expensive. A mistaken destination is costly.

Finally, I appreciate feedback, good and bad. Please let me hear from you via email at jpurner@100dollarhamburger.com. I personally answer every note that comes my way.

Fly someplace today. You've earned it!

Table of Contents

Legend

Symbols

🍽 Restaurant
⛺ Camping
🏛 Museum
🏨 Hotel
🏌 Golf

Star Ratings

★	Needs Improvement
★ ★	Adequate
★ ★ ★	Average
★ ★ ★ ★	Well Above Average
★ ★ ★ ★ ★	Outstanding

www.100dollarhamburger.com

FlyIn Alabama

⦿ BESSEMER, AL (BESSEMER - EKY)
Aprt Mgr: MIKE COLLINS PH: 205-428-9292
Field Elevation: 700 CTAF: 123.000 FUEL: 100LLA+
Runway: 05/23 Length: 6007 Width: 100 Surface: ASPH-F

★ ★ ★ Little D's Bar & Grill - (205) 424-0601
Proprietor: Diane Wilcox
Open:
> Mon - Thu: 11:00 am - 10:00 pm
> Fri - Sat: 11:00 am - 11:00 pm
> Sun: 1:00 pm - 9:00 pm

Restaurant Website: www.facebook.com
Restaurant Email: littledsbarandgrill@gmail.com
PIREP:
This is a pretty standard by the runway burger and breakfast joint with three big exceptions. First they've got a really cool out door area that is large and covered with sand. It makes me feel that I've gone to a beach spot. At one end of the beach is a band stand. That brings us to exception number two; live music on the weekends. The final difference is beer. Let's summarize. You can sit on the beach, eat a burger, drink beer and listen to live music. Oh yeah!

⦿EUFAULA, AL (WEEDON FIELD - EUF)
Aprt Mgr: ERIC LANGHAM PH: 334-687-2051
Field Elevation: 285 CTAF: 122.800 FUEL: 100LLA+
Runway: 18/36 Length: 5000 Width: 100 Surface: ASPH-G

★ ★ ★ Lakeside at the Airport - (334) 687-3132
Proprietor: Hope Thomas
Open: Open daily for lunch and dinner
PIREP:
The lunch fare is "southern home cooking", served buffet style, and it is **OUTSTANDING**!! Nothing fancy mind you, but they do have a nice view of the airport ramp, great folks at the FBO and the best fried chicken I have had in a long, long while. All the desserts are home-made.

Just a great stop!!!

⦿FLORALA, AL (FLORALA MUNI - 0J4)
Aprt Mgr: FLORALA AIRPORT AUTHORITY PH: 334-858-6173

Field Elevation: 314 **CTAF:** 123.000 **FUEL:**
Runway: 04/22 **Length:** 3197 **Width:** 75 **Surface:** ASPH-G

★ ★ ★ **Sunshine Aero Industries - (334) 858-6173**
Open:
        Daily: Lunch
Restaurant Email: ddavis@gtcom.net
PIREP:
The FBO has a buffet loaded with BBQ, dogs and burgers. Dave
smokes the pork right at the airport.
Watch out for military choppers, these guys flock to this place for lunch
and fuel. It's open seven days a week, year around. They're really setup
to cater to the military choppers (they hot fuel on site, fun to watch),
and the Navy trainers out of Pensacola. It's a very friendly bunch and
GA is always welcome.

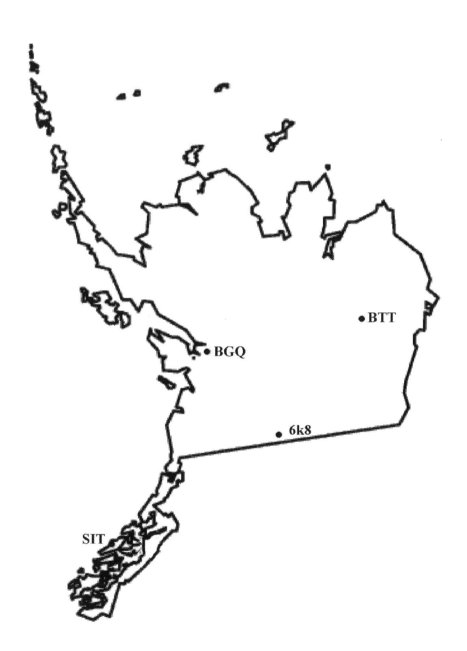

$100 Hamburger 2014/15

FlyIn ALASKA

⟨◉⟩BETTLES, AK (BETTLES - BTT)
Aprt Mgr: JEREMY WORRALL **PH:** 907-451-5230
Field Elevation: 647 **CTAF:** 122.900 **FUEL:** 100LLA1+ B
Runway: 01/19 **Length:** 5190 **Width:** 150 **Surface:** TURF-GRVL-G

★★★Bettles Lodge - (907) 692-5111
Proprietor: Dan and Lynda Klaes
Open:
　　　　　Daily: Breakfast, Lunch & Dinner
Restaurant Website: www.bettleslodge.com
Restaurant Email: info@bettleslodge.com
PIREP:
One of the best places to get a burger above the Arctic Circle is in the fly-in only community of Bettles, Alaska (50 residents) in the foothills of the Brooks Range (180 nm north of Fairbanks). The airstrip officially enjoys the most clear weather days out of anywhere in the State and is a well-maintained 5,200 foot gravel strip with nearby 5,000 foot float pond. A historic lodge acts as a pilot roadhouse and has a full service kitchen with many hamburgers on the menu. Stay overnight for the Midnight Sun in the summer or spend an afternoon exploring the unique and friendly community where everything (mail, fuel, food) is flown in daily. Visiting pilots enjoy talking with bush pilots and seeing the diverse amount of aircraft (from Cubs on tundra tires to DC-4 fuel carriers) that arrive daily. Pilots from as far away as Florida make the trip to Bettles annually.

⟨◉⟩BIG LAKE, AK (BIG LAKE - BGQ)
Aprt Mgr: NEAL HENSLEE **PH:** 907-745-2159
Field Elevation: 158 **CTAF:** 122.800 **FUEL:**
Runway: 07/25 **Length:** 2435 **Width:** 70 **Surface:** GRAVEL-G
★★★The Hangar Lounge - (907) 892-9230
Proprietor: Cindy and Mark Riley
Open:
　　　　　Daily: Breakfast, Lunch & Dinner
PIREP: The 2,400 foot gravel runway is well maintained and has pilot controlled lighting at 122.8 There is no fuel for sale on the field but is available at Wasilla approximately 10 miles west of BGQ. **The Hangar Lounge** is located across the street. It is a favorite with locals. The food is great and the service is friendly.

⟨◉⟩SITKA, AK (SITKA ROCKY GUTIERREZ - SIT)

www.100dollarhamburger.com

Aprt Mgr: DAVE LUCHINETTI PH: 907-966-2960
Field Elevation: 21 CTAF: 123.600 FUEL: 100 A1+
Runway: 11/29 Length: 6500 Width: 150 Surface: ASPH-G

★★★Nugget Restaurant & Bakery - (907) 966-2480
Proprietor: Patty Colton
Open:
> Mon – Sun: 8:00am - 8:00pm

Restaurant Website: www.facebook.com
Restaurant Email: nuggetsitkaak@yahoo.com
PIREP:
The Nugget is in the terminal. The ocean view is really nice. This place is famous for pie, so famous in fact that they have put in a vending machine to sell their pie slices quickly to airline passengers that must have a slice for their flight. Breakfast is also pretty good here but the service is spotty.

⦿TOK, AK (TOK JUNCTION - 6K8)
Aprt Mgr: DENNIS BISHOP PH: 907-883-5128
Field Elevation: 1639 CTAF: 122.800 FUEL: 100LLA
Runway: 07/25 Length: 2509 Width: 50 Surface: ASPH-E

★★★Fast Eddies - (907) 883-4411
Proprietor: Ed Young
Open:
> Summer Hours: 6am – 11pm
> Winter Hours: 6am – 10pm

Restaurant Website: www.fasteddysrestaurant.com
Restaurant Email: edyoung@aptalaska.net
PIREP:
This is a nice, clean, well decorated restaurant. The service is professional and food just one notch below excellent. I was lucky enough to be here when the Prime Rib Sandwich was the lunch special. It was really good.

FlyIn Arizona

ⒾCHANDLER, AZ (CHANDLER MUNI - CHD)
Aprt Mgr: CHRISTINE MACKAY **PH:** 480-782-3540
Field Elevation: 1243 **CTAF:** 126.100 **FUEL:** 100LLA
Runway: 04L/22R **Length:** 4401 **Width:** 75 **Surface:** ASPH-G
Runway: 04R/22L **Length:** 4870 **Width:** 75 **Surface:** ASPH-G

★★★**Hanger Cafe – (480) 899-6965**
Proprietor: Lillian George
Open:
> Mon – Sun: 7am - 2pm

PIREP:
The Hanger Cafe is a very typical airport café. It is on the ramp with a good view.

ⒾELOY, AZ (ELOY MUNI - E60)
Aprt Mgr: JOE BLANTON **PH:** 520-466-9201
Field Elevation: 1513 **CTAF:** 122.800 **FUEL:** 100LLA
Runway: 02/20 **Length:** 3900 **Width:** 75 **Surface:** ASPH-G

★★★**Bent Prop Saloon & Cookery - (520) 466-9268**
Open:
> Hours of operation vary according to season
> Daily: breakfast, lunch & dinner

Restaurant Website: www.skydiveaz.com/skydiving-Facilities/food
Restaurant Email: jump@skydiveaz.com
PIREP:
The airfield is frequented primarily by both young and old but always energetic skydivers from around the world - to be sure. They are here because Skydive Arizona is here with its large fleet of jump planes: 7 Skyvans, 4 Super Twin Otters, and one each DC3, Beech 18 and Pilatus Porter. The Bent Prop is right in the central business square of this old west styled skydiving village. Eat inside *(cool A/C!)* or on the porch *(later in the winter)*. It is large, clean and fun. The service at the Bent Prop restaurant was as outstanding as possible, decent burger bordering on unique, and a menu with a wide variety and very reasonable prices.

Be careful! Skydive Arizona is extremely active most of the year. Approach from the west and do not overfly. Skydivers land on the east. Watch out for skydivers and skydiver aircraft neither follow the regular rules. Listen carefully to traffic advisories on the way in.

◉KINGMAN, AZ (KINGMAN - IGM)
        Aprt Mgr: DAVID FRENCH **PH:** 928-757-2134
        Field Elevation: 3449 **CTAF:** 122.800 **FUEL:** 100LLA
        Runway: 17/35 **Length:** 6725 **Width:** 75 **Surface:** ASPH-G
        Runway: 03/21 **Length:** 6827 **Width:** 150 **Surface:** ASPH-G

        ★★★★**Kingman Airport Cafe - (928) 757-4420**
Proprietor: Henery Desoausa
Open:
        Tue – Sun: 6am to 2pm
PIREP:
Kingman Airport Café is by the pumps. The food is good and inexpensive. I've been here for breakfast and enjoyed it.

◉LAKE HAVASU CITY, AZ (LAKE HAVASU CITY - HII)
        LAKE HAVASU CITY, AZ (LAKE HAVASU CITY - HII)
        Aprt Mgr: STEVE JOHNSTON **PH:** 928-764-3330
        Field Elevation: 783 **CTAF:** 122.700 **FUEL:** 100LLA
        Runway: 14/32 **Length:** 8001 **Width:** 100 **Surface:** ASPH-G

        ★★★**Waldo's BBQ – (928) 764-FOOD**
Proprietor: Clay Caldwell
Open:
        Mon – Sun: 10:30am - 9:00pm
Restaurant Website: waldosbarbeque.com
Restaurant Email: waldosbbqhavasu@frontier.com
PIREP:
I am first a pilot and second a BBQ guy. For me it's all about cow not pig. I start with the sliced beef sandwich and finish with the Bread Pudding.

◉NOGALES, AZ (NOGALES INTL - OLS)
        Aprt Mgr: LAWRENCE TIFFIN **PH:** 520-287-9120
        Field Elevation: 3955 **CTAF:** 122.800 **FUEL:** 100LLA
        Runway: 03/21 **Length:** 7200 **Width:** 100 **Surface:** ASPH-G

        ★★★ **Nogales Airport Café - (520) 287-9120**
Proprietor: Jose Duran
Open:
        Mon – Sun: 7:30am to 2:00pm
PIREP:
The Nogales Airport Café is in the Tiffin Aviation Services building. The airport, like most in Arizona, has a long runway to compensate for high density altitude days. It features a pretty good downhill slope, and some rising terrain to the northeast which will make your first arrival

interesting. Don't make your first trip here at night. The food is strictly airport coffee shop fare; neither good nor bad.

⦿PAYSON, AZ (PAYSON - PAN)
Aprt Mgr: BETH MYERS **PH:** 928-472-4748
Field Elevation: 5157 **CTAF:** 122.800 **FUEL:** 100LLA
Runway: 06/24 **Length:** 5500 **Width:** 75 **Surface:** ASPH-G

★ ★ ★ The Crosswinds Café - (928) 474-1613
Proprietor: Darla & Roger Annabel
Open:

Mon - Tue: 6:00 am - 3:00 pm
Wed - Sat: 6:00 am - 8:00 pm
Sun: 6:00 am - 6:00 pm

Restaurant Website: www.facebook.com/crosswindsrest
PIREP:
The surrounding terrain is beautiful making this one of my favorite flights for scenic views. **The Crosswinds Café** is overrun by locals. They love the place. I love the pancakes and the friendly people. Pies are baked fresh daily. You can take a fruit pie home for less than 10 bucks.

⦿PHOENIX, AZ (PHOENIX DEER VALLEY - DVT)
Aprt Mgr: ART FAIRBANKS **PH:** 623-869-0975
Field Elevation: 1478 **CTAF:** 118.400 **FUEL:** 100LLA
Runway: 07L/25R **Length:** 4508 **Width:** 75 **Surface:** ASPH-G
Runway: 07R/25L **Length:** 8197 **Width:** 100 **Surface:** ASPH-G

★ ★ ★ Deer Valley Airport Restaurant - (602) 582-5454
Proprietor: Voula Papamatheakis
Open:

Mon – Sun: 6:30am to 9:00pm

Restaurant Website: www.deervalleyairportrestaurant.com
Restaurant Email: information@deervalleyairportrestaurant.com
PIREP:
Deer Valley Airport Restaurant is within walking distance of the ramp. Food, service, ambiance and prices are first-rate. I have been here more than once for breakfast. A good way to judge an airport restaurant is by the number of locals that show up. **Deer Valley Airport Restaurant** passes that test with flying colors.

⦿PHOENIX, AZ (PHOENIX-MESA GATEWAY - IWA)
Aprt Mgr: LYNN KUSY **PH:** 480-988-7600
Field Elevation: 1384 **CTAF:** 120.600 **FUEL:** 100LLA
Runway: 12C/30C **Length:** 10201 **Width:** 150 **Surface:** CONC-G

Runway: 12L/30R **Length:** 9300 **Width:** 150 **Surface:** CONC-G
Runway: 12R/30L **Length:** 10401 **Width:** 150 **Surface:** CONC-G

★ ★ ★ ★ **The Flight Deck Cafe - (480) 988-9517**
Proprietor: Leif Thompson
Open:
>Monday – Friday: 7:30-2:00
>Saturday-Sunday: Breakfast Buffet 7:30 -1:00
Restaurant Website: www.flightdeckcafe.com
PIREP:
The Flight Deck Cafe is located on the flight line in the general aviation center. I have only been here twice; once for breakfast and once for lunch. I left happy on both occasions. Be prepared to share the traffic pattern with military aircraft.

▮◉PRESCOTT, AZ (ERNEST A. LOVE FIELD - PRC)
>**Aprt Mgr:** BENJAMIN D VARDIMAN **PH:** 928-777-1114
>**Field Elevation:** 5045 **CTAF:** 125.300 **FUEL:** 100LLA
>Runway: 12/30 **Length:** 4408 **Width:** 75 **Surface:** ASPH-G
>Runway: 03L/21R **Length:** 4848 **Width:** 60 **Surface:** ASPH-G
>Runway: 03R/21L **Length:** 7616 **Width:** 150 **Surface:** ASPH-G

★ ★ ★ **Susie's Skyway Restaurant - (928) 445-6971**
Proprietor: Susan Sullivan
Open:
>Mon – Sun: 7am – 4pm
PIREP:
Suzie's has a great view of the airport and the mountains beyond. It offers the typical airport diner menu but executes it better than most. The atmosphere is warm and friendly. The décor is straight out of the fifties.

▮◉SEDONA, AZ (SEDONA - SEZ)
>**Aprt Mgr:** EDWARD MC CALL **PH:** 928-282-4487
>**Field Elevation:** 4830 **CTAF:** 123.000 **FUEL:** 100LLA
>Runway: 03/21 **Length:** 5132 **Width:** 100 **Surface:** ASPH-G

★ ★ ★ ★ ★ **The Mesa Grill - 928-282-2400**
Proprietor: Marc Battistini
Open:
>Mon – Fri: 7am – 9pm
>Sat – Sun: 7am – 9:30pm
Restaurant Website: www.mesagrillsedona.com
Restaurant Email: marc@mesagrillsedona.com
PIREP:

The Sedona Airport is awesome. For that matter Sedona is awesome. This is a wonderful place to fly and watch your passengers press their noses against the window as they strain to get the best view possible. **The Mesa Grill** fits the locale. It too is perfect. Get this, it is even pet friendly so you can bring your furry flying buddies and sit outdoors on their patio. The ambiance is state of the art. The food? Some of the best you'll ever enjoy!

⦿SCOTTSDALE, AZ (SCOTTSDALE - SDL)

Aprt Mgr: GARY MASCARO **PH:** 480-312-7735
Field Elevation: 1510 **CTAF:** 119.900 **FUEL:** 100LLA
Runway: 03/21 **Length:** 8249 **Width:** 100 **Surface:** ASPH-G

★★★Zulu Caffe - (480) 636-1634
Proprietor: Dee Dee Maza
Open:
　　　　　Mon - Fri: 11am - 2pm
Restaurant Website: www.zulucaffe.com
Restaurant Email: deedee@ciaobabycatering.com
PIREP:
Think upscale. Think floor to ceiling windows. Think right on the ramp, so close that you can see not just your airplane but the instruments in its panel. Think GREAT food. I ate the BEST BLT I have ever had right here. All that said there is a HUGE problem with this place. It is only open for lunch and it is not open on weekends. If they added breakfast and weekend service I'd give it four stars.

⦿TUCSON, AZ (MARANA RGNL - AVQ)

Aprt Mgr: ORVILLE SALING **PH:** 520-437-6220
Field Elevation: 2031 **CTAF:** 123.000 **FUEL:** 100LLA
Runway: 03/21 **Length:** 3892 **Width:** 75 **Surface:** ASPH-G
Runway: 12/30 **Length:** 6901 **Width:** 100 **Surface:** ASPH-G

★★ Sky Rider Coffee Shop - (520) 682-3046
Proprietor: Brenda Carter
Open:
　　　　　Tue – Sun: 7am – 2pm
Restaurant Website: www.marana.com/index.aspx?nid=330
Restaurant Email: jmangialardi@marana.com
PIREP:
I come here for one reason, the Chicken Fried Steak. They do a really good job with it. Other than that it is a pretty standard airport restaurant. The décor could use an update.

⦿TUCSON, AZ (RYAN FIELD - RYN)

Aprt Mgr: SCOTT R. DRIVER **PH:** 520-883-9800
Field Elevation: 2417 **CTAF:** 125.800 **FUEL:** 100LLA
Runway: 15/33 **Length:** 4000 **Width:** 75 **Surface:** ASPH-F
Runway: 06L/24R **Length:** 4900 **Width:** 75 **Surface:** ASPH-G
Runway: 06R/24L **Length:** 5500 **Width:** 75 **Surface:** ASPH-G

★ ★ ★ **Todd's Restaurant - (520) 883-7770**
Proprietor: Todd Scott
Open:
>   Mon – Sun: 8am – 2pm
Restaurant Website: www.toddsrestaurant.com
Restaurant Email: cheftodd@toddsrestaurant.com
PIREP:
Every seat is a window seat. That's good. The fact that the owner is an award winning chef is even better. Great views and great food is hard to beat. For any business time is the test. Todd's has been open for a dozen years; it has passed the test of time.

◉WINSLOW, AZ (WINSLOW-LINDBERGH RGNL - INW)
Aprt Mgr: JIM FERGUSON **PH:** 928-289-2423
Field Elevation: 4941 **CTAF:** 122.800 **FUEL:** 100LLA
Runway: 04/22 **Length:** 6236 **Width:** 75 **Surface:** ASPH-F
Runway: 11/29 **Length:** 7100 **Width:** 150 **Surface:** ASPH-G

★ ★ ★ ★ **E & O Kitchen- (928) 289-5352**
Proprietor: Oscar Barron
Open:
>   Mon - Thu: 11:00 am - 7:00 pm
>   Fri: 11:00 am - 8:00 pm
>   Sat: 11:00 am - 5:00 pm
Restaurant Website: www.facebook.com
PIREP:
E & O Kitchen is right on the ramp next to the FBO. It is short on looks but long on food and service. We're talking home cooked Mexican food. This must be the best place to get it north of the Baja. People DRIVE here from 100 miles away to eat the Menudo. The least we pilots can do is join 'em.

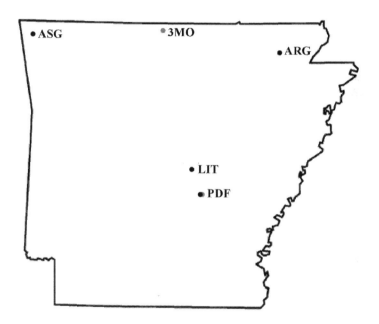

$100 Hamburger 2014/15

FlyIn Arkansas

⦿↩ LAKEVIEW, AR (GASTONS - 3M0)
    Aprt Mgr: JA GASTON **PH:** 870-431-5202
    Field Elevation: 479 **CTAF:** 122.800 **FUEL:** 100LL
    Runway: 06/24 **Length:** 3200 **Width:** 55 **Surface:** TURF-G

    ★★★★ Gaston's Restaurant - (870) 431-5202
Proprietor: Jim Gaston
Open:
        Daily: Breakfast, Lunch, Dinner
Restaurant Website: www.gastons.com
Restaurant Email: gastons@gastons.com
PIREP:
You come here to eat trout not steak and not breakfast. This is the
house that trout built. My favorite is the Pan Seared Boneless Rainbow
Trout. Guess where it comes from? I must mention that the approach
and the landing strip are among my personal favorites. I love the sound
that tires make as they kiss the grass.

    ★★★★★ Gaston's White River Resort - (870) 431-5202
Proprietor: Jim Gaston
Open:
        Year-Round
Restaurant Website: www.gastons.com
Restaurant Email: gastons@gastons.com
PIREP:
If you are a pilot and a fisherman this should be on your bucket list.
Certainly, there are better fishing holes in Canada and Alaska but this
one is almost dead center in the middle of America. That means you
can get here with a Cherokee from about anywhere in the USA. The
landing strip is 3,200 feet of manicured turf with an easy approach.
Once on the ground, you'll find everything you need including guides,
boats, training and rental fishing gear. The plus factor is the setting, the
cabins, the Lodge and the restaurant. Do this. You'll thank me a
thousand times for recommending it.

⦿ LITTLE ROCK, AR (ADAMS FIELD - LIT)
    Aprt Mgr: RON MATHIEU **PH:** 501-372-3439
    Field Elevation: 266 **CTAF:** 0.000 **FUEL:** 100LLA
    Runway: 18/36 **Length:** 6224 **Width:** 150 **Surface:** CONC-G
    Runway: 04R/22L **Length:** 8251 **Width:** 150 **Surface:** CONC-G
    Runway: 04L/22R **Length:** 8273 **Width:** 150 **Surface:** CONC-G

★★★Flight Deck - (501) 975-9315
Proprietor: Pearl Rodgers
Open:

Mon – Fri: 6:30am to 3:00pm

Sat: 10:00am - 2:00pm

Restaurant Website: www.central.aero/flight-deck
Restaurant Email: pearl@central.aero marketing@central.aero
PIREP:

The Flight Deck at Bill and Hillary Clinton/Adams Field (LIT) in Little Rock makes a great food stop. It is located inside the Central Flying Service FBO building on the GA ramp. They have a full restaurant menu with daily lunch specials. They lay claim to *"the best cheese burger in aviation history"* and they may be right as the burgers are really very good. The ambiance is clean and modern made better by large floor to ceiling windows overlooking a very active field. You will be very impressed by the service both on the ramp and in the restaurant – fast and friendly!

🍴PINE BLUFF, AR (GRIDER FIELD - PBF)
Aprt Mgr: DOUG HALE **PH:** 870-534-4131
Field Elevation: 206 **CTAF:** 123.000 **FUEL:** 100LLA
Runway: 18/36 **Length:** 5998 **Width:** 150 **Surface:** ASPH-G

★★★Grider Field Restaurant - (870) 534-4131
Proprietor: Doug Hale
Open:

Mon - Fri: 11am - 2pm

Restaurant Website:
www.cityofpinebluff.com/pbairport/?page_id=236
Restaurant Email: doug.grider@yahoo.com
PIREP:

The Grider Field Restaurant is in the main terminal building. You can literally taxi up to the front door. The food, especially the fried chicken, is first rate. They offer a meat and three, buffet which I always enjoy. Everything is cooked from scratch according to the manager. Great airport; Great restaurant!! Give it a try. I'm glad I did.

🍴SPRINGDALE, AR (SPRINGDALE MUNI - ASG)
Aprt Mgr: JAMES SMITH **PH:** 479-750-8585
Field Elevation: 1353 **CTAF:** 118.200 **FUEL:** 100LLA
Runway: 18/36 **Length:** 5302 **Width:** 76 **Surface:** ASPH-F

★★★★★Flaps Down Grill – 479-361-8032
Open:

Mon - Sun: 10:00 am - 2:00 pm
Mon - Sun: 4:30 pm - 9:00 pm
Restaurant Website: www.flaps-down.com
Restaurant Email: bill@flaps-down.com
PIREP:

The Flaps Down Grill is first class in every way. Wonderful menu, expertly prepared plus micro brewed beers plus live entertainment plus an amazing deck plus wonderful service plus ambiance that makes you feel good about being here. Take a friend, that's how I found this spot and I have been grateful ever since.

📷🏛 **WALNUT RIDGE, AR (WALNUT RIDGE RGNL - ARG)**
Aprt Mgr: MITCH WHITMIRE **PH:** 870-886-5432
Field Elevation: 279 **CTAF:** 122.800 **FUEL:** 100LLA
Runway: 04/22 **Length:** 6001 **Width:** 150 **Surface:** ASPH-G
Runway: 18/36 **Length:** 5001 **Width:** 150 **Surface:** CONC-F
Runway: 13/31 **Length:** 5003 **Width:** 150 **Surface:** CONC-F

★★★**Parachute Inn – (870) 886-5918**
Proprietor: Donna Robertson
Open:

Tue - Thurs: 7:00am - 2:00pm
Fri: 7:00am - 8:00pm
Sat: 11:00am -8:00pm

Restaurant Website: www.parachuteinnrestaurant.com
PIREP:

You can literally taxi within 20 ft. of the front door. The FBO is about 100 ft. away. They have cleverly connected a 737 fuselage to the dining room. Part of the plane's interior has been converted into roomy booths, or you sit in the original airline chairs. It's unique. The food and service are very good. I try to show-up for lunch on Friday. It's a catfish buffet.... hushpuppies, french-fries, pinto beans, slaw, salad bar, iced tea and great desserts.

★★★ **Wings of Honor Museum – (800) 584-5575**
Proprietor: Donna Robertson
Open:

Mon - Sat: 9:00am - 5:00pm

Museum Website: www.wingsofhonor.org
Museum Email: harold@wingsofhonor.org
PIREP:

"The wings they wore...the wings that carried them to victory"

The Wings of Honor Museum is located across the road from the Walnut Ridge Regional Airport. It was established in 1999 to preserve the history of the Walnut Ridge Army Flying School, the Marine Corps Air Facility at Walnut Ridge, the War Assets Administration's Warbird Storage, Sales and Scrapping Facility, and the USAF 725th Radar Squadron; and to remember and honor those civilian and military personnel who served to maintain our freedom.

www.100dollarhamburger.com

FlyIn California

ARCATA/EUREKA, CA (ARCATA - ACV)
    Aprt Mgr: JACQUELYN HULSEY **PH:** 707-839-5401
    Field Elevation: 222 **CTAF:** 123.000 **FUEL:** 100LLA
    Runway: 01/19 **Length:** 4501 **Width:** 150 **Surface:** ASPH-G
    Runway: 14/32 **Length:** 6046 **Width:** 150 **Surface:** ASPH-G

    ★ ★ ★ **The Silver Lining - 707-839-0304**
Proprietor: Mandala, Damian and Joshua Lakey
Open:
        Mon: 8:30 am - 8:30 pm
        Tue: 8:30 am - 11:45 pm
        Wed - Thu: 8:30 am - 8:30 pm
        Fri - Sat: 8:30 am - 11:00 pm
        Sun: 8:30 am - 8:30 pm
Restaurant Website: www.facebook.com/silverliningrestaurant
PIREP:
A view of the runway on one side of the dining area and a view of the ocean on the other side gives The Silver Lining a definite edge over most ramp side Cafes. After lunch take a walk down to the beach via the Hammond trail. Dinner features live music and Karaoke for the brave. The food is very, very good with a menu that includes prime rib and chocolate mousse.

AUBURN, CA (AUBURN MUNI - AUN)
    Aprt Mgr: MS. BERNIE SCHROEDER **PH:** 530-386-4211
    Field Elevation: 1539 **CTAF:** 122.700 **FUEL:** 100LL80 A
    Runway: 07/25 **Length:** 3700 **Width:** 75 **Surface:** ASPH-G

    ★ ★ ★ ★ **Wings Grill & Espresso Bar - (530) 885-0428**
Proprietor: Connie Horning
Open:
        Mon – Sun: 7am – 2pm

PIREP:
Auburn is a very scenic airport best viewed from the deck of **Wings.** The locals discovered this place many years ago so be prepared to wait; it's worth it! I have been here twice for breakfast and once for lunch. At breakfast, go with any omelet you like. They're all good and come with a rasher of bacon (4 pieces) and a mountain of hash browns (homemade).

BAKERSFIELD, CA (BAKERSFIELD MUNI - L45)
    Aprt Mgr: STUART PATTESON **PH:** 661-326-3105
    Field Elevation: 378 **CTAF:** 122.800 **FUEL:** 100LL
    Runway: 16/34 **Length:** 4000 **Width:** 75 **Surface:** ASPH-G

    ★★★**Rocket Shop Cafe Sports Bar & NASCAR Store - (661) 832-4800**
Proprietor: John Harmon
Open:
        Mon – Thurs: 7am – 8:30pm
        Friday: 7am – 9pm
        Saturday: 7am – 10pm
        Sunday: 7am – 3m
Restaurant Website: www.rocketshopcafe.com
Restaurant Email: rocketshopcafe@att.net
PIREP:
Taxi to the extreme northwest corner of the field and look for the only building with windows in the area. NASCAR memorabilia makes up most of the décor. A combination coffee shop, sports bar with a NASCAR store as well as a banquet room.

BIG BEAR CITY, CA (BIG BEAR CITY - L35)
    Aprt Mgr: JAMES GWALTNEY **PH:** 909-585-3219
    Field Elevation: 6752 **CTAF:** 122.725 **FUEL:** 100LLA
    Runway: 08/26 **Length:** 5850 **Width:** 75 **Surface:** ASPH-G

    ★★★Barnstormer - **909 585-9339**
Proprietor: Renee Wagner
Open:
        Mon – Sun: 7am – 3pm
        Fri – Sat: 5pm – 9pm
Restaurant Website: www.barnstormrestaurant.com
Restaurant Email: reneew@Charter.net
PIREP:
The scenery up here is spectacular, especially after the first snowfall. Just be sure to watch that mixture! The altitude is 6,700' so count on eating up 1/3 to ½ of the 5,800' runway on takeoff especially in the summer. The restaurant is worth the trip so are the views of the mountains, the lake and the forest. On the weekends you can pretty much count on waiting in line behind the locals. Be patient, its worth the wait.

BORREGO SPRINGS, CA (BORREGO VALLEY - L08)
    Aprt Mgr: PETER DRINKWATER **PH:** 760-767-7415

Field Elevation: 520 **CTAF:** 122.800 **FUEL:** 100LL
Runway: 08/26 **Length:** 5011 **Width:** 75 **Surface:** ASPH-G
Airport Website: www.co.san-diego.ca.us/dpw/airports/borrego.html

---

★ ★ ★ ★ **Asssagio Ristorante Italiano - (760)767-3388**
Open:

       Tue – Sat: 11am - 9:30pm
       Sun: 11am - 8:30pm

Restaurant Website: www.assaggioitalian.com/borrego.html
PIREP:
Asssagio Ristorante Italiano is a very upscale Italian restaurant, with a extensive menu. The ambiance, food and service are top drawer. They have a rooftop patio with very nice views. Price? Well it goes to value I suppose. Good food cost more than bad food. Here's the question to ask. What's bad food worth?

⦿CALEXICO, CA (CALEXICO INTL - CXL)
       Aprt Mgr: LUIS ESTRADA **PH:** 760-768-2175
       Field Elevation: 4 **CTAF:** 122.800 **FUEL:** 100LLA
       Runway: 08/26 **Length:** 4679 **Width:** 75 **Surface:** ASPH-G

★ ★ ★ **Rosa's Plane Food – (760) 357-6660**
Proprietor: Rosa Maria Barajas
Open:

       Mon-Thu: 10 am - 8 pm
       Fri: 10 am - 9 pm
       Sat-Sun: 9:30 am - 8 pm

Restaurant Website: facebook.com
PIREP:
Mexican Seafood sounds like a bad combination. It isn't. One trip to Rosa's and you'll know how well this combination can work at the direction of a master chef. Landing at CXL is interesting the runway is wash-boarded but not unusable. The restaurant itself could go unnoticed. It is a little brown building sitting next to the Customs office. It isn't much to look at but the food is really good.

⦿CAMARILLO, CA (CAMARILLO - CMA)
       Field Elevation: 77 **CTAF:** 128.200 **FUEL:** 100LLA
       Runway: 08/26 **Length:** 6013 **Width:** 150 **Surface:** ASPH-CONC-G
       Aprt Mgr: AARON WALSH **PH:** 805-388-4246

★ ★ ★ ★ **Waypoint Café – (805) 388-2535**
Proprietor: Greg Hunter
Open:

       Mon –Fri: 7am – 3pm

Sat: 7am- 4pm

Sun: 8am – 4pm

Restaurant Website: thewaypointcafe.com

PIREP:

Clean, pleasant efficient and friendly with food and service that rewards the effort it took to get here. Excellent tie downs adjacent to the restaurant. The **Waypoint Café** is a nice place to go in the summer and enjoy the cool ocean breeze from the patio. I came here for breakfast and was intrigued by the Enchilada Omelet. It is made with one cheese enchilada buried in the omelet and one top side. It was really good.

CHINO, CA (CHINO - CNO)

Aprt Mgr: JAMES JENKINS **PH:** 909-597-3910

Field Elevation: 650 **CTAF:** 118.500 **FUEL:** 100LLA

Runway: 08L/26R **Length:** 4858 **Width:** 150 **Surface:** ASPH-G

Runway: 03/21 **Length:** 4919 **Width:** 150 **Surface:** ASPH-G

Runway: 08R/26L **Length:** 7000 **Width:** 150 **Surface:** ASPH-G

★ ★ ★ **Flo's Airport Café - (909) 597-3416**

Proprietor: Paul and Donna Hughes

Open:

Mon – Sun: 5:30am-8:00pm

Restaurant Website: www.floscafes.com

Restaurant Email: FlosRestaurants@gmail.com

PIREP:

Flo's Airport Café is the oldest ramp side restaurant in the world having celebrated its 50th anniversary in 2013. They must be doing something right. The menu is filled with made from scratch comfort food. There slogan says it all, *"Pie Fixes Everything".* This is not a place for dieters! It is packed with SoCal aviators and locals alike.

CHIRIACO SUMMIT, CA (CHIRIACO SUMMIT - L77)

Airport Website: skyvector.com/airport/L77/Chiriaco-Summit-Airport

Aprt Mgr: DARYL SHIPPY **PH:** 760-955-9722

Field Elevation: 1713 **CTAF:** 122.900 **FUEL:**

Runway: 06/24 **Length:** 4600 **Width:** 50 **Surface:** ASPH-P

★ ★ ★ ★ Chiriaco Summit Café - 760-227-3227

Proprietor: Margit Chiriaco Rusche

Open:

Mon – Sun: 6am -11pm

Restaurant Website: www.chiriacosummit.com/facilities.php

PIREP:

The word that comes to mind is eclectic. I came to visit the museum and have breakfast. Before leaving, I tried and liked the date shake. Tiedowns are at the west end of the field near the Patton Museum and the restaurant. If your takeoff is westbound, you'll have to taxi east on the runway. I was able to find some chains on the tiedown cables, but it would be a good idea to bring tie down ropes in case there are more than a couple of planes on the ramp. There's room for perhaps 10 planes. I was one of two. California Highway Patrol aircraft stop here often for meals. Overall this is an easy flight from the Los Angeles area with good food waiting at a very out-of-the-way, back-in-time diner.

★★★General Patton Memorial Museum
Open:
> Mon – Sun: 9:30am - 4:30pm

Museum Website: www.generalpattonmuseum.com
Museum Email: gpmm@wildblue.net
PIREP:
This museum touches the west ramp of the airport. One million American soldiers were trained here for WWII at what was called the Desert Training Center. The spot was personally selected by "Old Blood and Guts" himself, General George Patton. Eventually it was set aside by the Bureau of Land Management as a spot to honor General Patton and the soldiers who followed him into battle against German General Rommel in North Africa. The museum opened November 11, 1988 at 11 in the morning. It would have been General Patton's one hundredth birthday. A crowd of over 5000 attended the opening. Here you will see, explore and touch the tanks and other artifacts of that period. The museum includes a large tank yard with tanks ranging from World War II through the Vietnam War.

⦿◗⤳COALINGA, CA (HARRIS RANCH - 3O8)
Aprt Mgr: JACK BROWN **PH:** 559-935-0717
Field Elevation: 470 **CTAF:** 122.900 **FUEL:** 100LL
Runway: 14/32 **Length:** 2820 **Width:** 30 **Surface:** ASPH-G

★★★★★ Harris Ranch Restaurant - (599) 935-0717
Chef: Erasmo Rodriguez
Open:
> 7 days lunch and dinner

Restaurant Website: harrisranch.com/dine_steakhouse.php
Restaurant Email: service@harrisranch.com
PIREP:
It does not get any better period! It's been here since 1937 so they've had plenty of time to get it right. They have used their time well. It is the best fly-in restaurant you will ever visit. The airstrip's large parking

ramp is literally adjacent to the restaurant. The menu is overwhelming with beef choices from steaks and filets to pot roast (which is elegant). The service is superb, the decor compliments the menu, and the prices are very reasonable given the quality of the food. Worth the trip even if it is out of the way. I diverted 45 minutes from my flight path to come here the first time. Don't miss this one.

★ ★ ★ ★ ★ **Harris Ranch Inn - (599) 935-0717**
Proprietor: The Harris Family
Open:
      Always
Restaurant Website: harrisranch.com
PIREP: service@harrisranch.com
The Inn claims to be of a "higher quality". It is. On the grounds you'll find a 25 meter Olympic style, heated pool and three spas. Once inside, your last visit to a Ritz-Carlton property will come to mind. It is premium class. Thankfully the rates aren't. My advice is to check-in enjoy your dinner paired with the wine or cocktail of your choice knowing that you won't be in the cockpit until you are rested and refreshed. The great restaurant and great hotel are made better by the Harris Ranch Store where you can buy beef to go!

CORONA, CA (CORONA MUNI - AJO)
    Aprt Mgr: RICHARD BRODEUR PH: 951-736-2289
    Field Elevation: 533 CTAF: 122.700 FUEL: 100LLA
    Runway: 07/25 Length: 3200 Width: 60 Surface: ASPH-G

Corona Airport Cafe - (951) 273-1643
Proprietor: Jorge Gomez
Open:
      Mon - Sun: 6:00 am - 3:00 pm
Restaurant Website: www.coronaairportcafe.com
PIREP:
This is a very basic airport restaurant that shows what a difference great service can make. On my recent visit the manager came out to say hello and no he didn't know who we were and we didn't tell him.

EL MONTE, CA (EL MONTE - EMT)
    Aprt Mgr: CHRIS BROOKS **PH:** 626-448-6129
    Field Elevation: 296 **CTAF:** 121.200 **FUEL:** 100LLA
    Runway: 01/19 **Length:** 3995 **Width:** 75 **Surface:** ASPH-G

★ ★ ★ **Annia's Kitchen - (626) 401-2422**
Proprietor: Flavio Bugarin
Open:

Mon - Thu: 7:00 am - 8:00 pm
Fri - Sat: 6:00 am - 8:00 pm
Sun: 6:00 am - 3:00 pm

Restaurant Website: anniaskitchen.net
PIREP:
Right next to the ramp/transient parking. I came here to enjoy watch the sunset from the terrace while eating a burger and fries and enjoying the view. Great ambiance from this family run haven.

⦿FRESNO, CA (FRESNO CHANDLER EXECUTIVE - FCH)
Aprt Mgr: RICK DUNCAN **PH:** 559-621-7677
Field Elevation: 279 **CTAF:** 123.000 **FUEL:** 100LLA
Runway: 12/30 **Length:** 3630 **Width:** 75 **Surface:** ASPH-G

★★ **Tailspin Tommy's – (559) 268-2880**
Proprietor: Geneva and Bruce McJunkin
Open:
Tue – Thurs: 10am - 2pm
Fri – Sat: 7am - 2pm
Restaurant Website: tailspintommys.com
PIREP:
Taxi to the main terminal building, tie-down and go inside. I haven't personally been here. The reports from our volunteer Burger Patrol Pilots are mixed. I give it a definite maybe for now.

⦿HALF MOON BAY, CA (HALF MOON BAY - HAF)
Aprt Mgr: MARK LARSON **PH:** 650-573-3700
Field Elevation: 66 **CTAF:** 122.800 **FUEL:** 100LL
Runway: 12/30 **Length:** 5000 **Width:** 150 **Surface:** ASPH-CONC-G

★★★★**Three Zero Café – (650) 728-1411**
Proprietor: Mark Smith
Open:
Mon – Fri: 8am – 2pm
Sat – Sun: 7am – 3pm
Restaurant Website: www.3-zerocafe.com
PIREP:
Fog! Watch out for the fog. The marine layer rolls in quickly. That said this is my favorite California airport and one of my favorite restaurants. Most come here for breakfast and I have too. It's good but for me lunch is the better option. My reason is the GRILLED salmon. I pair it with a Double Vanilla Malt.

⦿HEMET, CA (HEMET-RYAN - HMT)
Aprt Mgr: DARYL SHIPPY **PH:** 951-955-9722

Field Elevation: 1512 **CTAF:** 123.000 **FUEL:** 100LLA
Runway: 04/22 **Length:** 2045 **Width:** 25 **Surface:** ASPH-G
Runway: 05/23 **Length:** 4314 **Width:** 100 **Surface:** ASPH-G

★ ★ ★ ★ **Hangar One Cafe - (951)766-5460**
Proprietor: Willie Cliff
Open:

        Mon - Sat 6:30am - 2:30pm
        Sun: 7:30am - 2:30pm

PIREP:
You can taxi all the up and tiedown in front of the rear deck. The restaurant is very small and the crowd can sometimes be large. The food and service is good. The big problem is that there is only one restroom; plan on standing in line to use it.

HESPERIA, CA (HESPERIA - L26)
    Aprt Mgr: GARRY ABBOTT **PH:** 760-947-0807
    Field Elevation: 3390 **CTAF:** 123.000 **FUEL:** 100LL
    Runway: 03/21 **Length:** 3910 **Width:** 50 **Surface:** ASPH-F

★ ★ ★ **Mile High Cafe – (760) 947-8844**
Proprietor: Bennie and Michele
Open:

        Mon – Sun: 6am – 2pm

Restaurant Website: www.milehighcafe.com
Restaurant Email: michelelyell@msn.com
PIREP:
It's a sports bar complete with pool tables, darts and HD TVs as well as an airport café. The first time I came here I was impressed with the outside patio because it has an awning covering it so you can sit outside even at noon in the summer without being roasted. Breakfast was being served and I went with the polish sausage and eggs because it was the first time I had ever seen polish sausage available for breakfast at an airport. Man was it good.

KERNVILLE, CA (KERN VALLEY - L05)
    Aprt Mgr: RON BREWSTER **PH:** 661-391-1800
    Field Elevation: 2614 **CTAF:** 122.800 **FUEL:**
    Runway: 17/35 **Length:** 3500 **Width:** 50 **Surface:** ASPH-G

★ ★ ★ **The Airport Café - (760) 376-2852**
Open:

        Mon – Sun: 7am – 6pm

Restaurant Website: www.kernvalleyairport.com/page6.html
PIREP:

The restaurant is very rustic having a log cabin appearance. The restaurant is right on the ramp with two rows of parking available. Be warned that it slopes and your plane can roll if not chocked and tied down. Also be aware that this airport can draw a crowd on the weekends. The scenery is excellent and the airport is very laid back. You can listen to UNICOM on the patio. The old crusty local pilots will grade the landings and takeoffs. The food and service are more than adequate. You'll be happy but not overjoyed.

★★Kern Valley Airport Campground
Open:
> Always

Camping Website: www.kernvalleyairport.com/page8.html
PIREP:
The campground is managed by the Airport Café. It is adjacent to the runway and has paved tie-downs for about 10 aircraft. The campground itself is a large grassy area shaded by many large trees. A picnic table and a fire pit are located at each camping space. Water is available from a spigot and a hose is provided for filling a black barrel above a shower enclosure for taking a *"solar shower."* The sanitary facility is only a portable potty but it is adequate. Tie-down/space rental is $15 per day. It's a long walk from the campground to the café since the campground is at the north end of the runway and the café is at the south end, but it's only a short walk over to the Kern River which is the reason to camp here. The town of Kernville is within walking distance if you're in good shape. The airport has a beater car available to borrow.

‖●‖LANCASTER, CA (GENERAL WM J FOX AIRFIELD - WJF)
Aprt Mgr: STEVE IRVING **PH:** 661-940-1709
Field Elevation: 2351 **CTAF:** 120.300 **FUEL:** 100LLA
Runway: 06/24 **Length:** 7201 **Width:** 150 **Surface:** ASPH-G

★Foxy's Landing - (661) 949-2284
Proprietor: Joudi Alsady
Open:
> Mon – Sun: 7am – 3pm

PIREP:
It's an airport restaurant offering a good view of the runway. The food is risky and the service is spotty. Expect little and you won't be disappointed.

‖●‖LA VERNE, CA (BRACKETT FIELD - POC)
Aprt Mgr: CYLE WOODRUFF **PH:** 909-593-1395

Field Elevation: 1014 **CTAF:** 118.200 **FUEL:** 100LLA
Runway: 08L/26R **Length:** 3661 **Width:** 75 **Surface:** ASPH-G
Runway: 08R/26L **Length:** 4841 **Width:** 75 **Surface:** ASPH-G

★★★Norm's Hangar - (909) 596-6675
Open:
        Mon – Sun: 7am – 3pm
Restaurant Website: www.normshangar.com
PIREP:
The view from the patio is awesome; ramp, taxiway, runway and mountains. You see them all in that order. This is a busy place on the weekends. Plan to come late if not you'll wait to be seated and served and you'll be unhappy. Come later and you'll feel that you got the royal treatment complete with princely food.

⦿LODI, CA (LODI - 1O3)
        Airport Website: www.lodiairport.com
        Aprt Mgr: ROBERT KUPKA **PH:** 209-369-9126
        Field Elevation: 60 **CTAF:** 122.900 **FUEL:** 100LL80 A
        Runway: 12/30 **Length:** 2073 **Width:** 26 **Surface:** ASPH-F
        Runway: 08/26 **Length:** 3735 **Width:** 42 **Surface:** ASPH-F

★★★★Lodi Airport Café - (209) 369-6144
Proprietor: Joann Sturgeon
Open:
        Mon – Sun: 7am – 2pm
Restaurant Website:
www.lodiairport.com/RESTAURANT/restaurant.html
PIREP:
The cafe sits right on the flight line which makes it easy to find. There is a good view of the flight line but the real show is overhead. There is a skydiving operation here. Bring along some folding chairs. After your meal spend some time here and watch. It is very, very entertaining. It can get very, very crowded here on the weekend.

What about the food? The restaurant is chef owned and operated. She provides some of the best food I have every eaten. The ambiance is crisp and clean with appropriate decoration. On one wall hangs a piece of nose art apparently clipped from the bomber that once displayed it.

⦿MOJAVE, CA (MOJAVE - MHV)
        Airport Website: mojaveairport.com
        Aprt Mgr: STU WITT **PH:** 661-824-2433
        Field Elevation: 2801 **CTAF:** 127.600 **FUEL:** 100LLA
        Runway: 12/30 **Length:** 12503 **Width:** 200 **Surface:** ASPH-E

www.100dollarhamburger.com

Runway: 08/26 **Length:** 7049 **Width:** 100 **Surface:** ASPH-G
Runway: 04/22 **Length:** 3946 **Width:** 50 **Surface:** ASPH-P

★ ★ ★ Voyager Restaurant - (661) 824-2048
Proprietor: Joudi Alsaady
Open:
> Mon – Fri: 7am – 3pm
> Sat: 8am – 3pm
> Sun: 8am – 2pm

Restaurant Website: mojaveairport.com/visit/voyager
PIREP:
Mohave is a museum of the future which celebrates the past. **The Voyager Restaurant** is located on the flight line in the terminal under the old tower. After you land request taxi instruction to the old tower. Get a table next to the window. The runway before you is all about the history and the future of flight. Yesterday's record holders jumped off of this pavement just as tomorrows dreams of private space flight are being launched today. The tower radio is piped to each table so you'll know when to look. The food is good not special but good. The service is caring and friendly. Come here if you can. You'll leave happy to know that the best days of aviation are ahead of us. We can still dream of going where no man has gone before with the encouragement that we can be that man just as others have been before us. One day we can all be astronauts because of the men and women who call Mohave home.

ＭONTEREY, CA (MONTEREY PENINSULA - MRY)
Airport Website: www.montereyairport.com
Aprt Mgr: THOMAS E. GREER **PH:** 831-648-7000
Field Elevation: 257 **CTAF:** 118.400 **FUEL:** 100LLA
Runway: 10R/28L **Length:** 7616 **Width:** 150 **Surface:** ASPH
Runway: 10L/28R **Length:** 3513 **Width:** 60 **Surface:** ASPH-G

★ ★ ★ The Golden Tee Restaurant and Bar - (831) 373-1232
Proprietors: Melinda Scardina, Michael & George Reta
Open:
> Mon – Wed: 9am – 9pm
> Thurs – Sun: 8:30am – 9pm

Restaurant Website: www.goldenteemonterey.com
PIREP:
The Golden Tee Restaurant and Bar is located on the second floor of the terminal building and offers great views of Monterey Bay and the airport. You'll watch takeoffs and landings if they're using Runway 10, and taxiing airplanes if they're using Runway 28. I come here for the **Monterey Combo** – Sand Dabs and Calamari. Amazing!!!!

🍴OROVILLE, CA (OROVILLE MUNI - OVE)
    Aprt Mgr: RICK WALLS **PH:** 530-538-2420
    Field Elevation: 194 **CTAF:** 122.800 **FUEL:** 100LLA
    Runway: 12/30 **Length:** 3540 **Width:** 100 **Surface:** ASPH-G
    Runway: 01/19 **Length:** 6020 **Width:** 100 **Surface:** ASPH-G

★★★**The Restaurant at Table Mountain Golf Club - (530) 533-3922 ext. 101**
Open:
    Mon - Fri: 8am – 3pm
    Sat – Sun: 7am – 3pm
Restaurant Website: www.tablemountaingolf.com/restaurant.html#
PIREP:
The restaurant is at the golf course which adjoins the Oroville. The decor is typical golf club. Don't worry that the restaurant is on the opposite side of the airport from the FBO as you can taxi right to the golf club where there are tie-downs. They have sit-down service. The food is good and the service enthusiastic.

★★★**Table Mountain Golf Club – (530) 533-3922 ext. 100**
Open:
    Daily
Golf Club Website: www.tablemountaingolf.com
PIREP:
This is a very, very flat 18 hole course that is also a great flyin. You can literally tie-down in their parking lot. The green fee with cart is about fifty bucks. If you show up after 3PM they offer a $25 Twilight Special.

🍴PALO ALTO, CA (PALO ALTO ARPT OF SANTA CLARA CO - PAO)
    Aprt Mgr: CHRIS NUCCI **PH:** 408-918-7700
    Field Elevation: 7 **CTAF:** 118.600 **FUEL:** 100LLA
    Runway: 13/31 **Length:** 2443 **Width:** 70 **Surface:** ASPH-G

★★★**Abundant Air Café – (650) 858-1003**
Proprietors: Harpik Avetian & Dennis Mcknew
Open:
    Mon – Fri: 7:30am – 4pm
Restaurant Website: www.abundantair.com
PIREP:
This is a deli a very good deli but a deli. You stand in line to order and pick up your food. They have really good Panini sandwiches. I have enjoyed the Chipotle Roast Beef more than once. That and a lemon drop smoothie and I'm good to go.

www.100dollarhamburger.com

⊚PERRIS, CA (PERRIS VALLEY - L65)
    Aprt Mgr: PAT CONATSER **PH:** 951-943-9673

    Field Elevation: 1413 **CTAF:** 122.775 **FUEL:** 100LLA
    Runway: 15/33 **Length:** 5100 **Width:** 50 **Surface:** ASPH-P

    ★ ★ ★ ★The Bombshelter Bar & Grill – (951) 943-4863
    Proprietor: Ben Conatser
    Open:
        Mon – Sun: 8am - Sunset
    Restaurant Website: www.skydiveperris.com/facilities.aspx
    Restaurant Email: bombshelter@skydiveperris.com
    PIREP:
When you fly in, remain west of the field and call Unicom at least 5 miles out. The jump zone is east of the field and the ultralights remain generally south. The runway is in good condition and paved for at least 3,000 feet and then extends to 5,100 with smooth dirt. **The Bombshelter Bar & Grill** is on the **Skydive Perris** property. Typically I grab my grub and head for the outside patio and pull up a lounge chair by the pool. That's right they have a pool for their guest and yes you can use it. I can sit here for hours on a Saturday watching the Skydivers do their thing. This is probably the best skydive facility in the world. They have the usual planes in the fleet plus a DC-9 jet. By the way, this is the place to skydive if you're up for it because you don't have to jump from a plane. They have a terrific indoor skydive setup. It is way cool!

⊚PETALUMA, CA (PETALUMA MUNI - O69)
    Aprt Mgr: BOB PATTERSON **PH:** 707-778-4404
    Field Elevation: 90 **CTAF:** 122.700 **FUEL:** 100LLA
    Runway: 11/29 **Length:** 3601 **Width:** 75 **Surface:** ASPH-F

    ★ ★ ★ The Two Niner Diner - 707-765-2900
    Proprietor: Joan Kelly
    Open:
        Wed – Sun: 8am – 3pm
    PIREP:
The restaurant is right on the ramp and offers indoor and outdoor dining. Stay outside if you can. The views of the hills and the runway are worth it. The food is a very good example of airport diner fare. I have been here for breakfast and had the Country Pilot which includes eggs, sausage and biscuits with gravy. It was very good.

⊚PORTERVILLE, CA (PORTERVILLE MUNI - PTV)

Aprt Mgr: JIM MCDONALD **PH:** 559-782-7540
Field Elevation: 443 **CTAF:** 122.800 **FUEL:** 100LL80 A
Runway: 12/30 **Length:** 5960 **Width:** 150 **Surface:** ASPH-G

★★★**Airway Cafe - (559) 784-8208**
Proprietor: Richard & Tami Chilcutt
Open:
      Wed – Mon: 8am – 2pm
Restaurant Website: facebook.com/pages/Airway-Cafe/253902174626697?rf=113159518713456
Restaurant Email: rtchilcutt@aol.com
PIREP:
Transient parking is well marked and plentiful right in front of the terminal building. The restaurant is right inside. The terminal has some nice murals of vintage aircraft and firefighting planes. Overall, this is a good *"blue plate"* restaurant. The service is very efficient and friendly.

⦿RED BLUFF, CA (RED BLUFF MUNI - RBL)
Aprt Mgr: MARTIN NICHOLS **PH:** 530-527-2605
Field Elevation: 352 **CTAF:** 123.000 **FUEL:** 100LLA
Runway: 15/33 **Length:** 5431 **Width:** 100 **Surface:** ASPH-G

★★★**Valeigh's Airpark Restaurant - (530) 529-6420**
Proprietor: Leigh Dougdale
Open:
      Mon - Sun: 7am – 2pm
PIREP:
Valeigh's Airpark Restaurant is located upstairs in the terminal. It provides a view of the runway and the surrounding mountains. The best thing about this restaurant is the service. The waitresses are the nicest I have ever encountered. The food is good and the prices low.

⦿REDDING, CA (REDDING MUNI - RDD)
Aprt Mgr: ROD DINGER **PH:** 530-224-4321
Field Elevation: 505 **CTAF:** 119.800 **FUEL:** 100LLA
Runway: 12/30 **Length:** 5067 **Width:** 150 **Surface:** ASPH-G
Runway: 16/34 **Length:** 7003 **Width:** 150 **Surface:** ASPH-G

★★★**Peter Chu's Skyroom - (530) 222-1364**
Proprietor: Peter Chu
Open:
      Mon - Sat: 11:00 am - 9:00 pm
      Sun: 12:00 pm - 8:00 pm
Restaurant Website: www.peterchus.com
PIREP:

Peter Chu's Skyroom is upstairs above the terminal. It has huge windows so you can watch air operations and a nice, friendly atmosphere. The staff is efficient and courteous. The best part is the home style Chinese food. It offers a great escape from the usual burgers and fried things found at virtually every other airport restaurant.

⁑RIVERSIDE, CA (RIVERSIDE MUNI - RAL)
Aprt Mgr: MARK RIPLEY **PH:** 951-351-6113
Field Elevation: 819 **CTAF:** 121.000 **FUEL:** 100LLA
Runway: 16/34 **Length:** 2850 **Width:** 50 **Surface:** ASPH-F
Runway: 09/27 **Length:** 5401 **Width:** 100 **Surface:** ASPH-G

★★D&D Cafe - (951) 688-3337
Proprietor: Dave and Delmy
Open:
Mon-Sat: 6:30am-7:00pm
Sun: 6:30am-4:00pm
Restaurant Website: facebook.com/pages/DD-Airport-Cafe/192400990785101
Restaurant Email: dndcafe@juno.com
PIREP:
This is a very standard airport restaurant with an extra dose of friendly. It is on the ramp, has an outside patio and the obligatory runway view. The food is really uninspired and unimpressive. I have been back because I like the people.

⁑RIVERSIDE/RUBIDOUX/, CA (FLABOB - RIR)
Aprt Mgr: LEO L DOIRON **PH:** 951-683-2309
Field Elevation: 764 **CTAF:** 122.800 **FUEL:** 100LL80
Runway: 06/24 **Length:** 3200 **Width:** 50 **Surface:** ASPH-F

★★★ Flabob Airport Café - (951) 686-6660
Open:
Mon - Sun: 6:30am-3:00pm
PIREP:
The airport is a step back in time and that's probably worth the trip. The restaurant is on the ramp and has a great view of the runways and the brown desert mountains. The food is very standard airport café faire. The service is good. What makes this place work for me is the customers. This is a great place to hangar fly and learn things you never knew you never knew.

⁑SACRAMENTO, CA (SACRAMENTO EXECUTIVE - SAC)
Aprt Mgr: JOHN DOWNEY **PH:** 916-875-9035

Field Elevation: 24 **CTAF:** 119.500 **FUEL:** 100LLA
Runway: 16/34 **Length:** 3485 **Width:** 150 **Surface:** ASPH-G
Runway: 12/30 **Length:** 3836 **Width:** 100 **Surface:** ASPH-G
Runway: 02/20 **Length:** 5503 **Width:** 150 **Surface:** ASPH-G

★★★Aviator's Restaurant - (916) 424-1728
Open:

> Mon – Sun: 7am - 3pm
>
> Fri - Sat: 5pm - 9pm

Restaurant Website:
www.sacramento.aero/sac/facilities_services/businesses/
PIREP:
Aviator's Restaurant is on the second floor of the terminal building and provides the great runway view you would expect from that vantage point. The décor is a nice mix of brick and wood. It has a very folksy feel. I came here for breakfast and was glad I did. Imagine eggs and hash browns set beside a gravy covered chicken fried steak. It cannot get any better than that. Breakfast and lunch on one plate!

🍴SALINAS, CA (SALINAS MUNI - SNS)
Aprt Mgr: GARY PETERSEN **PH:** 831-758-7214

Field Elevation: 85 **CTAF:** 119.400 **FUEL:** 100LLA
Runway: 14/32 **Length:** 1900 **Width:** 50 **Surface:** ASPH-G
Runway: 13/31 **Length:** 4825 **Width:** 150 **Surface:** ASPH-G
Runway: 08/26 **Length:** 6003 **Width:** 150 **Surface:** ASPH-G

★★★Landing Zone - (831) 758-9663
Proprietor: James Clemis
Open: Daily: Breakfast & Lunch Closed Sunday
PIREP:
This is California and the views you get while flying are their own payoff. You can often see the Sierras about 120+ miles away as you slide into Salinas. The controllers in the tower are nice guys and when you taxi up, there is someone from the FBO to greet you and direct you to a tie down. The restaurant is a short talk down the ramp. The food is good, the service fine and the view adequate. It is a small place and it can get really crowded. It feels cramped to me.

🍴SAN CARLOS, CA (SAN CARLOS - SQL)
Aprt Mgr: MARK LARSON **PH:** 650-573-3700
Field Elevation: 5 **CTAF:** 119.000 **FUEL:** 100LLA
Runway: 12/30 **Length:** 2600 **Width:** 75 **Surface:** ASPH-G

★★★★★Izzy's Steakhouse - (650) 654-2822

Open:

        Mon – Fri: 11:30am – 10pm

        Sat – Sun: 5pm – 10pm

Restaurant Website: www.izzyssteaks.com

PIREP:

We don't hand out five stars lightly. This is a great place. Park by the Hiller Museum. It is a very short walk from there to **Izzy's**. The original **Izzy's** is in the San Francisco Marina district. It is a steakhouse. Yes they serve fish but pass on that come here for MEAT! For a steak to be good it has to be aged and that is what Izzy's does. They buy the best Midwestern beef that's available and then they age it for 21 days. Next they cook it to perfection in accordance with your taste. Bring a client here for lunch. Bring your significant other here for dinner. I look forward to my next visit.

★ ★ ★ ★ Sky Kitchen Cafe - 650-595-0464

Proprietor: Ben Abolmoluki

Open:

        Mon – Sun: 6am – 3pm

Restaurant Website: www.skykitchencafe.com

PIREP:

This too is one of my favorites. It is a very California kind of place. Clean and modern with a menu filled with fresh, healthy items. They offer 40 different kinds of omelets for breakfast. If none of them float your boat number 41 is titled U-Do-It. I like the Chili and Cheese which exposes my Texas roots.

★ ★ ★ Hiller Aviation Museum - 650-595-0464

Director: Jeffery Bass

Open:

        Mon – Sun: 10am – 5pm

Museum Website: www.hiller.org

Museum Email: jeff@hiller.org

PIREP:

After clearing the runway contact the Ground Frequency and ask for the Northwest Transient parking. There is a walkthrough gate that leads out behind **Izzy's** restaurant. It is a short walk to the museum. (Remember the gate code. You'll need it to re-enter). There are several wonderful exhibits here my two favorites are the **1945 Hiller 360** *(first inherently-stable helicopter to be licensed by the FAA)* and the fully accessible Boeing 747 cockpit.

🍴SAN DIEGO/EL CAJON, CA (GILLESPIE FIELD - SEE)
    Aprt Mgr: ROGER GRIFFITHS **PH:** 619-956-4805

Field Elevation: 388 **CTAF:** 120.700 **FUEL:** 100LLA
Runway: 09R/27L **Length:** 2738 **Width:** 60 **Surface:** ASPH-G
Runway: 17/35 **Length:** 4145 **Width:** 100 **Surface:** ASPH-G
Runway: 09L/27R **Length:** 5342 **Width:** 100 **Surface:** ASPH-G

★★★**Gillespie Field Cafe - (619) 448-0415**
Proprietor: Roxanne & Peter Oliver
Open:
> Mon – Sun: 7am – 3pm

Restaurant Website: www.gillespiecafe.com
Restaurant Email: cafe@gillespiecafe.com
PIREP:
A nice place to talk airplanes, watch airplane and grab a decent meal. The food is the basic sandwich-and-fries fare. The service is always excellent. There is outdoor seating, as well as a few tables inside for those 2 days a year when the weather isn't perfect.

🍴**SAN DIEGO, CA (MONTGOMERY FIELD - MYF)**
Aprt Mgr: ERNIE GESELL **PH:** 858-573-1440
Field Elevation: 427 **CTAF:** 119.200 **FUEL:** 100LLA
Runway: 05/23 **Length:** 3400 **Width:** 150 **Surface:** ASPH-G
Runway: 10R/28L **Length:** 3401 **Width:** 60 **Surface:** ASPH-G
Runway: 10L/28R **Length:** 4577 **Width:** 150 **Surface:** ASPH-G

★★★★★**94th Aero Squadron - (858) 560-6771**
Open:
> Mon-Thurs: 11:00 am-9:00 pm
> Fri: 11:00 am-11:00 pm
> Sat: 11:00 am-10:00 pm
> Sun: 9:00 am.-3:00 pm

Restaurant Website: www.94thaerosquadron.signonsandiego.com
Restaurant Email: 94thsd@sbcglobal.net
PIREP:
If you've never eaten at a **94th AERO Squadron** you need to. If you've visited another location you'll be shocked at how much better this one is. Zagat rates it, as one of America's Top Restaurants with "very good to Excellent" review for 2013. I agree. It is probably the BEST place in San Diego county for Brunch.

★★**Casa Machado - (858) 292-4716**
Open:
> Mon – Sun: 11:00am - 9:00pm

Restaurant Website: casamachadomex.com
Restaurant Email:
PIREP:

Casa Machado is easy to find right at transient parking next to the terminal. I'm a huge Mexican food fan and this is good Mexican food. For me, breakfast is best. I like the Machaca.

☜SAN DIEGO, CA (BROWN FIELD MUNI - SDM)
  Aprt Mgr: CHRIS COOPER **PH:** 619-424-0456
  Field Elevation: 526 **CTAF:** 126.500 **FUEL:** 100LLA
  Runway: 08L/26R **Length:** 7972 **Width:** 150 **Surface:** ASPH-CONC-G
  Runway: 08R/26L **Length:** 3180 **Width:** 75 **Surface:** ASPH-G

★The Landing Strip Café & Bar - (619) 661-6038
Open:
   Mon – Sat: 6:30am – 8pm
   Sun: 8am – 2pm
Restaurant Website: facebook.com/pages/The-Landing-Strip/116285551729735
Restaurant Email: bbrown923©yahoo.com
PIREP:
It's on the airport so I am including it but……. This is not I place I would ever go to. It seems to be a down market bar with a small restaurant tacked on. So the ambiance is someplace between really bad to none existent. The food is reported to be pretty good. The offset is the service which is often described as rude.

☜SAN LUIS OBISPO, CA (SAN LUIS COUNTY RGNL - SBP)
  Aprt Mgr: RICHARD HOWELL **PH:** 805-781-5205
  Field Elevation: 212 **CTAF:** 124.000 **FUEL:** 100LLA
  Runway: 07/25 **Length:** 2500 **Width:** 100 **Surface:** ASPH-G
  Runway: 11/29 **Length:** 6100 **Width:** 150 **Surface:** ASPH-G

★★★The Spirit of San Luis - (805) 549-9466
Proprietor: Doug and Julie Wagnon
Open:
   Mon - Sat: 9:00 am - 8:00 pm
   Sun: 9:00 am - 3:00 pm
Restaurant Website: sloairport.com/airport_dining.html
PIREP:
The Spirit of San Luis Restaurant is located to the east of the terminal building. The outdoor patio has a great view of the runways. The food and the service are very good. The menu is a step above the normal airport burger and fries place.

★★Runway Cafe - (805) 781-0633
Open:

48

Mon - Fri: 4:30am - 5:00pm
Sat & Sun: 5:00am - 4:30pm
Restaurant Website: sloairport.com/airport_dining.html
PIREP:
The Runway Cafe is located in the terminal lobby to the right of the entrance doors. Fortunately, it is before TSA so you can slip in and slip out. This is not really a restaurant. It is a step above an airport terminal grab and go kiosk.

⦿SANTA MONICA, CA (SANTA MONICA MUNI - SMO)
Aprt Mgr: ROBERT TRIMBORN **PH:** 310-458-8591
Field Elevation: 177 **CTAF:** 120.100 **FUEL:** 100LLA
Runway: 03/21 **Length:** 4973 **Width:** 150 **Surface:** ASPH-G

★ ★ ★ **Spitfire Grill - (310) 397-3455**
Proprietor: John Clarizio
Open:
Sunday – Thursday 7:30am ~ 10:00pm
Friday – Saturday 7:30am ~ 10:00pm
Restaurant Website: www.spitfiregrill.net
Restaurant Email: Team@spitfiregrill.net
PIREP:
The Spitfire offers a broader menu than typical for an airport place but the food is mediocre. It has a cute aviation theme & art but **no view of airport**. It is actually across the street and behind a building.

★ ★ ★ ★ **Typhoon Restaurant - (310) 390-6565**
Open:
Lunch:
Sunday 11:30am – 2:30pm
Monday – Friday 12:00pm - 2:30pm
Dinner:
Sunday 5:00pm – 9:00pm
Monday – Thursday 5:30pm – 10:00pm
Friday – Saturday 5:30pm – 10:30pm
Restaurant Website: www.typhoon.biz
Restaurant Email: Team@typhoon.biz
Transient Parking for singles and light-twins is available right in front of **Typhoon** and the airport administration building on the south side of the field. The views from the Typhoon and the attached upper level observation deck are amazing. The food and service are very, very good here. The plus factor is the music. Check the website for the upcoming playbill. Expect to find great blues and jazz at two evening shows with a small cover.

www.100dollarhamburger.com

📷SANTA ROSA, CA (SONOMA COUNTY - STS)
    Aprt Mgr: JON G. STOUT **PH:** 707-565-7243
    Field Elevation: 128 **CTAF:** 118.500 **FUEL:** 100LLA
    Runway: 01/19 **Length:** 5004 **Width:** 100 **Surface:** ASPH-G
    Runway: 14/32 **Length:** 5119 **Width:** 150 **Surface:** ASPH-G

★★★**Skylounge Steak House and Raw Bar** – **(707) 542-9400**
Open:
    Mon – Sun: 7:30 am-10:00 pm
PIREP:
Skylounge Steak House and Raw Bar is right at the terminal. It's a short walk from Sonoma Jet Center where you can park for free. You can watch the runways and the commuter airline service from the patio. The food is good but not great. It is served quickly and with a smile. Avoid the sushi.

📷SOUTH LAKE TAHOE, CA (LAKE TAHOE - TVL)
    Aprt Mgr: SHERRY MILLER **PH:** 530-542-6182
    Field Elevation: 6269 **CTAF:** 122.950 **FUEL:** 100LLA
    Runway: 18/36 **Length:** 8541 **Width:** 100 **Surface:** ASPH-E

★★★**The Flight Deck Restaurant and Bar - 530-542-3325**
Proprietor: Tom & Diane Miller
Open:
    Mon-Fri: 11 am - 10 pm
    Sat-Sun: 8 am - 10 pm
Restaurant Website:
www.cityofslt.us/DocumentCenter/Home/View/943
PIREP:
The flight in is beautiful though somewhat challenging. It is in the mountains after all. Park the plane at Mountain West Aviation and go out the door to the building next door. You look directly over the airport and the mountains beyond. During the summer they have dining on the deck. The owner is a personable guy who will make you feel welcome. The food is very good and they have a full bar and an OK wine list.

📷STOCKTON, CA (STOCKTON METROPOLITAN - SCK)
    Aprt Mgr: PATRICK CARRENO **PH:** 209-468-4700
    Field Elevation: 33 **CTAF:** 120.300 **FUEL:** 100 100LLA
    Runway: 11R/29L **Length:** 4448 **Width:** 75 **Surface:** ASPH-G
    Runway: 11L/29R **Length:** 10650 **Width:** 150 **Surface:** ASPH-G

★★★**Top Flight Grill and Catering - (209) 944-7780**
Proprietor: Tommy Joyce

Open:

    Mon 10:30 am - 8 pm

    Tue-Sat 10:30 am - 5 pm

Restaurant Website: www.facebook.com/TopFlightGrillandCatering

PIREP:

It's a burger and fries on the ramp airport restaurant with an unusual interior and an outdoor seating area.

⭐TRUCKEE, CA (TRUCKEE-TAHOE - TRK)

Aprt Mgr: KEVIN SMITH **PH:** 530-587-4119

Field Elevation: 5901 **CTAF:** 122.800 **FUEL:** 100LLA A1+

Runway: 01/19 **Length:** 4650 **Width:** 75 **Surface:** ASPH-G

Runway: 10/28 **Length:** 7000 **Width:** 100 **Surface:** ASPH-G

★★★ **Red Truck on the Runway - (530) 587-1394**

Proprietor: Larry Abney

Open:

    Mon – Sun: 11am – 2pm

Restaurant Website: www.redtrucktahoe.com/cafe.html

Restaurant Email: yum@redtrucktahoe.com

PIREP:

Chef Larry Abney prepares and serves sustainable organic eats with bold flavors. For four years prior to opening his restaurant at the airport Chef Abney has been serving the same food out of a Big Red Food Truck which wonders the streets of Tahoe and caterings local events. If you are into sustainable organic eats with bold flavors, this is your place. If you're looking for a cheese burger – keep on flying.

⭐UPLAND, CA (CABLE - CCB)

Aprt Mgr: CHARLES R BARNETT **PH:** 909-982-6021

Field Elevation: 1444 **CTAF:** 123.000 **FUEL:** 100LLA

Runway: 06/24 **Length:** 3863 **Width:** 75 **Surface:** ASPH-E

★★★ **Maniac Mike's - (909) 982-9886**

Open:

    Mon – Sun: 7am - 3pm

Restaurant Website: www.maniac-mikes.com

Restaurant Email: maniac@ maniac-mikes.com

PIREP:

I like the place you will too. It has all of the dishes that you would expect at an airport diner for breakfast and lunch and a few that will surprise you. I think I may have gone a little too Californian because my favorite item is the salmon burger. It is really good.

⭐VAN NUYS, CA (VAN NUYS - VNY)

Aprt Mgr: JESS ROMO **PH:** 424-442-6500
Field Elevation: 802 **CTAF:** 119.300 **FUEL:** 100LLA
Runway: 16L/34R **Length:** 4011 **Width:** 75 **Surface:** ASPH-G
Runway: 16R/34L **Length:** 8001 **Width:** 150 **Surface:** ASPH-G

★ ★ ★ ★ ★ **The 94th Aero Squadron - (818) 994-7437**
Proprietor: David Mashagh
Open:

Lunch:

Mon - Thur: 11am - 4pm
Fri & Sat: 11am - 4pm

Dinner:

Mon - Thur: 4pm - 9pm
Fri & Sat: 4pm - 10pm
Sun: 4pm - 9pm

Brunch:

Sun: 9:00am - 3pm
Restaurant Website: www.94thvannuys.com
PIREP:
You come here because its fun and you'll enjoy your meal ass you overlook Runway 16R, the most famous runway in general aviation. It was the movie that immortalized it that brought me in for Sunday Brunch. Van Nuys is also the world's busiest GA airport with about 1,000 operations each day. You won't be bored. I like the food. The service is unhurried. Many believe it is over-priced and that's probably true but it is a very nice aviation themed restaurant with an amazing view. I think it's worth every penny they ask. The issue here is getting to it. The restaurant does not have a ramp so you MUST park at one of the FBOs and get a ride to the restaurant.

★ ★ ★ ★ **The Landing - 818-997-7412**
Proprietor: Executive Chef Desi Szonntagh
Open:

Mon-Sun: 6 am - 9 pm
Restaurant Website: www.airtelplaza.com
Restaurant Email: jdunn@airtelplaza.com
PIREP:
The Landing Restaurant is located in the **Airtel Plaza Hotel** which has its own ramp. Taxi over, tie-down and walk to the lobby. **The 94th Aero Squadron** wins the ambiance battle but The Landing scores on food service and price. I had dinner here and thoroughly enjoyed a New York Strip steak which was cooked by a person that knew what to do.

★ ★ ★ ★ ★ The Airtel Plaza Hotel - 818-997-7412
Open:
> **Always**

Hotel Website: www.airtelplaza.com
Hotel Email: jdunn@airtelplaza.com
If you are flying into the LA area on business this is where you stay, no question about it. I like the hotel and I like the restaurants in it. I am also a huge fan of this airport. The hotel is right on the runway so there is noise. I love the sound of airplanes. It puts me to sleep.

WATSONVILLE, CA (WATSONVILLE MUNI - WVI)
Aprt Mgr: DON FRENCH **PH:** 831-728-6064
Field Elevation: 163 **CTAF:** 122.800 **FUEL:** 100LLA
Runway: 08/26 **Length:** 3999 **Width:** 100 **Surface:** ASPH-G
Runway: 02/20 **Length:** 4501 **Width:** 150 **Surface:** ASPH-G

★ ★ ★ Props Restaurant & Lounge - 831-724-7767
Proprietor: Andrew and Kryss Crocker
Open:
> Mon - Thu: 11:00 am - 9:00 pm
> Fri - Sat: 11:00 am - 10:00 pm
> Sun: 11:00 am - 9:00 pm

Restaurant Website: www.propsrestaurant.com
Restaurant Email: ContactProps@gmail.com
PIREP:
Props Restaurant & Lounge is one half airport diner and one half sports bar. It is a good mix. Located right off the ramp, nice ambience with standard airplane paraphernalia, outdoor patio looking over the ramp and runway, and a well-stocked bar with plenty of wide screens for sporting events.

WILLOWS, CA (WILLOWS-GLENN COUNTY - WLW)
Aprt Mgr: ANNETTE CHAVEZ **PH:** 530-934-6546
Field Elevation: 141 **CTAF:** 122.800 **FUEL:** 100LL
Runway: 13/31 **Length:** 3788 **Width:** 60 **Surface:** ASPH-F
Runway: 16/34 **Length:** 4125 **Width:** 100 **Surface:** ASPH-G

★ ★ ★ ★ Nancy's Airport Cafe - (530) 934-7211
Open:
> Mon – Sun: 8am – 7pm

Restaurant Website: www.nancysairportcafewillows.com
PIREP:
This is a well-established, family run, airport diner. The food is really very good and the service is tops. I come here for the airport. Things happen here. The Forest Service runs their fire control operations out of

Willows during fire season. They have an amazing arsenal of aircraft. On weekends many private aviators head here for breakfast. I hope to be among them again very soon. On the flight line you will find, LSAs, Experimentals, certified machines and warbirds sporting propellers and jet engines.

▌◉▌WOODLAKE, CA (WOODLAKE - O42)

Aprt Mgr: CRUZ DOMINGUEZ **PH:** 559-564-8055
Field Elevation: 425 **CTAF:** 122.900 **FUEL:** 100LL
Runway: 07/25 **Length:** 2203 **Width:** 50 **Surface:** ASPH-TRTD-G

★ ★ ★ The Runway Café - (559) 564-3986
Proprietor: Thelma Venturella
Open:
> Mon – Sun: 7am – 2pm

PIREP:

Woodlake is a small *(3320ft X 50ft)* airport nestled at the foot of the Sierras about 15 min. north of Porterville. They offer Chevron self-serve and plenty of parking right in front of the restaurant. The restaurant is rustic. It resembles an old wooden cabin. The food is good with a wide selection. I have been here for breakfast which is my favorite meal of the day probably because it is difficult to mess-up. I had biscuits and am pleased to report that they were expertly made on site.

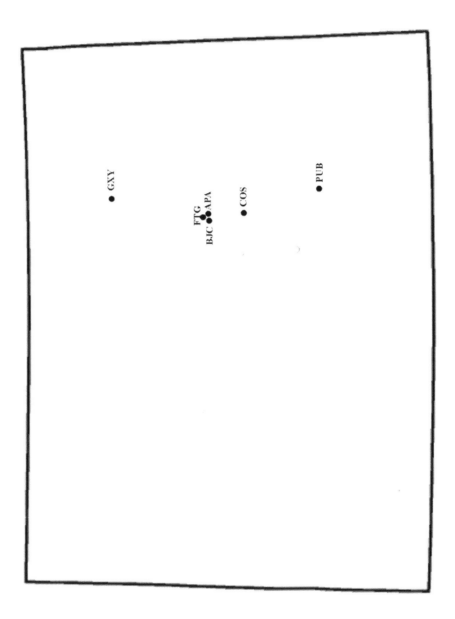

FlyIn Colorado

๏COLORADO SPRINGS, CO (COLORADO SPRINGS MUNI - COS)
Aprt Mgr: MARK N. EARLE PH: 719-550-1900
Field Elevation: 6187 CTAF: 0.000 FUEL: 100LLA
Runway: 13/31 Length: 8269 Width: 150 Surface: ASPH-G
Runway: 17R/35L Length: 11022 Width: 150 Surface: ASPH-G
Runway: 17L/35R Length: 13501 Width: 150 Surface: CONC-G

★★★The Airplane Restaurant - (719) 570-7656
Proprietor: Steve Kanatzar
Open:
> Mon - Thurs: 11:00 am - 9:00pm
> Fri – Sun: 11:00 am - 10:00pm

Restaurant Website: www.solosrestaurant.com
Restaurant Email: Solosrestaurant@aol.com
PIREP:
The Airplane Restaurant is a short walk from the Colorado Jet Center and is immediately adjacent to the Radisson. The decor is wonderful. A mammoth Boeing KC-97 tanker is glued onto the restaurant's main building. You can actually dine on it if you like. The servers introduce themselves as "flight attendants". The food very good, I highly recommend the Rueben paired with the onion rings.

๏DENVER, CO (ROCKY MOUNTAIN METROPOLITAN - BJC)
Aprt Mgr: KENNETH MAENPA PH: 303-271-4850
Field Elevation: 5673 CTAF: 118.600 FUEL: 100LLA
Runway: 02/20 Length: 3600 Width: 75 Surface: ASPH-F
Runway: 11R/29L Length: 7002 Width: 75 Surface: ASPH-G
Runway: 11L/29R Length: 9000 Width: 100 Surface: ASPH-G

★★★★The Bluesky Bistro - 720-628-5213
Proprietor: Dan and Sherise
Open:
> Mon – Fri: 7:00am-2:00pm

Restaurant Website: www.blueskybistro.com
Restaurant Email: info@blueskybistro.com
PIREPS:
The Bluesky Bistro is located in the Main Terminal. It offers fantastic views of the Flatirons and the runways from the patio or upper level of the Terminal. The food is just south of awesome. Plan to show up Wednesday through Friday so you may have the option of enjoying their BBQ.

★ ★ ★ **Runway Grill - 720-887-1004**
Open:
> Tues – Sat: 7:30am - 9:00pm
> Sun – Mon: 7:30am - 3:00pm

Restaurant Website: www.therunwaygrill.com
Restaurant Email: Runwaygrill@gmail.com
PIREP:
The Runway Grill is also located in the Main Terminal. Like the **Bluesky Bistro** it offers fantastic views of the Flatirons and the runways. The food to my taste is a cut below the **Bluesky Bistro** the service is equal. Here's the plus point, it stays open later. If you're looking for a late lunch or dinner this is your place.

⦿DENVER, CO (CENTENNIAL - APA)

Aprt Mgr: ROBERT OLISLAGERS **PH:** 303-790-0598
Field Elevation: 5885 **CTAF:** 0.000 **FUEL:** 100LLA
Runway: 10/28 **Length:** 4800 **Width:** 75 **Surface:** ASPH-G
Runway: 17R/35L **Length:** 7000 **Width:** 77 **Surface:** ASPH-G
Runway: 17L/35R **Length:** 10001 **Width:** 100 **Surface:** ASPH-G

★ ★ ★ ★ ★ **The Perfect Landing - (303) 649-4478**
Proprietor: Jim and Sean Carter
Open:
> Sun – Mon: 7am-9pm
> Tue – Sat: 7am to 10pm

Restaurant Website: www.theperfectlanding.com
PIREP:
Food good, service fast, drinks for your passengers and wonderful airport and mountain views. Park at the Jet Center, fuel is priced well and they will put you right in front of the restaurant's window. This is one of the great on-field restaurants. Go on a Friday night and get a few dances in by the piano. In the evening the ambiance changes considerably. The white table clothes come out, candles are placed on each table and the piano bar fires up. It is a great place to take a date. **The Perfect Landing** is my favorite restaurant in the mountain states.

⦿DENVER, CO (FRONT RANGE - FTG)

Aprt Mgr: ROBERT OLISLAGERS **PH:** 303-790-0598
Field Elevation: 5885 **CTAF:** 0.000 **FUEL:** 100LLA
Runway: 10/28 **Length:** 4800 **Width:** 75 **Surface:** ASPH-G
Runway: 17R/35L **Length:** 7000 **Width:** 77 **Surface:** ASPH-G
Runway: 17L/35R **Length:** 10001 **Width:** 100 **Surface:** ASPH-G

★ ★ ★ **Aviator Bar & Grill – (303) 261-4054**

Proprietor: Robert Bradley\
Chef: Giovanni Lanzante & Katie Place
Open:
>Mon – Sat: 9:30am - 2:30pm

Restaurant Website: www.ftg-airport.com/aviator_cafe.php
Restaurant Email: info@AviatorBarandGrill.com
PIREP:

⦿GREELEY, CO (GREELEY-WELD COUNTY - GXY)

Aprt Mgr: GARY CYR **PH:** 970-336-3000
Field Elevation: 4697 **CTAF:** 122.800 **FUEL:** 100LLA
Runway: 09/27 **Length:** 5801 **Width:** 100 **Surface:** ASPH-G
Runway: 16/34 **Length:** 10000 **Width:** 100 **Surface:** ASPH-G

★★★**Barnstormer Restaurant – (970) 336-3020**
Proprietor: Linda Belleau
Open:
>Mon – Sat: 7:00am - 2:30pm
>Sun: 7:00am- 12:00pm

Restaurant Website:
Restaurant Email: lindabelleau@comcast.net
PIREP:
The **Barnstormer Restaurant** has been in business since 1990. Clearly, they're doing something right. Initially it goes to location. They are in the airport terminal, right in front of the ramp area. I like seeing my plane while I eat breakfast. I can do that here. Next it's the food and service which are good if not spectacular. Expect airport diner fare and you won't be disappointed. Finally, it's the view which is spectacular. You can see the runway which is pretty standard but you can also see the mountains.

⦿PUEBLO, CO (PUEBLO MEMORIAL - PUB)

Aprt Mgr: MARK LOVIN **PH:** 719-553-2760
Field Elevation: 4729 **CTAF:** 119.100 **FUEL:** 100LLA
Runway: 08R/26L **Length:** 3767 **Width:** 75 **Surface:** ASPH-G
Runway: 17/35 **Length:** 8310 **Width:** 150 **Surface:** ASPH-G
Runway: 08L/26R **Length:** 10498 **Width:** 150 **Surface:** ASPH-G

★★★ **The Spitfire Grill Airfield Diner - (719) 948-4185**
Proprietor: Max Howells
Open:
>Mon – Sun: 8:00am - 2:30pm

Restaurant Website: www.spitfiregrillpueblo.com
PIREP:

The Spitfire Grill Airfield Diner is located in the terminal. It's an easy stroll from either of the FBOs. The owner/chef grew up here and has a vested interest in the community. His friends and family live close by. The food is good, the service is attentive. You'll be glad you came.

$100 Hamburger 2014/15

FlyIn Connecticut

HARTFORD, CT (HARTFORD-BRAINARD - HFD)
    Aprt Mgr: "SENDLEIN, KURT" **PH:** 860-566-7037
    Field Elevation: 18 **CTAF:** 119.600 **FUEL:** 100LLA
    Runway: 11/29 **Length:** 2314 **Width:** 71 **Surface:** ASPH-G
    Runway: 02/20 **Length:** 4417 **Width:** 150 **Surface:** ASPH-G
    Runway: NE/SW **Length:** 2309 **Width:** 150 **Surface:** TURF

★ **Wings - (218) 828-0206**
Proprietor: Tammy and Guy
Open:
        Mon – Fri: 6am – 2pm
        Sat: 7am – 2pm
        Sun: 8am – 2pm
Restaurant Website: brainerdairport.com/wings-cafe.html
PIREP:
Park at Atlantic Aviation it is connected to Wings. The ambiance is that of a slightly down market sports bar with multiple monitors and a pool table. The patrons, who are mostly locals, mirror the setting. The food is very good and the service about what you'd expect.

OXFORD, CT (WATERBURY-OXFORD - OXC)
    Aprt Mgr: MATTHEW J. KELLY **PH:** 203-264-8010
    Field Elevation: 726 **CTAF:** 118.475 **FUEL:** 100LLA
    Runway: 18/36 **Length:** 5800 **Width:** 100 **Surface:** ASPH-G

★ ★ ★ ★ ★ **121 Restaurant Bar - 203-262-0121**
Proprietor: The 121 group
Open:
        Tue – Thur: 11:30 am– 9:00 pm
        Fri – Sat: 12:00 pm – 10:00 pm
        Sun: 12:00 pm – 9:00 pm
Restaurant Website: 121group.com/restaurants/oxford-airport/about
Restaurant Email: catering@121atoxc.com
PIREP:
DOUBLE WOW!
A truly upscale restaurant that is almost on the runway. It's almost too good to be an airport restaurant, I would expect to find it in NYC. **121** is without a doubt the nicest airport restaurant that you can fly into in the Northeast. It is also the priciest airport restaurant in the Northeast. **121** will not let you down.

WINDSOR LOCKS, CT (BRADLEY INTL - BDL)

> **Aprt Mgr:** "ERIC WALDRON, A.A.E. ACE" **PH:** 860-292-2001
> **Field Elevation:** 173 **CTAF:** 0.000 **FUEL:** 100LLA
> **Runway:** 06/24 **Length:** 9510 **Width:** 200 **Surface:** ASPH-E
> **Runway:** 01/19 **Length:** 4268 **Width:** 100 **Surface:** ASPH-F
> **Runway:** 15/33 **Length:** 6847 **Width:** 150 **Surface:** ASPH-F

★ ★ ★ ★ New England Air Museum - (860) 623-3305
Open:

> Mon – Sun: 10:00am - 5:00pm

Restaurant Website: www.neam.org
Restaurant Email: staff@neam.org
PIREP:

Park at either **Signature Flight Support** or **Tac Air**, both provide courtesy shuttle service to and from the museum. I used Signature and was pleased that they provided passes to the museum and waived the tiedown fee for a small fuel purchase. They are very nice people. This is a great museum with some wonderful exhibits including a Lockheed 10A Electra. Three times each year this Museum has an Open Cockpit Day. You will be invited to climb into the pilot's seat of 12 aircraft selected from their collection of WWII fighters, jet fighters, airliners, helicopters, and civilian aircraft. This is a great chance to get some photos of these old birds interior. You may never have a chance like this again, don't let it pass you by. What about food? They have a small dining area with vending machines offering snacks and beverages. You won't starve.

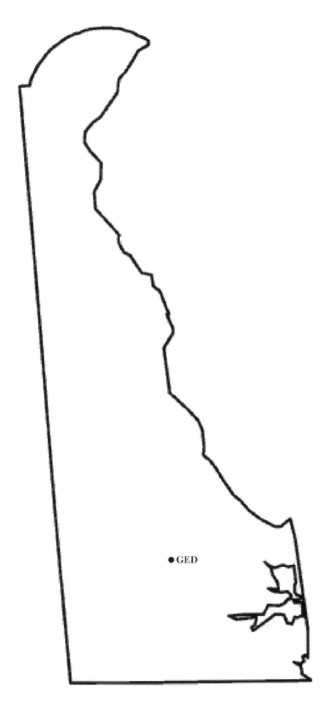

www.100dollarhamburger.com

FlyIn Delaware

◉ **GEORGETOWN, DE (SUSSEX COUNTY - GED)**
Aprt Mgr: JIM HICKIN **PH:** 302-855-7774
Field Elevation: 53 **CTAF:** 123.000 **FUEL:** 100LLA
Runway: 10/28 **Length:** 3109 **Width:** 75 **Surface:** ASPH
Runway: 04/22 **Length:** 5000 **Width:** 150 **Surface:** ASPH-G

★ ★ ★ ★ **Arena's at the Airport - 302-856-3297**
Open:

>   Mon-Thurs: 11am-9pm
>   Friday: 11am-10pm
>   Sat: 9am-10pm
>   Sun: 9am- 9pm

Restaurant Website: www.arenasdeli.com
PIREP:

Come on the weekend and enjoy breakfast. **Arena's** is a five location deli that has been in the area for over 20 years. Deli's do breakfast right and this one is no exception. For me it's a corn beef and cheese omelet with an onion bagel.

64

www.100dollarhamburger.com

FlyIn Florida

¶ DAYTONA BEACH, FL (SPRUCE CREEK - 7FL6)
    Aprt Mgr: VERN HENDERSHOTT **PH:** 386-872-1430
    Field Elevation: 24 **CTAF:** 0.000 **FUEL:** 100LLA A+
    Runway: 05/23 **Length:** 4000 **Width:** 176 **Surface:** ASPH-G

    ★ ★ ★ ★ The Downwind Cafe - (386) 756-8811
    Proprietor: Kenny Garguilo
    Open:
            Tue - Sun: 8am – 9pm
    Restaurant Website: www.thedownwind.com
    Restaurant Email: downwindcafe@gmail.com
    PIREP:
You MUST phone **The Downwind** for permission to land before
going, (386) 756-8811 as Spruce Creek is a private airport. Be certain
to ask were you can park. They have a large area for transient aircraft
near the restaurant. The food is really very, very good and the service is
the well above average. There is an outside seating area but you can't
see the runway from it. That's OK there are airplanes everywhere.
Spruce Creek is the largest and nicest flyin community in the world
with every amenity you can imagine including an 18 hole golf course, a
tennis club and much, much more. You're likely to meet several very
nice people while you're here. The problem with going to Spruce Creek
is that it's hard to leave Spruce Creek as it is where every pilot wants to
live.

¶ DELAND, FL (DELAND MUNI-SIDNEY H TAYLOR FIELD - DED)
    Aprt Mgr: NICKOLIS LANDGRAFF **PH:** 386-740-6955
    Field Elevation: 80 **CTAF:** 123.075 **FUEL:** 100LLA
    Runway: 05/23 **Length:** 4301 **Width:** 75 **Surface:** ASPH-G
    Runway: 12/30 **Length:** 6001 **Width:** 100 **Surface:** ASPH-G

    ★ ★ ★ Airport Restaurant and Gin Mill – (386) 734-9755
    Proprietor: John DeWitt & Scott Pollitt
    Open:
            Mon - Sat: 11:00 am - 2:00 am
            Sun: 11:00 am - 10:00 pm
    Restaurant Website: www.airportginmill.com
    Restaurant Email: bestburger@airportginmill.com
    PIREP:
Great little airport bar and grill with a rustic pilot atmosphere. Excellent
cheeseburgers but also have chicken or fried fish sandwiches - all the

same price. It is set back off runway 5 behind some tall bushes, but the glowing neon beer signs in the windows give it away. Watch the skydivers all day long and listen to live music when the sun goes down. Try it out, you will like it.

🍽 **FORT LAUDERDALE, FL (FT LAUDERDALE EXECUTIVE - FXE)**
Aprt Mgr: CLARA BENNETT **PH:** 954-828-4955
Field Elevation: 13 **CTAF:** 0.000 **FUEL:** 100LLA
Runway: 13/31 **Length:** 4000 **Width:** 100 **Surface:** ASPH-G
Runway: 08/26 **Length:** 6001 **Width:** 100 **Surface:** ASPH-G

★ ★ ★ ★ ★ **Jet Runway Cafe - 954 958 9900**
Proprietor: Don Campion
Open:
> Monday- Friday: 7:30am - 3pm
> Saturday: 7:30am - 2pm

Restaurant Website: www.jetrunwaycafe.com
Restaurant Email: info@ jetrunwaycafe.com
PIREP:
This is my second Florida favorite. If I get to choose this is where we go for lunch. The reason is the Honey Lime Salmon. Great ambiance, great food and great service and a BIG plus factor; Banyan Air Service. They are the BEST FBO I've ever found. They have an amazing pilot shop and they have amazing service. When you get ready to fly to the Bahamas, this is where you leave from. They will walk you through the process and fill out all of the forms for you. If you need life vests (which you must have) or a life raft (which you should have) they can sell or rent them to you.

🍽 **FORT PIERCE, FL (ST LUCIE COUNTY INTL - FPR)**
Aprt Mgr: TODD COX **PH:** 772-462-1732
Field Elevation: 23 **CTAF:** 128.200 **FUEL:** 100LLA
Runway: 10L/28R **Length:** 4000 **Width:** 75 **Surface:** ASPH-G
Runway: 14/32 **Length:** 4755 **Width:** 100 **Surface:** ASPH-G
Runway: 10R/28L **Length:** 6492 **Width:** 150 **Surface:** ASPH-G

★ ★ ★ ★ **The Airport Tiki - (772) 489-2285**
Proprietor: Errol Houck
Open:
> Mon- Sun: 7am – 5pm

PIREP:
When you land just say, *"Taxi to Tiki"* and the controller will get you to the correct ramp. That's important. There are three great reasons to go to **The Airport Tiki.** First, it's the food and the food here measures up. Next it's the service, and the service here is what you'd want even

when it's really busy. Here's the PLUS factor. When you return from the Bahamas *(it's on your bucket list isn't it?)* you will most likely clear customs at Ft. Pierce and custom's at Ft. Pierce is right next door to **The Airport Tiki.**

🍽 LAKELAND, FL (LAKELAND LINDER RGNL - LAL)

Aprt Mgr: "EUGENE B. CONRAD, III" **PH:** 863-834-3298
Field Elevation: 142 **CTAF:** 124.500 **FUEL:** 100LLA
Runway: 05/23 **Length:** 5005 **Width:** 150 **Surface:** ASPH-G
Runway: 09/27 **Length:** 8499 **Width:** 150 **Surface:** ASPH-G

★ ★ ★ ★ **Earhart's - 863-937-8900**
Proprietor: Paul Layman
Open:

> Mon - Tue: 11:00am-3:00pm
> Wed -Thur: 11:00am-8:00pm
> Fri: 11:00am-11:00pm
> Sat: 8:00am-8:00pm
> Sun: 8:00am-3:00pm

Restaurant Website: www.earhartsrunwaygrill.com
Restaurant Email: downwindcafe@gmail.com
PIREP:
This is the home airport of the 2nd greatest show in aviation, **Sun 'n Fun.** On the opposite side of the field from the show site is a very nice, very modern terminal. **Earhart's** is on the 2nd floor. It is well attended by locals, airport employees and transient pilots. Come on Sunday for the Prime Rib Brunch.

🍽 LAKE WALES, FL (CHALET SUZANNE AIR STRIP - X25)

Aprt Mgr: ERIC HINSHAW **PH:** 863-676-6011
Field Elevation: 130 **CTAF:** 122.800 **FUEL:**
Runway: 18/36 **Length:** 2313 **Width:** 50 **Surface:** TURF-G

★ ★ ★ ★ ★ **Chalet Suzanne – (863) 676-6011**
Proprietor: The Hinshaw Family
Open:

> Tue – Sun: 8:00 - 8:00

Restaurant Website: www.chaletsuzanne.com
Restaurant Email: info@ chaletsuzanne.com
PIREP:
The runway is a short *(2,300'),* well maintained and well lit *(for our night departure)* somewhat bumpy turf strip. Quaint eclectic ambiance with great gourmet food. **The Chalet Suzanne** has been charming visitors for generations. They also operate a soup cannery on the

premises. They are sso good that NASA packed one of away for the lunar bound astronauts.

🍽 MIAMI, FL (MIAMI INTL - MIA)

Aprt Mgr: "JOSE ABREU, P.E." **PH:** 305-876-7077
Field Elevation: 9 **CTAF:** 0.000 **FUEL:** 100 A
Runway: 08L/26R **Length:** 8600 **Width:** 150 **Surface:** ASPH-G
Runway: 12/30 **Length:** 9355 **Width:** 150 **Surface:** ASPH-G
Runway: 08R/26L **Length:** 10506 **Width:** 200 **Surface:** ASPH-G
Runway: 09/27 **Length:** 13016 **Width:** 150 **Surface:** ASPH-G

★★★ **The 94th Aero Squadron - (305) 261-4220**
Proprietor: Pamela Ambroci
Open:

Mon - Sat: 11am - 11pm

Restaurant Website: www.94thvannuys.com/94thmiami
PIREP:

There are several **94th Aero Squadron's** across the country and I have visited all of them. They are all aviation themed restaurants centered on the WWI period. The restaurants are all fashioned to look like a French farmhouse of that period. All are located to overlook the runway at an airport and all have superior food and service priced to match. None of them have ramp access. This one is no exception. You must pick the FBO that suits you and they will shuttle you to and from the restaurant. Miami International is not my first pick as a piston powered GA friendly place. It is a busy place. That is the reason we rate the Miami **94th Aero Squadron** as a three rather than four star stop.

🍽 NEW SMYRNA BEACH, FL (NEW SMYRNA BEACH MUNI - EVB)

Aprt Mgr: RHONDA WALKER **PH:** 386-424-2199
Field Elevation: 10 **CTAF:** 119.675 **FUEL:** 100LLA
Runway: 02/20 **Length:** 4000 **Width:** 100 **Surface:** ASPH-F
Runway: 11/29 **Length:** 4319 **Width:** 100 **Surface:** ASPH-G
Runway: 07/25 **Length:** 5000 **Width:** 75 **Surface:** ASPH-G

★★★ **Airgate Café - 386-478-0601**
Open:

Mon – Sun: 6am - 2pm

PIREP:

The Airgate Café is located at the north side of **Airgate Aviation's** (FBO) hangar. It is best to park on the ramp just south of the self-serve fuel facility. The café is small and somewhat plain inside with four outdoor tables also available. The food and service are first rate. It is pricey.

OKEECHOBEE, FL (OKEECHOBEE COUNTY - OBE)
Aprt Mgr: KATHY SCOTT **PH:** 863-467-5505
Field Elevation: 33 **CTAF:** 123.000 **FUEL:** 100LLA
Runway: 14/32 **Length:** 4001 **Width:** 75 **Surface:** ASPH-G
Runway: 05/23 **Length:** 5000 **Width:** 100 **Surface:** ASPH-G

★ ★ ★ **The Landing Strip - (863) 467-6828**
Open:
Mon-Sun: 6 am - 3 pm
PIREP:
Nice cross runways, easy landing in any wind. Great seats outside where we could watch the traffic. Park on their ramp right. Cheap self-serve fuel. OK cheap is a relative term. They serve breakfast all day which works for me as breakfast is my favorite meal of the day.

ORMOND BEACH, FL (ORMOND BEACH MUNI - OMN)
Aprt Mgr: STEVEN LICHLITER **PH:** 386-615-7019
Field Elevation: 29 **CTAF:** 119.075 **FUEL:** 100LLA
Runway: 17/35 **Length:** 3702 **Width:** 100 **Surface:** ASPH-G
Runway: 08/26 **Length:** 4003 **Width:** 75 **Surface:** ASPH-G

★ ★ ★ ★ **Manatee Bar & Grill @ River Bend Golf Club - 386-673-6000 ext. 14**
Head Chef: Gary Bennett
Open:
Tue - Sun: 11am – 3pm
Restaurant Website: www.riverbendgolf.info
Restaurant Email: proshop@playriverbendgolf.com
PIREP:
This is one of the most delightful flyin spots I have found in Florida. It is a short (100 yard) walk from the ramp to the Club House. On the other side of the pro shop you'll find a large, well-attended restaurant. The menu is varied and includes a soup and salad bar if you are in the mood. The service is crisp. The ambiance is somewhere between muni golf course and country club.

★ ★ ★ ★ **River Bend Golf Club - 386-673-6000 ext. 14**
Head Pro: Ken Van Leuven
Open:
Tue - Sun:
Restaurant Website: www.riverbendgolf.info
Restaurant Email: proshop@playriverbendgolf.com
PIREP:

From the air, it looks like a very well laid out course. Golf and flying in the same day is hard to beat. There is one little problem and be aware of it. Daytona area flight schools flock to Ormond as a practice destination. It is a good field and it is towered. Keep a smile on your face and your head on a swivel. All things considered, you'd have to work at being unhappy with this destination. Green fees and cart rentals very by time of day and season. Together they max out at less than 50 bucks.

⬤ PUNTA GORDA, FL (PUNTA GORDA - PGD)
Aprt Mgr: GARY QUILL **PH:** 941-639-1101
Field Elevation: 26 **CTAF:** 119.550 **FUEL:** 100LLA A+
Runway: 15/33 **Length:** 5688 **Width:** 150 **Surface:** ASPH-G
Runway: 04/22 **Length:** 7193 **Width:** 150 **Surface:** ASPH-G
Runway: 09/27 **Length:** 2636 **Width:** 60 **Surface:** ASPH-P

★ ★ ★ Skyview Cafe - 941 637-6004
Proprietor: Edward Gallagher
Open:
>
> Mon – Thu: 7:00am - 2:00pm
> Fri: 7:00am - 8:00pm
> Sat – Sun: 7:00am - 2:00pm

PIREP:
This is a towered airport and that is served by one airline. The result is a TSA presence which means that you can't park in front of the restaurant and you can't walk across the redlines that are painted on the terminal ramp. So, you park at the FBO and use a little foot power to get to the restaurant. The walk from the FBO is short. The "crunchy" French Toast" is really, really good and you want it. You can sit outside but be warned that it is a smoking zone.

⬤ RIVER RANCH, FL (RIVER RANCH RESORT - 2RR)
Aprt Mgr: DEAN MADDUX **PH:** 863-692-0727
Field Elevation: 55 **CTAF:** 122.800 **FUEL:** 100LL
Runway: 16/34 **Length:** 4950 **Width:** 75 **Surface:** ASPH-F

★ ★ ★ ★ The Westgate Smokehouse Grill - (863) 692-1321
Open:
>
> Serving breakfast, lunch and dinner
> *(Seasonal hours; please call ahead)*

Restaurant Website:
www.westgatedestinations.com/florida/westgate-river-ranch/dining
PIREP:
Pick up a golf cart and a map at the FBO/Golf Course Pro Shop. It'll set you back 5 bucks for two hours but it'll save you a long walk. **The**

Westgate Smokehouse Grill overlooks the Kissimmee River. The menu offers steaks, seafood, baby back ribs, burgers, sandwiches and salads. You can eat on the large screened-in porch and watch the birds feeding and spot alligators. Days and hours of operation vary by season, so make sure to call ahead before making the flight.

🍽 **ST AUGUSTINE, FL (NORTHEAST FLORIDA RGNL - SGJ)**
Aprt Mgr: ED WUELLNER **PH:** 904-209-0090
Field Elevation: 10 **CTAF:** 127.625 **FUEL:** 100LLA
Runway: 06/24 **Length:** 2701 **Width:** 60 **Surface:** ASPH-E
Runway: 02/20 **Length:** 2610 **Width:** 75 **Surface:** ASPH-F
Runway: 13/31 **Length:** 8002 **Width:** 150 **Surface:** ASPH-G

★**Allison's Fly-by Cafe – 904-824-3494**
Proprietor: Allison Rogers
Open:

> Tues - Sat: 7 am - 8 pm
> Sun - Mon: 7 am - 6 pm
> Sunday Breakfast till 2 pm

PIREP:
This used to be a very good stop and perhaps it will be again. For the moment, things seem to have gone badly downhill both food and service.

🍽 **ST PETERSBURG, FL (ALBERT WHITTED – SPG)**
Aprt Mgr: RICH LESNIAK **PH:** 727-893-7657
Field Elevation: 7 **CTAF:** 127.400 **FUEL:** 100LLA A1
Runway: 18/36 **Length:** 2864 **Width:** 150 **Surface:** ASPH-G
Runway: 07/25 **Length:** 3677 **Width:** 75 **Surface:** ASPH-G

★ ★ ★ ★ **The Hangar Restaurant & Flight Lounge – 727-822-PROP**
Open:

> Mon - Sun: 8am – 10pm

Restaurant Website: www.thehangarstpete.com
PIREP:
Albert Whitted is everything a general aviation airport should be...convenient location, beautiful scenery, multiple runways and an very good restaurant. The restaurant is modern, clean and attractive with seating both outdoors and inside. Both the food and service are outstanding. For me it's the Grilled Ham & Cheese followed by the seven layer carrot cake. By the way, the ham is pit grilled and cheese is Brie. The spoiler is the FBO's insistence on a $15 ramp fee or a fuel purchase.

🍽 **SEBASTIAN, FL (SEBASTIAN MUNI - X26)**

Aprt Mgr: JOE GRIFFIN **PH:** 772-633-0151
Field Elevation: 21 **CTAF:** 123.050 **FUEL:** 100LL
Runway: 08/26 **Length:** 3200 **Width:** 75 **Surface:** ASPH-G
Runway: 04/22 **Length:** 4024 **Width:** 75 **Surface:** ASPH-G

★ZOOBAR - 772-388-5672
Proprietor: Jim Iannaccone
Open:
> Mon - Sun: 9am - sunset

Restaurant Website: www.skydiveseb.com/skydiving-facilities.htm
Restaurant Email: info@skydiveseb.com
PIREP:
The Zoo Bar and Restaurant is open for breakfast and lunch. It has more of a snack bar than restaurant feel. They serve beer and wine inside and on the observation deck. Sebastian is a skydiving center so keep your head on a swivel and listen closely for traffic advisories when arriving and departing. That said I really enjoy watching the antics of those who choose to jump out of planes as they return to earth.

🍴 SEBRING, FL (SEBRING RGNL - SEF)
Aprt Mgr: MIKE WILLINGHAM **PH:** 863-655-6444
Field Elevation: 62 **CTAF:** 122.700 **FUEL:** 100LLA MOGAS
Runway: 14/32 **Length:** 4990 **Width:** 100 **Surface:** ASPH-G
Runway: 18/36 **Length:** 5234 **Width:** 100 **Surface:** ASPH-G

★ ★ ★ JR's Runway Cafe - 863-655-0732
Proprietor: Michael Leone
Open:
> Monday – Friday: 8am - 2:30pm
> Saturday - Sunday: 7am - 2:30pm

Restaurant Website: www.sebring-airport.com/cafe.html
PIREP:
Sebring is a great destination. If you go on a weekend you are almost guaranteed and see and hear activity on the world famous race track which abuts the airport and is on the backside of the restaurant. Yes, you can easily walk over and have a look. The food and service at the restaurant are adequate – think **Denny's**. If you are interested in LSA's walk next door to Lockwood aviation they are a local dealer from some of the finest ones and they are renowned as a repair and service center for ROTAX engines.

🍴 TAMPA, FL (TAMPA NORTH AERO PARK - X39)
Aprt Mgr: CHARLES W. BRAMMER **PH:** 813-973-3703
Field Elevation: 68 **CTAF:** 123.050 **FUEL:** 100LLA
Runway: 14/32 **Length:** 3541 **Width:** 50 **Surface:** ASPH-F

★ ★ ★ **Happy Hangar Café - 813-973-3703**
Proprietor: Keith Carver
Open:
        Tue-Sun: 7am - 2pm
Restaurant Website: www.tampanorth.com
Restaurant Email: HappyHangar@gmail.com
PIREP:
The airport has new owners who are making serious efforts to improve and expand services. After landing taxi to the ramp area near the self-serve fuel pump and park in any space you like on the paved ramp or in the grass area behind it. Food and service are average airport fare at **The Happy Hangar Café**. Their plus factor is that everything is made from scratch including biscuits and pancakes. I've had the pancakes. They are very, very good. The restaurant's windows overlook the approach end of runway 32 as does the porch which has picnic tables.

🍽 **VENICE, FL (VENICE MUNI - VNC)**
    Aprt Mgr: "CHRIS ROZANSKY, C.M." **PH:** 941-486-2711
    Field Elevation: 18 **CTAF:** 122.725 **FUEL:** 100LLA
    Runway: 13/31 **Length:** 4999 **Width:** 150 **Surface:** ASPH-F
    Runway: 04/22 **Length:** 5000 **Width:** 150 **Surface:** ASPH-P

★ ★ **Suncoast Cafe - 941-484-0100**
Open:
        Mon - Sun: 7:30am – 3:30pm
Restaurant Website: www.suncoastcafe.com
Restaurant Email: dduboulay@suncoastcafe.com
PIREP:
This is your basic airport restaurant. The menu and the food it represents are very standard. The wait staff provides yeoman like service. It's worth the stop only if you're heading this way.

🍽 **VERO BEACH, FL (VERO BEACH MUNI - VRB)**
    Aprt Mgr: MR. ERIC MENGER **PH:** 772-978-4930
    Field Elevation: 24 **CTAF:** 126.300 **FUEL:** 100 A
    Runway: 11L/29R **Length:** 3504 **Width:** 75 **Surface:** ASPH-G
    Runway: 04/22 **Length:** 4974 **Width:** 100 **Surface:** ASPH-G
    Runway: 11R/29L **Length:** 7314 **Width:** 100 **Surface:** ASPH-G

★ ★ ★ ★ ★ **CJ Cannon's - 772-567-7727**
Proprietor: Charles J Cannon III
Open:
        Mon – Sat: 7:00am till 9:00pm
        Sun: 7:00am till 2:00pm

Restaurant Website: www.cjcannonsrestaurant.com
PIREP:
I have been coming here for many years. It is consistently wonderful.
Park your airplane and walk right up to the door. Great food and
ambiance. Can't be beat for quality and convenience. Call Piper before
you go and see if they can arrange a plant tour for you. Their plant is
further down the ramp.

$100 Hamburger 2014/15

FlyIn Georgia

⦿ ATLANTA, GA (COBB COUNTY-MC COLLUM FIELD - RYY)
Aprt Mgr: KARL A VON HAGEL **PH:** 770-528-1615
Field Elevation: 1041 **CTAF:** 125.900 **FUEL:** 100LLA1+
Runway: 09/27 **Length:** 6311 **Width:** 100 **Surface:** CONC-G

★ ★ ★ ★ Elevation Chophouse - (770) 485-7469
Proprietor: Michael Bowman
Open:
>Tue–Fri 5pm–10pm
>Sat 11am–10pm
>Sun 11am–9pm

Restaurant Website: www.elevationatlanta.com
Restaurant Email: info@elevationgeorgia.com
PIREP:
Elevation is certainly a cut above most airport cafes. The food choices vary between ordinary and unusual. My test is always a simple medium rare, New York Strip steak which is easy to screw up. The one I was presented was excellent. Test passed – grade A. The service is attentive. They also make their own ice cream using liquid nitrogen. Is it good? I really don't know – I passed.

⦿ ATLANTA, GA (DEKALB-PEACHTREE - PDK)
Aprt Mgr: LEE REMMEL **PH:** 770-936-5440
Field Elevation: 1003 **CTAF:** 120.900 **FUEL:** 100 A A1
Runway: 09/27 **Length:** 3383 **Width:** 150 **Surface:** ASPH-G
Runway: 02L/20R **Length:** 3746 **Width:** 150 **Surface:** ASPH-G
Runway: 16/34 **Length:** 3967 **Width:** 150 **Surface:** ASPH-G
Runway: 02R/20L **Length:** 6001 **Width:** 100 **Surface:** CONC-G

★ ★ ★ ★ The Downwind - 770/452-0973
Proprietor: Andreas Mammas and Jenifer Hardee
Open:
>Monday - Friday: 11am - 10pm
>Saturday - noon - 10pm

Restaurant Website: www.downwindrestaurant.com
Restaurant Email: downwindrest@aol.com
PIREP:
Park at Mercury, they don't charge a ramp fee or require a fuel purchase if you're there less than two hours. That's plenty of time to wolf down a burger. PDK is BUSY! Pay attention to the controller's instructions and make certain he knows what your intentions are. I love

using this airport as there is a Metra stop just outside its gate, that's the quickest way to get into town, do your business and get back to the 'port. Atlanta has killer traffic. The Metra save you the trouble. The Downwind really does have the *"Best Hamburger in Town"*. Get one!

⍟ JEKYLL ISLAND, GA (JEKYLL ISLAND - 09J)
Aprt Mgr: RONNIE SMITH **PH:** 912-635-4091
Field Elevation: 11 **CTAF:** 123.000 **FUEL:**
Runway: 18/36 **Length:** 3715 **Width:** 75 **Surface:** ASPH-G

★ ★ ★ ★ ★ **Jekyll Island Club Grand Dining Room - (912) 635-5155**
Proprietor: Executive Chef Abigail Hutchinson
Open:
Monday – Saturday: 7:00am – 10:00pm
Sunday Brunch: 10:45am – 2:00pm
Restaurant Website: www.jekyllclub.com/dining/
Restaurant Email: concierge@jekyllclub.com
PIREP:
The Jekyll Island Club was once a Rockefeller resort. It shows. The landing strip is in great shape and is a short stroll along a picturesque lane lined with moss draped oaks to the hotel. Come for Sunday Brunch. Everything you might care to eat is elegantly presented and perfectly prepared.The ambiance is white table clothes with service to match and the food matches up nicely. Don't miss this one.

⍟ LAWRENCEVILLE, GA (GWINNETT COUNTY - LZU)
Aprt Mgr: MATT SMITH **PH:** 770-822-5196
Field Elevation: 1062 **CTAF:** 124.100 **FUEL:** 100LLA1+
Runway: 07/25 **Length:** 6000 **Width:** 100 **Surface:** ASPH-G

★ ★ ★ **The Flying Machine - (770) 962-2262**
Proprietor: Hokey Sloan
Manager: Joy Hoge
Open:
Mon – Thurs: 11 am - 9 pm
Fri & Sat: 11 am - 10 pm
Sun: 11 am - 3 pm
Restaurant Website: www.theflyingmachine.com
Restaurant Email: mail@ theflyingmachine.com
PIREP:
If you're close, you should put this on your list. It is really, really a great restaurant. Downhome comfort food served by people that seem genuinely glad that you dropped by. Come on Wednesday, Friday or Saturday nigh and you'll hear some wonderful music. The last time I

was here I went with the $100 Hamburger *(what else)* and finished up with the Cobbler of the day *(lucky me it was apple)*. I'll be back.

⦿ WILLIAMSON, GA (PEACH STATE - GA2)

Aprt Mgr: RON ALEXANDER **PH:** 770-467-9490
Field Elevation: 926 **CTAF:** 122.800 **FUEL:** 100LL
Runway: 13/31 **Length:** 2400 **Width:** 100 **Surface:** TURF-F

★★ Barnstormer's Grill - (770) 227-9989
Proprietor: Trudy Gill
Open:

> Mon – Thurs: – 11:30am – 9:00pm
> Fri: 11:30am – 9:30pm
> Sat: 9:00am – 9:30pm
> Sun: 11:00am – 3:00pm

Restaurant Website: www.barnstormersgrill.com
Restaurant Email: barnstormersgril@bellsouth.net
PIREP:

This is a great airport restaurant with wonderful service and one **BIG** problem. The runway is a bit hilly and rough. It's fine for tail draggers or high wing planes with plenty of prop clearance but "puckering" for a low wing with limited prop clearance like a Mooney or an Aztec. Wonderfully improvements are being made at this airport surrounding the development of the Candler Field Museum. They're rebuilding the Atlanta's principal airport as it was in the days of the Barnstormer. They have and will add more wonderful exhibits. So why only two stars? Our focus is on flyin venues. If you can't operate comfortably out of the airport we have a problem. This landing strip is marginal for most of us and close to dangerous for a few.

$100 Hamburger 2014/15

FlyIn Idaho

🍽 **CALDWELL, ID (CALDWELL INDUSTRIAL - EUL)**
Aprt Mgr: ROB OATES **PH:** 208-459-9779
Field Elevation: 2432 **CTAF:** 122.700 **FUEL:** 100LLA
Runway: 12/30 **Length:** 5500 **Width:** 100 **Surface:** ASPH-G

___

★ ★ ★ **Caldwell Airport Café - (208) 546-2233**
Proprietor: Carol Cameron
Open:
> Mon – Sat: 7:00am - 2:30pm
> Sun: 7:00am - 1:30pm

Restaurant Website: facebook.com
PIREP:
A reasonably long, wide turf strip brings you to the rustic back country building that houses **The Caldwell Airport Café**. Mountain men fly in here for a breakfast of homemade biscuits and gravy. Expect to do some hanger flying.

🍽 **COOLIN, ID (CAVANAUGH BAY - 66S)**
Aprt Mgr: DIVISION ADMIN **PH:** 208-334-8775
Field Elevation: 2484 **CTAF:** 122.900 **FUEL:**
Runway: 15/33 **Length:** 3100 **Width:** 120 **Surface:** TURF-G

___

★ ★ ★ **Cavanaugh Bay Resort & Marina - (208) 443-2095**
Proprietor: Mike Belles
Open:
> **Fall Hours**
> Sun: 11am - 8pm
> Monday – Wednesday: CLOSED
> Thursday & Friday: 4pm - 9pm
> Saturday: 11am - 9:30pm

Restaurant Website: www.cavbay.com
Restaurant Email: cavanaughs@cavbay.com
PIREPS:
The restaurant is just across the road from the airstrip which is the usual turf that you expect in the back country. The deck is right on the Priest Lake. The Prime Rib sandwich is very good, and the onion rings are about the best I ever had.

🍽 **DRIGGS, ID (DRIGGS-REED MEMORIAL - DIJ)**
Aprt Mgr: TOM HUNTER **PH:** 208-313-5077

Field Elevation: 6231 **CTAF:** 122.700 **FUEL:** 100LLA
Runway: 03/21 **Length:** 7300 **Width:** 100 **Surface:** ASPH-E

★ ★ ★ ★ Warbirds Cafe - (208) 354-2550
Proprietor: Michael Bowman
Open:
        Tue – Sun: 11am – 9pm
Restaurant Website: www.tetonaviation.com/warbirds-cafe
Restaurant Email: info@tetonaviation.com
PIREP:
This is the place we've all been looking for. The restaurant is clean, well-staffed, large, bright , new and sparkling. In the summer, sit outside along the taxiway with your handheld radio on CTAF and eat gourmet food in full view of the Tetons in all of their majesty. The Warbirds Museum is under the same roof and is free. What a treat!!!

⦿ NAMPA, ID (NAMPA MUNI - MAN)
Aprt Mgr: COLLEEN HARTNETT **PH:** 208-468-5820
Field Elevation: 2537 **CTAF:** 122.700 **FUEL:** 100LLA
Runway: 11/29 **Length:** 5000 **Width:** 75 **Surface:** ASPH-G

★ ★ ★ The Picnic Basket Eatery - (208) 467-9633
Open:
        Mon - Sun: 7:00am - 3:00pm
Restaurant Website: www.picnicbasketeatery.com
PIREP:
Good flyin restaurants stops begin with good airports. Nampa is a great one. They have 3 crew cars and overnight shade hangars available plus two maintenance facilities for oxygen recharging, avionics sales, installation and repair; hangars. The restaurant changes hands more often than I like to see. Here's hoping the latest one succeeds. They serve good food at fair prices. Fingers crossed.

⦿ WARREN, ID (WARREN /USFS/ - 3U1)
Aprt Mgr: PAYETTE FOREST AIR OFFICER **PH:** 208-634-0746
Field Elevation: 5902 **CTAF:** 122.900 **FUEL:**
Runway: 11/29 **Length:** 2765 **Width:** 50 **Surface:** DIRT-G

★ ★ Baum Shelter - (208) 382-4336
Proprietor: Ernest Cooper
Open:
        Thurs - Sat: noon until early evening
Restaurant Website: www.secesh.net/WinterInn.htm
Restaurant Email: Becky@secesh.net
PIREP:

This is a real back country spot. I love them all. It makes you remember all of the wonderful places we get to go that people without airplanes can't. The hamburger and fries are homemade from scratch. They cook 'em after you order 'em.

$100 Hamburger 2014/15

FlyIn Illinois

🍴 BLOOMINGTON/NORMAL, IL (BLOOMINGTON-NORM - BMI)
Aprt Mgr: CARL G. OLSON **PH:** 309-663-7383
Field Elevation: 871 **CTAF:** 124.600 **FUEL:** 100LLA
Runway: 11/29 **Length:** 6525 **Width:** 150 **Surface:** ASPH-CONC-G
Runway: 02/20 **Length:** 8000 **Width:** 150 **Surface:** CONC-G

★★ ★★★ **CJ's Restaurant & Catering - 309-663-4444**
Proprietor: C J & Doug Stolfa
Open:
> Tues – Sat: 7:30 am – 9:30 pm
> Sun: 7:30 am – 9:30 pm

Restaurant Website: www.cjsrestaurantandcatering.com
PIREP:
Ground control directed us to parking on the GA ramp directly in front of the restaurant. CJs is vey large for an airport restaurant. It is sparkling clean and well furnished. Floor to ceiling windows provide great views onto the field. They have a huge outdoor patio with tables and umbrellas that will make for a summer stop next year. If you're here for lunch, go with the Rueben. I don't know if it's better than Pilot Pete's but it is certainly as good and it doesn't have the frenzied Chicago traffic.

🍴 BOLINGBROOK, IL (BOLINGBROOK'S CLOW INTL - 1C5)
Aprt Mgr: JOSEPH DE PAULO **PH:** 630-378-0479
Field Elevation: 670 **CTAF:** 122.900 **FUEL:** 100LLA
Runway: 18/36 **Length:** 3362 **Width:** 50 **Surface:** ASPH-G

★★ ★ **Charlie's - (630) 771-0501**
Proprietor: Chris King
Open:
> Mon – Sun: 7:00 am – 3:00 pm

Restaurant Website: www.charliesrestaurant.net
Restaurant Email: donnayoung129@gmail.com
PIREP:
Clow International is a Class E asphalt strip southwest of Chicago and just outside O'Hare's class B. **Charlie's** has picture windows overlooking the ramp area. The menu is extensive. You'll have no trouble finding a dish that interests you. The crowd is eclectic from mothers with kids to businessmen to senior aviators swapping stories.

🍴 CHICAGO/WEST CHICAGO, IL (DUPAGE - DPA)
www.100dollarhamburger.com

Aprt Mgr: DAVID BIRD **PH:** 630-584-2211
Field Elevation: 758 **CTAF:** 0.000 **FUEL:** 100LLA
Runway: 15/33 **Length:** 3399 **Width:** 100 **Surface:** ASPH-G
Runway: 10/28 **Length:** 4750 **Width:** 75 **Surface:** ASPH-G
Runway: 02R/20L **Length:** 5101 **Width:** 100 **Surface:** CONC-G
Runway: 02L/20R **Length:** 7571 **Width:** 100 **Surface:** CONC-G

★ ★ ★ **Kitty Hawk Cafe - (630) 208-6189**
Proprietor: Erin
Open:
> Mon - Fri: 9:00 am - 2:00 pm

Restaurant Website: facebook.com/pages/Kitty-Hawk-Cafe/244249793933
PIREP:
The Kitty Hawk in January 2014. The new terminal building is nice and I hope the restaurant will equal it. I am including the **Kitty Hawk** and trusting to luck.

🍽 **CHICAGO/SCHAUMBURG, IL (SCHAUMBURG RGNL - 06C)**
Aprt Mgr: JUNE E. JOHNSON **PH:** 847-923-3859
Field Elevation: 801 **CTAF:** 123.000 **FUEL:** 100LLA
Runway: 11/29 **Length:** 3800 **Width:** 100 **Surface:** CONC-G

★ ★ ★ ★ **Pilot Pete's - (847) 891-5100)**
Proprietor: J.R. Hutson and Mike Coughlan
Open:
> Mon – Sun: 11am – 9pm

Restaurant Website: www.pilot-petes.com
PIREP:
One of our $100 Hamburger website subscribers said it better than I ever could. So here's his review not mine:

Pilot Pete's deserves 6 stars if you ask me! I flew myself and a date there and for once dinner was as exciting as the flight! The atmosphere is a Jimmy Buffet meets the 'classic international' Juan Trippe/PanAm era with a mix of every aviation generation to follow! A funky mix of mood lighting creatively illuminates all of the wall murals and both large and small model airplanes hanging from the ceiling! The food was excellent – Pete's has a traditional American menu with its own unique twist. The prices are very reasonable and the proportions are not disappointing. I had no problem getting into the airport – I flew in from Michigan VFR – followed the lake shore from Gary north, right past the Chicago skyline – passengers are plastered to the window! I went direct DEERE-OBK-06C – north of PWK, no problems, Chicago ATC was friendly getting in and out. I highly recommend **Pilot Pete's** for a date with your lady or a trip with the guys – either way it's a great time!

🍴 DECATUR, IL (DECATUR - DEC)

Aprt Mgr: JOSEPH ATTWOOD **PH:** 217-428-2423
Field Elevation: 682 **CTAF:** 118.900 **FUEL:** 100LLA
Runway: 12/30 **Length:** 6799 **Width:** 150 **Surface:** ASPH-CONC-G
Runway: 06/24 **Length:** 8496 **Width:** 150 **Surface:** ASPH-CONC-G
Runway: 18/36 **Length:** 5298 **Width:** 150 **Surface:** ASPH-G

★ ★ ★ The Main Hangar – (217) 421-7452

Proprietor: Chris Cooper
Open:
>   Mon. - Thurs: 7:00am - 9:00pm
>   Fri./Sat: 7:00am - 10:00pm
>   Sunday All You Can Eat Brunch Buffet: 8:00am - 2:00pm

Restaurant Website: www.mainhangarrestaurant.net
Restaurant Email: info@mainhangarrestaurant.net
PIREP:
Taxi to the FBO by the control tower, go through the FBO and head for the main terminal building. **The Main Hangar** is inside the terminal. **The Main Hangar Restaurant** is a family owned and operated business serving authentic Sicilian and American Cuisines for breakfast, lunch, and dinner. Lunch is easy. You grab a plate and stand in the buffet line. Here's the deal. You build your own salad or baked potato & don't overlook the included soups, cold pasta and hot pastas for less than 10 bucks.

🍴 MATTOON/CHARLESTON, IL (COLES COUNTY - MTO)

Aprt Mgr: ANDREW FEARN **PH:** 217-234-7120
Field Elevation: 722 **CTAF:** 122.700 **FUEL:** 100LLA
Runway: 06/24 **Length:** 5799 **Width:** 100 **Surface:** ASPH-G
Runway: 11/29 **Length:** 6501 **Width:** 150 **Surface:** CONC-G
Runway: 18/36 **Length:** 1080 **Width:** 250 **Surface:** TURF

★ ★ ★ ★ The Airport Steakhouse - (217) 234-9433

Proprietor: Ron Bean
Open:
>   Mon - Sun: 7am – 8pm

Restaurant Website: charlestonairportsteakhouse.com
PIREP:
You can't park closer to a restaurant anywhere else. This is a solid 4 burger breakfast destination.   Best GIANT pork tenderloins anywhere. HUGE - hand breaded. They call it the Elephant Ear. Don't leave without one.

✈ MOLINE, IL (QUAD CITY INTL - MLI)
Aprt Mgr: BRUCE CARTER **PH:** 309-764-9621
Field Elevation: 590 **CTAF:** 119.400 **FUEL:** 100LLA
Runway: 13/31 **Length:** 7301 **Width:** 150 **Surface:** ASPH-CONC-F
Runway: 09/27 **Length:** 10002 **Width:** 150 **Surface:** CONC-E
Runway: 05/23 **Length:** 5015 **Width:** 150 **Surface:** CONC-G

★ ★ ★ Bud's Skyline Inn - (309) 764-5019
Proprietor: Bud Canfield
Open:

> Mon - Thurs: 11am - 9pm
> Fri: 11am - 10pm
> Sat: 4pm -10pm
> Sun: 4pm - 8pm

Restaurant Website: www.budsskylineinn.com
Restaurant Email: skylineinn@aol.com
PIREP:

It is on the north boundary of the airport right next to the threshold of runway 23. It has a great view of the airport and is decorated in an aviation theme. You can usually find local pilots here and always on Wednesdays at lunch. Bud bought this place as old tavern and cleaned it up expanding every couple of years as the business has grown. That was 30 years ago! Some folks come here just to play video poker. That's not me. I come here to eat the catfish. It's worth the trip.

✈ MOUNT VERNON, IL (MOUNT VERNON - MVN)
Aprt Mgr: CHRIS COLLINS **PH:** 618-242-7016
Field Elevation: 480 **CTAF:** 123.000 **FUEL:** 100LLA
Runway: 05/23 **Length:** 6496 **Width:** 150 **Surface:** ASPH-E
Runway: 15/33 **Length:** 3146 **Width:** 100 **Surface:** ASPH-G

★ ★ ★ ★ Wilkey's Airport Cafe - 618-242-1050
Proprietor: Donnie Wilkey
Open:

> Tue – Sat: 11 am – 7 pm
> Sunday "after service buffet": 11 am – ?

Restaurant Website: www.mtvernonairport.com
PIREP:

Family owned and operated since 1953. That's over half a century. My friend and $100 Hamburger website subscriber says it this way:
"Awesome Sunday buffet. Only $10 with beverage and the best fried chicken I have ever had. Get there early as church crowd really fills up the place fast."

Add to this the quality of the airport. The runway is 6,500 feet long with an ILS approach.

ROCHELLE, IL (ROCHELLE MUNI AIRPORT - RPJ)
Aprt Mgr: DON ELLIOT **PH:** 815-562-2494
Field Elevation: 781 **CTAF:** 122.800 **FUEL:** 100LLA
Runway: 07/25 **Length:** 4225 **Width:** 75 **Surface:** ASPH-G

★ ★ ★ Flight Deck Bar and Grill - (815) 561-3664
Proprietor: C J & Doug Stolfa
Open:
>Mon: 11:00am - 9:00pm
>Tue – Fri: 11:00am - 10:00pm
>Sat: 11:00am - 10:00pm
>Sun: 11:00am - 9:00pm
>Last Sunday of the month - Breakfast: 8:00am - 10:30am

Restaurant Website: www.flightdeckbar.com
Restaurant Email: info@ flightdeckbar.com
PIREP:
Arriving aircraft should check to see if the jump planes are up on CTAF 122.97. If they're not on that frequency, check 121.0 to see if their talking to Rockford Approach. **The Flight Deck Bar and Grill is** located in **Chicagoland Skydiving Center's** facilities just east of the T-hangars towards the approach end of runway 25. Park on the main ramp and use the sidewalk located on the south side of the airport that runs along the T-hangars. **The Flight Deck Bar and Grill** is not the normal snack shack that you find at skydiving centers. It is a large, clean, nicely decorated restaurant that provides very good food and friendly, efficient service. Your receipt from dining at the restaurant gets you a 10 cent per gallon discount on your fuel.

O5C ●

● EYE
4I7●

3I3 ●

●BAK

$100 Hamburger 2014/15

FlyIn Indiana

🍴 **COLUMBUS, IN (COLUMBUS MUNI - BAK)**
> **Aprt Mgr:** ROD BLASDEL **PH:** 812-376-2519
> **Field Elevation:** 656 **CTAF:** 118.600 **FUEL:** 100LLA
> **Runway:** 14/32 **Length:** 5000 **Width:** 100 **Surface:** ASPH-F
> **Runway:** 05/23 **Length:** 6400 **Width:** 150 **Surface:** ASPH-G

> ★ ★ ★ Blackerby's Hangar 5 Restaurant - 812-378-4010
> **Proprietor:** Wayne Blacherby
> **Open:**
>> Monday – Sunday: 6:30am-2:00pm
>
> **Restaurant Website:** www.hangarfiverestaurant.com
> **Restaurant Email:** info@ hangarfiverestaurant.com
> **PIREP:**
> The restaurant is right beside the tower. The FBO and the restaurant are in a fairly new building with all new decor. It's a good size restaurant with booths along the plate glass windows overlooking the runway. The menu is standard airport café breakfast and lunch selections. You won't be disappointed or impressed.

🍴 **GREENCASTLE, IN (PUTNAM COUNTY - 4I7)**
> **Aprt Mgr:** JOHN LAYNE **PH:** 765-653-1763
> **Field Elevation:** 842 **CTAF:** 122.800 **FUEL:** 100LLA1+
> **Runway:** 18/36 **Length:** 4987 **Width:** 100 **Surface:** ASPH-G

> ★ ★ ★ Final Approach Bar & Grill - (765) 655-1600
> **Open:**
>> Wed - Thur: 11am-2pm & 5pm-8pm
>> Fri: 11am-2pm & 5pm-8pm
>> Sat: 7am-11am & 5pm-9pm
>> Sun: 7am-10:30am & 11am-2pm
>
> **Restaurant Website:**
> www.dixiechopperhotel.com/final-approach-restaurant-pub
> **Restaurant Email:** info@ dixiechopperhotel.com
> **PIREP:**
> One of the lowest cost fuel stops in the Midwest. This restaurant rocks. I really like the food, the ambiance and the service. You can get a great sandwich for less than the price of a gallon of AVGAS. How about that? They also have a few new motel rooms upstairs you can rent.

🍴 **GRIFFITH, IN (GRIFFITH-MERRILLVILLE - 05C)**
> **Aprt Mgr:** CRAIG ANDERSON **PH:** 219-924-0207

www.100dollarhamburger.com

Field Elevation: 634 **CTAF:** 123.000 **FUEL:** 100LLA
Runway: 08/26 **Length:** 4899 **Width:** 75 **Surface:** ASPH-G

★ ★ ★ Mi Tierra - (219) 922-3633
Proprietor: Don Chuy
Open:
> Tue – Sat: 10:30am - 9:30pm

Restaurant Website: www.facebook.com/mitierrarestaurant
PIREP:
This is one of the spots that I have never been to so which is sad as I LOVE Mexican food. I am including a **PIREP** from one of the $100 Hamburger website subscribers.

"Great destination for those in the Chicago area. I flew on a Wednesday night, from the Wisconsin/Illinois border, skirting the Chicago class B airspace. The views of Chicago and Midway traffic were great. This is a good time to use VFR flight following. You will mix with heavy traffic and get good experience listening. I was handed off 4 times in 1.3 hours. The airport is well lit at night. No taxiway. Easy to find the huge general aviation parking area. Enter the FBO (fuel truck is available) and go down the hall to the restaurant. But get into your airplane by 8pm closing time. Looking for another excuse to have my dinner there, a $100 quesadilla!"

⦿ INDIANAPOLIS, IN (EAGLE CREEK AIRPARK - EYE)
Aprt Mgr: MICHAEL T. MEDVESCEK **PH:** 317-487-5024
Field Elevation: 823 **CTAF:** 122.800 **FUEL:** 100LLA
Runway: 03/21 **Length:** 4200 **Width:** 75 **Surface:** ASPH-G

★ ★ ★ ★ ★ Rick's Cafe Boatyard - (317) 290-9300)
Proprietor: Rick Albrecht
Open:
> Mon - Thurs: 11am to 10pm
> Fri - Sat: 11am to 11pm
> Sun: 10am to 10pm

Restaurant Website: www.rickscafeboatyard.com
Restaurant Email: info@rickscafeboatyard.com
PIREP:
Rick's is across the street from the FBO. It is a short 50 yard walk. If the weather is good go for a spot on the large deck. They run heaters if it's a little cool. You'll have a great view of boating activity on the lake as well as arriving and departing aircraft from the airport. The food is really near the top of anyone's expectations and the service is equal. I am a carnivore so I go for flamed kissed cow.

TERRE HAUTE, IN (SKY KING - 3I3)
Aprt Mgr: STEVE BROWN PH: 812-466-2229
Field Elevation: 496 CTAF: 122.800 FUEL: 100LL
Runway: 18/36 Length: 1978 Width: 50 Surface: ASPH-F
Runway: 08/26 Length: 3557 Width: 50 Surface: ASPH-F

★ ★ ★ Fox's Market - (812) 466-5825)
Proprietor: Richard Fox
Open:
　　　　Daily: Lunch
PIREP:
This is a grocery store/meat market that abuts the airport. They serve
dynamite sandwiches at lunch and you want one. Eating on the curb
outside of a small town grocery store brings me back to my youth in
Texas. Once you have landed at this airport back taxi to the office and
park on the ramp. The market is just a short walk across a two lane road
that is literally off the end of runway 26. Walk into **Fox's** for a
sandwich, a side and a drink. Be warned that this is a flight school.
During the school year it might be busier than many controlled airports.

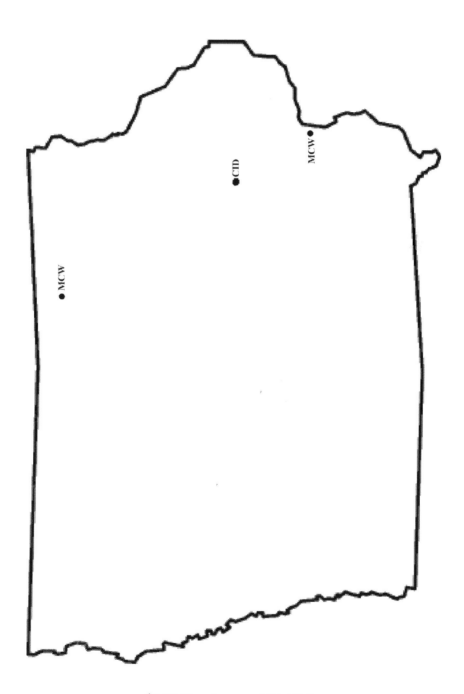

$100 Hamburger 2014/15

FlyIn Iowa

CEDAR RAPIDS, IA (THE EASTERN IOWA - CID)
Aprt Mgr: "MR. TIM BRADSHAW, A.A.E." **PH:** 319-362-3131
Field Elevation: 869 **CTAF:** 118.700 **FUEL:** 100LLA
Runway: 13/31 **Length:** 6199 **Width:** 150 **Surface:** ASPH-CONC-E
Runway: 09/27 **Length:** 8600 **Width:** 150 **Surface:** CONC-E

★ ★ ★ Tic Toc Restaurant - (515) 256-5342
Proprietor: Cedar Rapids Airport Commission
Operator: SSP America
Open:
> Daily: 4:30 a.m. to 8 p.m.

Restaurant Website: www.eiairport.org/at-the-airport/concessions/
Restaurant Email: info@eiairport.org
PIREP:
The Tic Toc Restaurant is located in the passenger terminal at the Cedar Rapids, IA airport. Fortunately it is in the lobby before the TSA screening area. As with any other TSA secured passenger terminal you cannot enter from the ramp and you cannot cross the red lines they have painted on the ramp around the passenger terminal. What you must do is enter through the front door. The FBO will shuttle you to and from the terminal. What about the food? Well, it's OK meaning nothing to write home about and nothing to run away from. It is wholesome and nourishing. You come here to relax and replenish not for a gourmet experience. The service like the food is OK.

CLINTON, IA (CLINTON MUNI - CWI)
Aprt Mgr: MICHAEL NASS **PH:** 563-242-3292
Field Elevation: 708 **CTAF:** 122.800 **FUEL:** 100LLA
Runway: 03/21 **Length:** 5204 **Width:** 100 **Surface:** ASPH-F
Runway: 14/32 **Length:** 4201 **Width:** 75 **Surface:** CONC-G

★ Airport Snack Machines - (563) 242-3292
PIREP:
We're talking about a microwave, a sandwich machine, a pop machine, and candy machine. Obviously this isn't a dining destination. If you are here for fuel or for some other reason and you are starving food is available. It is a very low quality food but it is food. 'Nuff said

MASON CITY, IA (MASON CITY MUNI - MCW)
Aprt Mgr: MS PAMELA OSGOOD **PH:** 641-421-3397

Field Elevation: 1214 **CTAF:** 123.000 **FUEL:** 100LLA
Runway: 12/30 **Length:** 5502 **Width:** 150 **Surface:** ASPH-E
Runway: 18/36 **Length:** 6501 **Width:** 150 **Surface:** ASPH-G

★ ★ ★ **Bumbleberry Bakery** - **(641) 530-0255**
Proprietor: Roxi
Open:
> Tues - Fri: 6am – 2pm
> Sat: 6am – 12pm

Restaurant Website: www.flymcw.com
Restaurant Email: bumbleberrybakery@yahoo.com
PIREP:
Bumbleberry Bakery is located in the passenger terminal. This presents no problem with TSA as there are no longer passenger flights to or from Mason City hence there is no TSA security. AT this time it is still necessary to enter the terminal only from the front door.
Bumbleberry Bakery has daily lunch specials. They also have drunken brats, crispy chicken sandwiches, tenderloins, and a grilled bacon and Swiss cheese on sourdough sandwich.

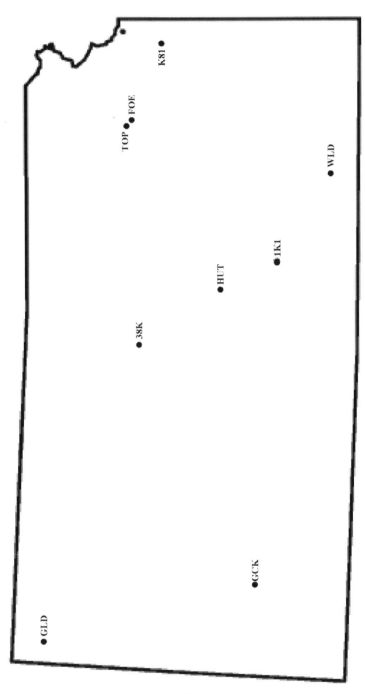

www.100dollarhamburger.com

FlyIn Kansas

🍽 **BENTON, KS (LLOYD STEARMAN FIELD - 1K1)**
　　Aprt Mgr: DWAYNE CLEMENS **PH:** 316-648-0132
　　Field Elevation: 1364 **CTAF:** 123.075 **FUEL:** 100LLA
　　Runway: 17/35 **Length:** 5106 **Width:** 60 **Surface:** ASPH-G

　　★ ★ ★ ★ ★ **Stearman Field Bar & Grill – (316) 778-1612**
　　Proprietor: Dwayne Clemens
　　Open:
　　　　Mon - Sun: 7am - 10pm.
　　Restaurant Website: www.stearmanfield.com
　　Restaurant Email: stearmanfield@gmail.com
　　PIREP:
　　The restaurant is at the very north end of the runway, right by the self-service fuel pumps. The food and service are very standard.

🍽 **GARDEN CITY, KS (GARDEN CITY RGNL - GCK)**
　　Aprt Mgr: MS. RACHELLE POWELL **PH:** 620-276-1190
　　Field Elevation: 2891 **CTAF:** 118.150 **FUEL:** 100LLA
　　Runway: 17/35 **Length:** 7300 **Width:** 100 **Surface:** CONC-E
　　Runway: 12/30 **Length:** 5700 **Width:** 100 **Surface:** CONC-G

　　★ ★ ★ ★ ★ **Napoli's - (620) 271-1490**
　　Open:
　　　　Tue - Thur: 11:00am – 9:00pm
　　　　Fri - Sat: 11:00am – 10:00pm
　　　　Sun: 11:00am – 9:00pm
　　Restaurant Website: www.italianrestaurantgardencityks.com
　　Restaurant Email: info@italianrestaurantgardencityks.com
　　PIREP:
　　Really good Italian food. Garden City Regional is several miles outside of town, but there is always a crowd of local customers; a very good indication of the quality of the food.

🍽 **GOODLAND, KS (RENNER FLD /GOODLAND MUNI/ - GLD)**
　　Aprt Mgr: MR. JOHN COLLETT **PH:** 785-890-7531
　　Field Elevation: 3657 **CTAF:** 122.950 **FUEL:** 100LLA
　　Runway: 05/23 **Length:** 3501 **Width:** 75 **Surface:** ASPH-G
　　Runway: 12/30 **Length:** 5499 **Width:** 100 **Surface:** CONC-G
　　Runway: 17/35 **Length:** 1781 **Width:** 40 **Surface:** TURF-G

　　★ ★ ★ **The Butterfly Cafe - (785) 890-2085**

$100 Hamburger 2014/15

Proprietor: John and Marilyn Collett
Open:

        Mon – Fri: 6am to 3pm
        Sat/Sun: 6am to 2pm

Restaurant Website: www.butterflyaviation.net/Cafe.php
Restaurant Email: butterfly@st-tel.net
PIREP:
The Butterfly Cafe is located on the ramp in the old FSS Building.
Great food at very reasonable prices-- and lots of locals come out from
town for breakfast and lunch. I come here for the homemade breads and
pies. They are terrific. I have never left without two whole pies in the
baggage compartment.

HUTCHINSON, KS (HUTCHINSON MUNI - HUT)

    Manager: MR. PIETER MILLER **PH:** 620-694-2692
    Field Elevation: 1543 **CTAF:** 118.500 **FUEL:** 100LLA
    Runway: 13/31 **Length:** 7004 **Width:** 100 **Surface:** ASPH-E
    Runway: 17/35 **Length:** 4252 **Width:** 75 **Surface:** ASPH-F
    Runway: 04/22 **Length:** 6000 **Width:** 100 **Surface:** ASPH-F

★ ★ ★ ★ ★ **The Airport Steak House - (620) 662-4281**
Proprietor: Kevin & Ralph Bowen
Manager: Eddie Wells
Open:

        Mon – Thurs: 8:00am to 8:00pm
        Fri: 8:00am to 9:00pm
        Sat: 11:00am to 9:00pm
        Sun: 11:00am to 8:00pm

Restaurant Website: www.airportsteakhouse.com
Restaurant Email: info@airportsteakhouse.com
PIREP:
Steaks are never better than the ones you get here. They cook them in
front of you over an open charcoal pit using the same Kingsford®
Charcoal you probably use at home. The restaurant is in the terminal
building about fifty steps from the ramp. The entrance above the door
way leading into the eating area is the tail section of a 1/2 scale biplane
positioned as though it has just flown through the wall. Two words
apply – **TOP NOTCH!**

LUCAS, KS (LUCAS - 38K)

    Aprt Mgr: GARY BRETZ **PH:** 785-525-6425
    Field Elevation: 1485 **CTAF:** 122.900 **FUEL:**
    Runway: 17/35 **Length:** 2904 **Width:** 50 **Surface:** ASPH-G

★ ★ ★ **K-18 - (785) 525-6262**

Proprietor: Amanda Maupin
Open:

Mon - Sun: Breakfast & Lunch
PIREP:

K-18 is adjacent to the airstrip. It provides "home-cookin'" breakfast.
Don't overlook the cinnamon rolls and do expect a BIG flyin crowd on
Sunday Morning.

PAOLA, KS (MIAMI COUNTY - K81)
Aprt Mgr: WAYNE HARCLERODE **PH:** 913-755-2345
Field Elevation: 943 **CTAF:** 122.800 **FUEL:** 100LL
Runway: 03/21 **Length:** 3398 **Width:** 60 **Surface:** ASPH-E
Runway: 15/33 **Length:** 2572 **Width:** 60 **Surface:** TURF-F

★ ★ ★ ★ **We-B-Smokin' - (913) 256-6802**
Proprietor: Terry Bright
Open:

Tues- Fri: 11am – 8pm
Sat Breakfast: 7:30 am – 8pm
Sunday Breakfast: 7am – 1pm
Restaurant Website: www.websmokin.com
Restaurant Email: info@websmokin.com/
PIREP:

Be very careful at this airport. It attracts many pilots flying antique
aircraft without radios. Keep your head on a swivel and strictly follow
normal traffic procedures. What about the food? They have very good
BBQ. It is certainly worth the trip. They even made our **$100
Hamburger Best of the Best** list a few years ago. It is not quite as
good now as it was then but it is still worth a stop.

TOPEKA, KS (PHILIP BILLARD MUNI - TOP)
Aprt Mgr: ERIC M. JOHNSON **PH:** 785-862-2362
Field Elevation: 881 **CTAF:** 118.700 **FUEL:** 100LLA
Runway: 04/22 **Length:** 3002 **Width:** 100 **Surface:** ASPH-F
Runway: 18/36 **Length:** 4331 **Width:** 75 **Surface:** ASPH-G
Runway: 13/31 **Length:** 5099 **Width:** 100 **Surface:** ASPH-G

★ ★ ★ **Tammy's Billard Airport Restaurant - (785) 232-3669**
Proprietor: Tammy Bailey
Open:

Wed – Mon: 8:00 am - 2:00 pm
Restaurant Website: www.mtaa-topeka.org/billard-airport/billard-
amenities
PIREP:

The place is right next to the ramp, and as you walk inside, it looks a bit run down, but don't be discouraged! This restaurant has been serving good ole' hot American food for more than half a century. Don't expect fancy but do expect wonderful down home food. I love this place.

TOPEKA, KS (FORBES FIELD - FOE)
Aprt Mgr: MR ERIC M JOHNSON **PH:** 785-862-2362
Field Elevation: 1078 **CTAF:** 120.800 **FUEL:** 100LLA
Runway: 03/21 **Length:** 7001 **Width:** 150 **Surface:** CONC-F
Runway: 13/31 **Length:** 12803 **Width:** 200 **Surface:** CONC-G

★ ★ ★ **Jet-A-Way Café – (785) 862-0950**
Proprietor: Million Air FOE
General Manager: Walt Frederick
Open:
Sun -Sat: 8:00am - 6:00pm
Restaurant Website: www.millionair.com/FBO/foe.aspx#2
Restaurant Email: wfrederick@millionair.com
PIREP:
Forbes Field is home to two Military units. On the north end of the airport is the Kansas Air National Guard unit that actively flies KC-135 aircraft. On the south end of the airport is a Kansas Army National Guard unit that is supported by various helicopters and other Military aircraft. Million Air is located in the middle of the airport in the main terminal building. Huge BBQ pork BBQ Beef or turkey sandwiches with potato salad and BBQ beans. Get an ice cream float for dessert. Great FBO, quick turnarounds, good food.

WINFIELD/ARKANSAS CITY, KS (STROTHER FIELD - WLD)
Aprt Mgr: SHAWN MCGREW **PH:** 620-221-9280
Field Elevation: 1160 **CTAF:** 122.800 **FUEL:** 100LLA
Runway: 13/31 **Length:** 3137 **Width:** 75 **Surface:** ASPH-G
Runway: 17/35 **Length:** 5506 **Width:** 100 **Surface:** ASPH-G

★ ★ ★ **Landing Strip - (620) 442-2800**
Proprietor: Todd Byers
Open:
Mon – Fri: 7am – 2pm
PIREP:
Excellent food but they are only open for breakfast and lunch on WEEKDAYS. Bummer!

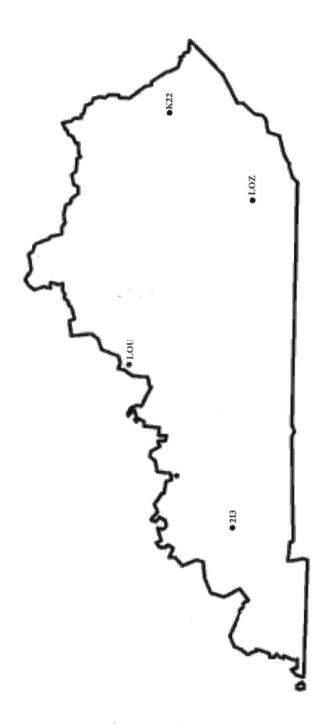

$100 Hamburger 2014/15

FlyIn Kentucky

ɪ●ɪ **FALLS-OF-ROUGH, KY (ROUGH RIVER STATE PARK - 2I3)**
    Aprt Mgr: CHUCK TEMPFER **PH:** 270-257-2311
    Field Elevation: 577 **CTAF:** 122.800 **FUEL:**
    Runway: 02/20 **Length:** 3200 **Width:** 75 **Surface:** ASPH-G

    ★ ★ ★ ★ ★ **Grayson's Landing Restaurant - (270) 257-2311**
    Proprietor: Chef Connell
    Open:
            Thurs: 4:30pm to 8:00pm
            Fri & Sat: 7:00am - 8:00pm
            Sun: 7:00am - 3:00pm
    Restaurant Website: www.parks.ky.gov/parks/resortparks/rough-river
    Restaurant Email: michael.ricks@ky.gov
    PIREP:
There are no instrument approaches so save this for a nice day. The landing strip is in very good shape and there is a pilot lounge. Be sure to bring your own chocks and tiedowns and remember the airport is unattended. The walk to the lodge is very short. You will eat overlooking a lake. A very pleasant experience all-and-all. The food is very good and the service is admirable.

ɪ●ɪ **LONDON, KY (LONDON-CORBIN ARPT-MAGEE FLD - LOZ)**
    Aprt Mgr: LARRY CORUM **PH:** 606-232-1452
    Field Elevation: 1212 **CTAF:** 123.000 **FUEL:** 100LLA+
    Runway: 06/24 **Length:** 5751 **Width:** 150 **Surface:** ASPH-G

    ★ ★ ★ **Hangar Restaurant - (606) 864-0530**
    Proprietor: Carol Gentry
    Open:
            Mon - Sun: 11am - Midnight
    Restaurant Website:
    www.london-corbinairport.com/the-hangar-restaurant.html
    PIREP:
Located next to the FBO so it is easy to find. It is a café with a bar, a few big screens and a late closing. I think of it as a cross between a sports bar and a mom and pop airport restaurant. The food is good but there are no surprises merely very ordinary offerings. The service is friendly.

ɪ●ɪ **LOUISVILLE, KY (BOWMAN FIELD - LOU)**
    Aprt Mgr: PH: 502-458-1475

Field Elevation: 546 **CTAF:** 119.500 **FUEL:** 100LLA
Runway: 06/24 **Length:** 4326 **Width:** 75 **Surface:** ASPH-F
Runway: 15/33 **Length:** 3579 **Width:** 75 **Surface:** ASPH-G

★ ★ ★ ★ ★ Bistro Le Relais - **502-451-9020**
Proprietor: Anthony Dike
Chef: Alexander Dulaney
Open:
>Fri: 11:30am – 2pm
>Tues – Sun: 5:30pm – 10pm

Restaurant Website: www.lerelaisrestaurant.com
Restaurant Email: lerelaisrst@bellsouth.net
PIREP:
Without doubt this is the best airport restaurant in Kentucky. It may be the best restaurant in Kentucky period. Come for dinner and plan on spending the night so you can enjoy a nice wine with your meal. The price is formidable but commensurate with the quality of the meal you will enjoy. It is located in the old terminal building. It's like going back in time to the 1930s. The food is French. The décor reminds you of Rick's Café in the movie Casablanca. Don't miss this one.

🍽 PRESTONSBURG, KY (BIG SANDY RGNL - K22)
Aprt Mgr: GARY COX **PH:** 606-298-5930
Field Elevation: 1221 **CTAF:** 123.050 **FUEL:** 100LLA+
Runway: 03/21 **Length:** 5000 **Width:** 100 **Surface:** ASPH-G

★ ★ ★ Cloud 9 Café - **(606) 298-2799**
Proprietor: Gary Cox
Open:
>Mon - Sun: 11am – 8pm

Restaurant Website: www.bigsandyregional.com/cafe.htm
PIREP:
This friendly café is located right next to the terminal. On the front porch you'll find several rocking chairs. Pick one out and sit a spell. It's kinda' like a mini Cracker Barrel! In the evening you may see some elk. There is a herd nearby and sometimes they show up.

FlyIn Louisiana

● JENNINGS, LA (JENNINGS - 3R7)
Aprt Mgr: DWAYNE BEBEE **PH:** 337-616-2370
Field Elevation: 23 **CTAF:** 122.800 **FUEL:** 100LLA
Runway: 13/31 **Length:** 3601 **Width:** 75 **Surface:** ASPH-E
Runway: 08/26 **Length:** 5002 **Width:** 75 **Surface:** ASPH-E
Runway: 17/35 **Length:** 1977 **Width:** 150 **Surface:** TURF-G

★ King Buffett - (337) 824-8848
Proprietor: Chef Connell
Open:
> Mon - Sun: 11am – 8pm

PIREP:
The King Buffet is an all you can eat Chinese buffet kinda' place. Park your plane on the east side of airport. Walk past the Quality Inn and the King Buffet is located inside the Days Inn. The reviews of this Days Inn range someplace between wretched and barely adequate. I have never stayed here and probably never will. The hosting facility gives you a view of what to expect at **The King Buffet**. If you're really hungry it will work. Don't expect much and you won't be disappointed.

● MONROE, LA (MONROE RGNL - MLU)
Aprt Mgr: CLEVE NORRELL **PH:** 318-329-2461
Field Elevation: 79 **CTAF:** 118.900 **FUEL:** 100LLA
Runway: 18/36 **Length:** 5001 **Width:** 150 **Surface:** ASPH-G
Runway: 04/22 **Length:** 7505 **Width:** 150 **Surface:** ASPH-G
Runway: 14/32 **Length:** 4999 **Width:** 150 **Surface:** ASPH-P

★★★ Spitfire Grill - (318) 324-8631
Proprietor: Terry LaPrarie
Open:
> Mon – Sun: 5am to 5:00pm

Restaurant Website: www.spitfiregrill.webs.com
Restaurant Email: tlaprarie@gmail.com
PIREP:
This is a pretty good Cajun style restaurant that also serves some pretty decent hamburgers. I eat one thing when I come here, the Shrimp PoBoy. While it certainly isn't the best one I've ever had. It is good and it is the best one I've ever had at an airport. They have other Cajun dishes. Next time I'll branch out.

● NEW IBERIA, LA (ACADIANA RGNL - ARA)

Aprt Mgr: F. JASON DEVILLIER **PH:** 337-365-7202
Field Elevation: 24 **CTAF:** 125.000 **FUEL:** 100LLA
Runway: 16/34 **Length:** 8002 **Width:** 200 **Surface:** CONC-G

★ ★ ★ ★ **Pelican Aviation - (337) 367-1401**
Proprietor: Edward Lasalle
Open:
> Mon - Sun: 7am - Sunset

Restaurant Website: www.pelican.us
Restaurant Email: gigi@pelican.us
PIREP:
The FBO, **Pelican Aviation**, provides a low cost, high quality meat and three type buffet every day at lunch. Its purpose is to draw in the military pilots and their fuel purchases. It works which make a stop here double fun. Good food and active military aircraft on the flight line. Call first as this can't go on forever.

$100 Hamburger 2014/15

FlyIn Maine

🍴 **AUGUSTA, ME (AUGUSTA STATE - AUG)**
    Aprt Mgr: JOHN GUIMOND **PH:** 207-626-2306
    Field Elevation: 352 **CTAF:** 123.000 **FUEL:** 100LLA
    Runway: 17/35 **Length:** 5001 **Width:** 150 **Surface:** ASPH-F
    Runway: 08/26 **Length:** 2703 **Width:** 75 **Surface:** ASPH-G

    ★ ★ ★ **Sweet Chili Thai Restaurant - (207) 621-8575**
Proprietor: Suparinya Anderson and Pringpanee Itthipalakornl
Open:
        Mon-Sat: 11:00am - 9:00pm
Restaurant Website: www.sweetchillithai.com
Restaurant Email: info@sweetchillithai.com
PIREP:
If you like Thai food and I do this is a must. It is one of only two Thai restaurants on an airport in the United States.

🍴 **BANGOR, ME (BANGOR INTL - BGR)**
    Aprt Mgr: REBECCA HUPP **PH:** 207-992-4600
    Field Elevation: 192 **CTAF:** 0.000 **FUEL:** 100LLA
    Runway: 15/33 **Length:** 11440 **Width:** 200 **Surface:** ASPH-G

    ★ ★ ★ **Red Baron - (207) 947-4375**
Proprietor: Jerry J. Caterer
Open:
        Mon – Sun: 7am – 9pm
PIREP:
Bangor International is a somewhat active commercial airport that also handles many transatlantic GA flights. When you land you'll be directed to the GA ramp. The FBO will be happy to give you a lift to the domestic terminal, where you can take refuge in the **Red Baron Lounge**. The food is pretty standard commercial airport fare as is the service. While this is not a destination Burger run, it is a great place to eat if you have another reason to be at Bangor International.

🏛 **ROCKLAND, ME (KNOX COUNTY RGNL - RKD)**
    Aprt Mgr: JEFF NORTHGRAVES **PH:** 207-594-4131
    Field Elevation: 56 **CTAF:** 123.050 **FUEL:** 100LLA
    Runway: 03/21 **Length:** 4000 **Width:** 100 **Surface:** ASPH-G
    Runway: 13/31 **Length:** 5007 **Width:** 100 **Surface:** ASPH-G

    ★ ★ ★ **Owl's Head Transportation Museum - (207) 594-4418**

www.100dollarhamburger.com

Proprietor: Kevin Bedford
Open:
>Mon - Sun: 10am – 5pm

Restaurant Website: www.ohtm.org
Restaurant Email: info@ohtm.org
PIREP:

Let's be clear, you do not come here for the food. It is merely a concession stand. You show-up to visit the Museum which is really pretty cool. Check out their website and plan accordingly. The aviation portion of the Museum is light but interesting.

⦿ SANFORD, ME (SANFORD RGNL - SFM)

Aprt Mgr: DANA H. PARRY **PH:** 207-432-0596
Field Elevation: 244 **CTAF:** 123.075 **FUEL:** 100LLA
Runway: 14/32 **Length:** 4999 **Width:** 100 **Surface:** ASPH-G
Runway: 07/25 **Length:** 6389 **Width:** 100 **Surface:** ASPH-G

★ ★ ★ The Cockpit Cafe - (207) 324-7332

Proprietor: Edward Lasalle
Open:
>Mon – Fri: 7am - 2pm
>Sat – Sun: 7am - Noon

Restaurant Website:
www.flyingsma.com/sanford-airport-fbo/cockpit-cafe/
Restaurant Email: info@flyingsma.com
PIREP:

The **Cockpit Cafe** is in the main terminal building, next to Southern Maine Aviation. There is plenty of no charge ramp parking. This is a good place to come for breakfast. Expect a crowd on the weekends as many locals show up. I always go with the lobster omelet as it is not something I can get anywhere else and it is very tasty.

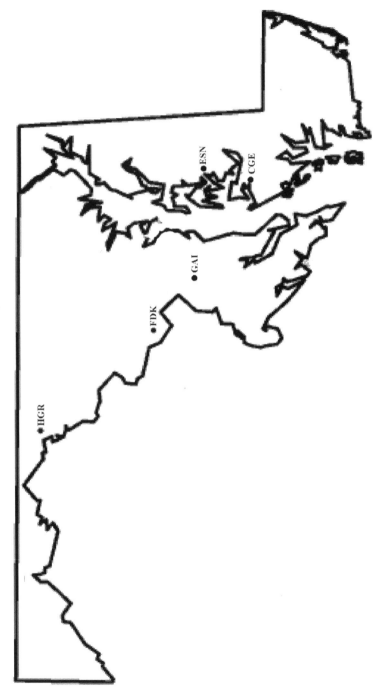

www.100dollarhamburger.com

FlyIn Maryland

⦿ CAMBRIDGE, MD (CAMBRIDGE-DORCHESTER - CGE)
Aprt Mgr: ROBERT TENANTY **PH:** 410-228-4571
Field Elevation: 20 **CTAF:** 122.700 **FUEL:** 100LLA
Runway: 16/34 **Length:** 4477 **Width:** 75 **Surface:** ASPH-G

★ ★ ★ ★ **Kay's At The Airport - (410) 901-8844**
Proprietor: Kay Rhea
Open:
>   Thu – Tue: 8:00 AM - 8:00 PM
>   Sunday – 8:00 AM - 3:00 PM

Restaurant Website: www.facebook.com/kaysattheairport
Restaurant Email: homecook99@gmail.com
PIREP:
Home cooked food, family atmosphere, and great service can all be found at this locally and operated restaurant located in the Dorcester County Airport Terminal. I have had the crab cakes here and they are pretty darn good. Well worth a stop.

⦿ EASTON, MD (EASTON/NEWNAM FIELD - ESN)
Aprt Mgr: MIKE HENRY **PH:** 410-770-8055
Field Elevation: 72 **CTAF:** 118.525 **FUEL:** 100LLA
Runway: 04/22 **Length:** 5500 **Width:** 100 **Surface:** ASPH-E
Runway: 15/33 **Length:** 4003 **Width:** 100 **Surface:** ASPH-G

★ ★ ★ **Sugar Buns Airport Cafe and Bakery- (410) 820-4220**
Proprietor: Susan Leonard
Open:
>   Monday-Saturday:
>   Lunch: 11:00 am to 3:00 pm
>   Dinner: 3:00 pm to 9:00 pm

Restaurant Website: www.sugarbuns.com
Restaurant Email: sugarbunscafe@yahoo.com
PIREP:
This is a small café and it gets crowded quickly on the weekends. No matter, the food is very good. The Lobster Roll is my lunch pick. It is served on a frankfurter roll which is odd but the bun is very good as they bake all of their own bread – all of it. This is more of a bakery than a restaurant so you can cart off bread and cakes if you desire.

⦿ FREDERICK, MD (FREDERICK MUNI - FDK)
Aprt Mgr: KEVIN DAUGHERTY **PH:** 301-600-2201

Field Elevation: 306 **CTAF:** 122.725 **FUEL:** 100LLA
Runway: 12/30 **Length:** 3600 **Width:** 75 **Surface:** ASPH-G
Runway: 05/23 **Length:** 5219 **Width:** 100 **Surface:** ASPH-G

★★★ Airways Inn of Frederick - (301) 228-2100
Proprietor: Jang Sewell
Open:
> Mon: 7:30am – 3pm
> Tues - Thurs: 7:30am – 8pm
> Fri: 7:30am - 9pm
> Sat: 7am – 9pm
> Sun: 7am – 7pm

Restaurant Website: www.airwaysinnoffrederick.com
Restaurant Email: airwaysinn@frederick.com
PIREP:
Many pilots like to come to Frederick because it is home to AOPA. I come here to visit **Airways Inn of Frederick**. It's that good. My choice is the steamed shrimp. I became aware of them when I was living in Newport News. I love them.

🍽 GAITHERSBURG, MD (MONTGOMERY COUNTY - GAI)
Aprt Mgr: JOHN LUKE III **PH:** 301-963-7100
Field Elevation: 539 **CTAF:** 123.075 **FUEL:** 100LLA
Runway: 14/32 **Length:** 4202 **Width:** 75 **Surface:** ASPH-G

★★★ The Airport Cafe - (301) 330-2222
Proprietor: Kerop Hadadian
Open:
> Mon - Sun: 8am – 9pm

Restaurant Website: www.theairportcafe.com
Restaurant Email: info@theairportcafe.com
PIREP:
The Airport Cafe is located in the terminal building and is a great place for breakfast especially on the weekends when they have Eggs Benedict for $6.95. Luckily they have a deck outside to be enjoyed when the weather is good. The view of the Chesapeake and all of its towns and harbors make for an interesting flight. I love flying over this part of the country.

🍽 HAGERSTOWN, MD (HAGERSTOWN RGNL - HGR)
Aprt Mgr: PHIL RIDENOUR **PH:** 240-313-2777
Field Elevation: 703 **CTAF:** 120.300 **FUEL:** 100LLA A1
Runway: 02/20 **Length:** 3165 **Width:** 100 **Surface:** ASPH-G
Runway: 09/27 **Length:** 7000 **Width:** 150 **Surface:** ASPH-G

★ ★ ★ ★ ★ **Nick's Airport Inn - (301) 733 8560**
Proprietor: Nick, Paul & Tina Giannaris
Open:

        Mon - Fri: 11:00am - 10:00pm
        Saturday: 11:00am - 10:30pm

Restaurant Website: www.nicksairportinn.com
Restaurant Email: info@ nicksairportinn.com
PIREP:

You'll have to park at Ryder Jet Center and borrow one of their three courtesy cars to drive to Nick's which is about a mile away. The car is FRE and there is no ramp fee if you buy 10 gallons. The FBO that used to be next is closed. Nick's is not your typical airport café. It is more like a fine downtown restaurant. Nick's is famous for crab cakes. I ordered them once and quickly understood why. Now I'm in a rut. When I go to Nick's that's what I eat. They have many other great choices that I never tried.

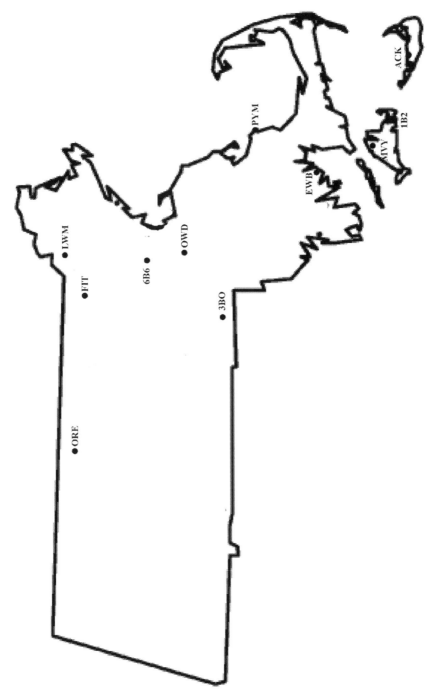

FlyIn Massachusetts

⭑◉⭑ EDGARTOWN, MA (KATAMA AIRPARK - 1B2)
Aprt Mgr: MICHAEL CREATO **PH:** 508-627-9018
Field Elevation: 18 **CTAF:** 122.800 **FUEL:** 100LL
Runway: 17/35 **Length:** 2600 **Width:** 50 **Surface:** TURF-G
Runway: 06/24 **Length:** 2700 **Width:** 50 **Surface:** TURF-G
Runway: 03/21 **Length:** 3700 **Width:** 50 **Surface:** TURF-G

★ ★ ★ Right Fork Diner - (508) 627-5522
Proprietor: Jamie Langley
Open:
> Seasonally for Breakfast, Lunch & Dinner
> Open Memorial Day through Columbus Day.

Restaurant Website: www.rightforkdiner.com
> www.facebook.com/rightforkdiner

Restaurant Email: rightforkdiner@hotmail.com
PIREP:

The season will commence on May 16th 2014. This is the airport that we ALL want to visit. It is a beautiful well maintained turf airport with three runways and two parking areas. I have come here twice to spent the day at the beach. Park at the opposite end of the airport from the restaurant and walk a path to the Atlantic. You'll have to cross the street. You should come early and stay a few hours at the sandy beach. There is a small fee that you pay at the restaurant, that is used to maintain the field. What about the food? Well, it's pretty darn good. Sit on their large deck and enjoy breakfast lunch or dinner.

⭑◉⭑ FITCHBURG, MA (FITCHBURG MUNI - FIT)
Aprt Mgr: ALFRED P. GUERTIN **PH:** 978-345-9580
Field Elevation: 348 **CTAF:** 122.700 **FUEL:** 100LLA
Runway: 02/20 **Length:** 3504 **Width:** 75 **Surface:** ASPH-G
Runway: 14/32 **Length:** 4510 **Width:** 100 **Surface:** ASPH-G

★ ★ ★ Gene Collette's Airport Restaurant - (978) 345-1580
Proprietor: Gene Collette
Open:
> Mon - Sun: 7:00 am - 2:00 pm

Restaurant Website: www.fitchburgairport.com/genes-restaurant/
PIREP:

Transient parking is right next to the terminal. The restaurant is just inside. It's a small café with very friendly service. The highlight of the menu is the homemade pies. Buy one to go and enjoy it all week.

ιΘι LAWRENCE, MA (LAWRENCE MUNI - LWM)
Aprt Mgr: MICHAEL MILLER **PH:** 978-794-5880
Field Elevation: 148 **CTAF:** 119.250 **FUEL:** 100LLA
Runway: 14/32 **Length:** 3900 **Width:** 100 **Surface:** ASPH-F
Runway: 05/23 **Length:** 5001 **Width:** 150 **Surface:** ASPH-G

★★★ Joe's Landing Café - (978) 682-8822
Proprietor: Joe Chedid
Open:
Mon - Sun: Breakfast and Lunch
PIREP:
The menu is filed with the ordinary American dishes that you expect plus a list of Mediterranean foods that will surprise and delight you. I am glad to come here when I need a break from hamburgers and pancakes.

ιΘι NANTUCKET, MA (NANTUCKET MEMORIAL - ACK)
Aprt Mgr: ALFRED G. PETERSON **PH:** 508-325-5300
Field Elevation: 47 **CTAF:** 118.300 **FUEL:** 100LLA
Runway: 12/30 **Length:** 2696 **Width:** 50 **Surface:** ASPH-F
Runway: 15/33 **Length:** 4000 **Width:** 100 **Surface:** ASPH-G
Runway: 06/24 **Length:** 6303 **Width:** 150 **Surface:** ASPH-G

★★★ Crosswinds Restaurant & Bar - 508-228-6005
Open:
Mon - Sun: 5:30am - 9:00pm
Restaurant Website: www.crosswindsnantucket.com
Restaurant Email: eat@crosswindsnantucket.com
PIREP:
The Nantucket Memorial Airport was home to the *"Wings"* television series. Some of which was shot in the restaurant. They claim to have a menu that will fill you up without emptying your wallet. I think that's true as the portions a HUGE and the prices are low. My lunch favorite is the chicken pot pie because you can't get it everywhere and the BLT because they use wonderful tomatoes that I suspect are grown locally.

ιΘι NEW BEDFORD, MA (NEW BEDFORD RGNL - EWB)
Aprt Mgr: THOMAS M. VICK **PH:** 508-991-6160
Field Elevation: 79 **CTAF:** 118.100 **FUEL:** 100LLA
Runway: 05/23 **Length:** 4997 **Width:** 150 **Surface:** ASPH-F
Runway: 14/32 **Length:** 5000 **Width:** 150 **Surface:** ASPH-F

★★★★ The Airport Grille - 508-994-7455
Proprietor: Robert Cassi

Open:

        Mon – Thurs: 11:30 am - 9:00 pm

        Fri – Sat: 11:30 am - 10:00 pm

        Sun: 11:30 am - 9:00 pm

Restaurant Website: www.airportgrille.com

Restaurant Email: info@airportgrille.com

PIREP:

Taxi to the terminal and park on its ramp, the controller tower sits right on top of it. Walk inside and work your way up to the second floor. **The Airport Grille's** elevated position and huge plate glass windows offer an expanse view of the airport. **The Grille** is an upscale modern American bistro providing a warm and relaxing environment. They use local produce and seafood and also have steaks and chops plus a pretty good wine. For lunch I recommend the wedge salad and the baked codfish.

⚬ NORWOOD, MA (NORWOOD MEMORIAL - OWD)

    Aprt Mgr: RUSS MAGUIRE **PH:** 781-255-5616

    Field Elevation: 49 **CTAF:** 126.000 **FUEL:** 100LLA

    Runway: 10/28 **Length:** 3995 **Width:** 75 **Surface:** ASPH-G

    Runway: 17/35 **Length:** 4008 **Width:** 100 **Surface:** ASPH-G

★ ★ ★ **Taso's Euro-Cafe – (781) 278-0001**

Proprietor: Christiana Kapsaskis

Open:

        Mon – Thurs: 11:00 am - 9:00 pm

        Fri – Sat: 11:00 am - 10:00 pm

Restaurant Website: www.tasoseurocafe.com

Restaurant Email: tasos42@gmail.com

PIREP:

This is a family owned and operated Greek restaurant. The food and service are amazing. It is well worth the trip. Go with the baked lamb. It is really, really good. Start with an order of calamari for the table. Be warned they are not opened on Sunday.

⚬ ORANGE, MA (ORANGE MUNI - ORE)

    Aprt Mgr: LEONARD BEDAW **PH:** 978-544-8189

    Field Elevation: 555 **CTAF:** 122.800 **FUEL:** 100LLA

    Runway: 14/32 **Length:** 4801 **Width:** 75 **Surface:** ASPH-G

    Runway: 01/19 **Length:** 5000 **Width:** 75 **Surface:** ASPH-G

★ ★ **Sharon's White Cloud Diner - (978) 544-6821**

Proprietor: Sharon Prue

Open:

        Mon – Sun: 6am - 2pm

PIREP:

The airport is a very active skydiving center so monitor CTAF and time your arrival to miss theirs. It takes about 5 minutes to walk from the tie-down through the airport office, down the drive and across the street to the restaurant. It's a big airport so be sure to tie down near the office off the taxiway parallel to 14/32. They make honest if not great food. The service is fast and genuinely friendly.

✈ PLYMOUTH, MA (PLYMOUTH MUNI - PYM)

Aprt Mgr: TOM MAHER **PH:** 508-746-2020
Field Elevation: 148 **CTAF:** 123.000 **FUEL:** 100LLA
Runway: 15/33 **Length:** 3351 **Width:** 75 **Surface:** ASPH-G
Runway: 06/24 **Length:** 4350 **Width:** 75 **Surface:** ASPH-G

★ ★ ★ ★ Plane Jane's Cafe - (508) 747-9396

Proprietor: Jane Grennell
Open:

> Mon – Wed: 6am to 3pm
> Thurs & Fri: 6am to 9pm
> Sat & Sun: 6am to pm

Restaurant Website: www.planejanesplace.com
Restaurant Email: info@planejanesplace.com
PIREP:

For 20 years this Mom and son owned and operated restaurant has been serving up the **BEST** breakfast in New England. Do no miss any opportunity to land here. Consider how good any airport restaurant has to be to survive for 20 years let alone thrive. These folks continue to expand and improve the place. I enjoy sitting on their deck and eating their Blueberry pancakes with a side of crisp bacon.

✈ SOUTHBRIDGE, MA (SOUTHBRIDGE MUNI - 3B0)

Aprt Mgr: JAMES LATOUR **PH:** 508-765-0226
Field Elevation: 699 **CTAF:** 122.800 **FUEL:** 100LL
Runway: 02/20 **Length:** 3501 **Width:** 75 **Surface:** ASPH-G
Runway: 10/28 **Length:** 1450 **Width:** 100 **Surface:** TURF-G

★ ★ ★ Jim's Fly-in Diner - (508) 765-7100

Proprietor: Paul and Louise Servant
Open:

> Seasonal – May through September
> Tue & Wed: 7:00 am – 2:00 pm
> Thurs & Fri: 7:00 am – 8:00 pm
> Sat & Sun: 6 am– 2:00 pm

PIREP:

South bridge offers a good paved runway and a short turf runway. Take your pick and taxi to within 10 feet of this small diner. They have a good cheese burger and a decent patio to eat it on. Be warned this is a seasonal stop.

🍴 STOW, MA (MINUTE MAN AIR FIELD - 6B6)
Aprt Mgr: DONALD MC PHERSON **PH:** 978-897-3933
Field Elevation: 268 **CTAF:** 122.800 **FUEL:** 100LL
Runway: 03/21 **Length:** 2770 **Width:** 48 **Surface:** ASPH-F
Runway: 12/30 **Length:** 1600 **Width:** 70 **Surface:** TURF-GRVL-F

★ ★ ★ ★ ★ **Nancy's Air Field Cafe - (978) 897-3934**
Proprietor: Nancy McPherson
Open:

Wed, Thur, Sun: 8am - 3pm
Fri – Sat: 8am - 9pm

Restaurant Website: www.nancysairfieldcafe.com
Restaurant Email: info@nancysairfieldcafe.com
PIREP:

This is a great place to come to fuel your body and your plane. The food at **Nancy's** is really good and deserving of the awards and accolades it has received. The fuel price is one of the lowest in the country and certainly the lowest in New England. All of that well earned praise acknowledged it is also true that you must take care with the runway. The FAA marks them *(turf or asphalt)* as Fair and that is generous. They are long overdue for repair. Do come here but do be careful.

🍴 VINEYARD HAVEN, MA (MARTHAS VINEYARD - MVY)
Aprt Mgr: SEAN FLYNN **PH:** 508-693-7022
Field Elevation: 67 **CTAF:** 121.400 **FUEL:** 100LLA
Runway: 15/33 **Length:** 3328 **Width:** 75 **Surface:** ASPH-G
Runway: 06/24 **Length:** 5504 **Width:** 100 **Surface:** ASPH-G

★ ★ ★ ★ **Plane View Restaurant - (508) 693-1886**
Proprietor: Robert Jackson
Open:

Mon – Sun: 7:00 am - 3:00 pm
Mon – Sun: 7:00 am - 7:00 pm (June 23 through September 5)

PIREP:
I like Martha's Vineyard. It is a good place to visit during the shoulder seasons. The food is good, the service is crisp and the prices are astoundingly low. Can you imagine getting a three egg cheese omelet for less than five bucks anywhere let alone on MV? This is one of my favorite New England flyin's. I come here eat breakfast, grab and bus

and wonder the island. The Martha's Vineyard Regional Transit Authority operates public buses from the airport to all of the island villages and many popular island locations. Bus routes also serve several **island beaches** including **State Beach**, **Oak Bluffs**, and **South Beach** in Edgartown. **The island's bus system is uncommonly clean and efficient and is a model of public transportation systems.** Sometimes I hang out at the beach all day but that's just me.

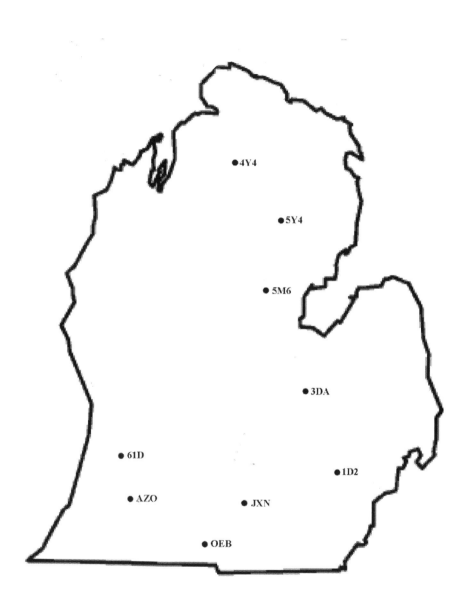

$100 Hamburger 2014/15

FlyIn Michigan

🍽 COLDWATER, MI (BRANCH COUNTY MEMORIAL - OEB)
Aprt Mgr: RON DOOLEY **PH:** 517-279-7050
Field Elevation: 959 **CTAF:** 122.700 **FUEL:** 100LLA
Runway: 07/25 **Length:** 5350 **Width:** 75 **Surface:** ASPH-F
Runway: 04/22 **Length:** 3500 **Width:** 75 **Surface:** ASPH-G
Runway: 16/34 **Length:** 2400 **Width:** 190 **Surface:** TURF-G

★ ★ ★ Prop Blast Café - 517-781-6000
Proprietor: Shawn Avra
Manager: Zach Van Stelle
Open:
> Mon - Sun: 11am to 8pm

Restaurant Website: www.propblastcafe.com
Restaurant Email: zach@propblastcafe.com
PIREP:
The café is located in the FBO building which is right on the taxiway with plenty of ramp space. This is one of those places that pays careful attention to the ingredients that they place before you. For instance, they serve only romaine lettuce in their salads and on their sandwiches; no iceberg is served here. It is a small homey place with good service. For lunch I suggest the chicken wrap.

🍽 FLUSHING, MI (DALTON - 3DA)
Aprt Mgr: ANTHONY SABOURIN **PH:** 810-624-4001
Field Elevation: 733 **CTAF:** 122.800 **FUEL:** 100LL
Runway: 18/36 **Length:** 2510 **Width:** 50 **Surface:** ASPH-F
Runway: 09/27 **Length:** 1633 **Width:** 130 **Surface:** TURF-G

★ ★ ★ Liberty Family Restaurant - (810) 867-4768
Proprietor: Art & John Panos
Open:
> Mon - Sat: 7am - 9pm
> Sun: 7am - 4pm

PIREP:
Dalton is an interesting little airport populated by airplane folks. There are a slew of hangars and a good number of homes with hangars -- some very nice and at least one single wide mobile home -- with hangar. This is truly an *"everyman's airpark."* Park in the grass at the north end of 18/36 and walk over to the diner. The food is about what you'd expect. The service is very good. The place fills up with locals on the weekends.

⦾ Ϯ GAYLORD, MI (LAKES OF THE NORTH - 4Y4)
　　Aprt Mgr: SCOTT BROWN **PH:** 231-585-6000
　　Field Elevation: 1286 **CTAF:** 122.900 **FUEL:**
　　Runway: 05/23 **Length:** 4285 **Width:** 40 **Surface:** ASPH-P

★ ★ Settings Restaurant - (231) 585-6000
Proprietor: Joe and Jan Lauka
Open:
　　　　　Mon - Sun: 7:00am - 10:00pm
Restaurant Website: www.settingsrestaurant.com
Restaurant Email: info@settingsrestaurant.com
PIREP:
LAKES OF THE NORTH is the getaway resort area for Michigan. It is scenic and fun with lakes, forest and recreational opportunities everywhere. '**Settings**' serves the golfers in the summer and the snowmobilers in the winter. Pilots are welcome year round. The food is what you'd expect for a muni. golf course clubhouse. I came here to play a round and munch a burger. Both were good but you don't really come here for the food.

★ ★ ★ Deer Run Golf Course – (800) 851-4653
Golf Pro: Mike Alpers
Open:
　　　　　Seasonal
Restaurant Website: settingsrestaurant.com
Restaurant Email: tcalpers@yahoo.com
PIREP:
You can cart your clubs over from the tie-down. A round with a cart will set you make about $35.00, which is a really good deal.

⦾ Ϯ GLADWIN, MI (SUGAR SPRINGS - 5M6)
　　Aprt Mgr: RICHARD SAGER **PH:** 989-426-9153
　　Field Elevation: 940 **CTAF:** 122.900 **FUEL:**
　　Runway: E/W **Length:** 3800 **Width:** 50 **Surface:** TURF

★ ★ ★ ★ ★ The Hearth Restaurant & Pub - (989) 426-9203
Proprietor: Nancy McPherson
Open:
　　　　　Sun: 9am - 8pm
　　　　　Mon - Thurs: 4pm - 8pm
　　　　　Fri: 4pm - 10pm
　　　　　Sat: 11am - 10pm
Restaurant Website: www.sugarsprings.net/Restaurant/dining.html
PIREP:

This is a terrific place to slip away to for a round of golf or a good meal. Remember, this is a PRIVATE airstrip and permission **MUST** be granted before you land. It's easy to obtain. Simply call the Property Owners Association Office at 989-426-4111, the Golf Pro Shop at 989-426-4391, or the Hearth Restaurant at 989-426-9203. Park at the west or east end *(the west end is easier and has an access road)*. Bring your own tie-downs and have a member or guest pass with you. The food, service, ambiance and setting are all excellent. I recommend fish not seafood but local lake fish; either the whitefish or yellow belly perch. They are really worth the trip.

★ ★ ★ ★ ★ **Sugar Springs Golf Club - (989) 426-9203**
Proprietor: Nancy McPherson
Open:
　　　　Seasonal
Restaurant Website:
www.sugarsprings.net/Golf/golfcoursehome.html
PIREP:
Sugar Springs Golf Club is 6,737 yards, par 72, 18 hole championship course, designed by Jerry Matthews. It weaves through a wooded front nine and a more open back nine with subtle elevation changes, water in play on five holes, & greens guarded with bunkers that creates an enjoyable challenge for golfers of all skill levels. The 18 hole green fee is about $30.00! The resort also offers many lakes, an Olympic size pool, archery and tennis.

JACKSON, MI (JACKSON COUNTY-REYNOLDS FIELD - JXN)
　　　Aprt Mgr: KENT L MAURER **PH:** 517-788-4225
　　　Field Elevation: 1001 **CTAF:** 128.475 **FUEL:** 100LLA
　　　Runway: 06/24 **Length:** 5349 **Width:** 150 **Surface:** ASPH-F
　　　Runway: 14/32 **Length:** 4000 **Width:** 100 **Surface:** ASPH-G

　　　★ ★ ★ **The Airport Restaurant & Spirits - (517) 783-3616**
　　　Proprietor: Dianne Weems
　　　Open:
　　　　　　Mon - Sun: 7am – 8pm
PIREP:
I have never made this stop but hope too soon. From all reports of the $100 Hamburger website subscribers, it is one of the best burger restaurants in the area made better by its proximity to Michigan International Speedway and all of the auto company proving grounds which are scattered nearby.

KALAMAZOO, MI (KALAMAZOO INTL - AZO)
　　　Aprt Mgr: CLIFTON MOSHOGINIS **PH:** 269-388-3668

Field Elevation: 874 **CTAF:** 118.300 **FUEL:** 100LLA
Runway: 09/27 **Length:** 2800 **Width:** 60 **Surface:** ASPH-G
Runway: 05/23 **Length:** 3438 **Width:** 100 **Surface:** ASPH-G
Runway: 17/35 **Length:** 6502 **Width:** 150 **Surface:** ASPH-G

★The Air Zoo "Kitty Hawk Cafe" - (866) 524-7966
Proprietor: EMA Enterprises
Open:
>Mon - Sun: Lunch

Restaurant Website: www.airzoo.org/page.php?page_id=80
Restaurant Email: airzoo@airzoo.org
PIREP:
There is a snack bar on the second floor of the museum. You don't come here for the food but you shouldn't starve if you're that hungry. 'Nuff said!

★ ★ ★ ★ ★The KALAMAZOO Air Zoo – (269) 382-6555
Open:
>Mon - Sat: 9:00am - 5:00pm
>Sun: 12:0 pm - 5:00pm

Restaurant Website: www.airzoo.org
Restaurant Email: airzoo@airzoo.org
PIREP:
The Air Zoo features more than 50 rare and historic aircraft, amusement park-style rides, full-motion flight simulators, RealD 3D/4D Missions Theater, as well as historical exhibits and educational activities. The **NEW** Air Zoo is a $19.50 multimedia and aviation experience. The **OLD** Air Zoo with its numerous WWII warbirds is still open and is right on the airport, the **NEW** Air Zoo is a short walk away. Park at Duncan Aviation. They'll show you what to do next.

◉ LUZERNE, MI (LOST CREEK - 5Y4)
Aprt Mgr: CLIFF OLSON **PH:** 734-775-1953
Field Elevation: 1051 **CTAF:** 122.900 **FUEL:**
Runway: 05/23 **Length:** 2200 **Width:** 100 **Surface:** TURF-F
Runway: 18/36 **Length:** 2600 **Width:** 100 **Surface:** TURF-F

★ ★ ★ Lost Creek Sky Ranch - (517) 826-9901
Proprietor: Dennis Kann and Debbie Coulon
Open:
>Mon - Tue: 4:00 pm - 9:00 pm
>Wed - Thu: 11:00 am - 9:00 pm
>Fri - Sat: 11:00 am - 10:00 pm
>Sun: 11:00 am - 9:00 pm

Restaurant Website: www.facebook.com/LostCreekSkyRanch

Restaurant Email: Lostcreekskyranch768@yahoo.com
PIREP:
I have never been here but one of my good friends and $100
Hamburger subscribers has. Here's what Victor Adamko says about
this place:
"The 'Lost Creek Sky Ranch' (5Y4) located in Luzerne, Michigan is an
excellent choice for just a meal or a weekend destination. The airport is
public use with two grass strips 2200' and 2600' in good shape. The
flying "R" ranch offers two restaurants, one upstairs serving anything
from burgers to steaks, prime rib, BBQ ribs and seafood. The lower
restaurant is a pizza joint. I have eaten there on several occasions; the
prices are reasonable ($8.00 - $20.00) the food and service has always
been very good! They also serve drinks and have a band on the
weekends.

Overnight accommodations are available at a very reasonable price!
Although I have not seen the rooms the rest of the place is kept up very
well! I believe tent camping is still available. The ranch also caters to
the horse crowd and horse rental is available for any one crazy enough
to ride one of those things! From a quick burger to a weekend getaway,
it is certainly a great destination and one of my personal favorites (five
burgers). No services are offered so plan your fuel and bring your own
tie downs with stakes."

⭐ PLAINWELL, MI (PLAINWELL MUNI - 61D)
Aprt Mgr: VIRGIL WILLIAMS **PH:** 269-685-6268
Field Elevation: 722 **CTAF:** 122.800 **FUEL:** 100LL
Runway: 09/27 **Length:** 2650 **Width:** 50 **Surface:** ASPH-F
Runway: 01/19 **Length:** 2550 **Width:** 150 **Surface:** TURF-G

★ ★ ★ Fly Inn Again - (269) 685-1554
Proprietor: Richard and Cathy Dunn
Open:
Mon - Sat: 6:30am – 2:30pm
Sun: 7am – 12:00pm
PIREP:
This is a small but wonderful café right on the ramp. These folks care
so much about the burgers they serve that they grow their own lettuce
and tomatoes, bake their own bread and grind their own meat. Now
that's dedication that deserves our support.

⭐ PLYMOUTH, MI (CANTON-PLYMOUTH-METTETAL - 1D2)
Aprt Mgr: DOUGLAS KITZE **PH:** 734-459-6627
Field Elevation: 696 **CTAF:** 122.700 **FUEL:** 100LL
Runway: 18/36 **Length:** 2303 **Width:** 75 **Surface:** ASPH-F

★ ★ ★ **Canton Coney Island - (734) 414-0890**
Proprietor: Fred and Fouad Hussein
Open:
        Daily: Breakfast, Lunch & Dinner
Restaurant Website: www.cantonconeyisland.com
Restaurant Email: info@cantonconeyisland.com
PIREP:
I come here for the Coney Island hot dogs and I get mine with Chili, Cheese and raw onions. Man are they good. They are easy just 300 feet away from the tie downs at the FBO. Consider that these guys have been at this location for almost thirty years. They also have some good looking Greek dishes.

FlyIn Minnesota

🍴 **BRAINERD, MN (BRAINERD LAKES RGNL - BRD)**
Aprt Mgr: RICK ADAIR **PH:** 218-825-2166
Field Elevation: 1232 **CTAF:** 122.700 **FUEL:** 100LLA
Runway: 12/30 **Length:** 4080 **Width:** 75 **Surface:** CLOSED
Runway: 16/34 **Length:** 7100 **Width:** 150 **Surface:** CONC-E
Runway: 05/23 **Length:** 6514 **Width:** 150 **Surface:** CONC-G

★ ★ ★ ★ Wings Cafe - (218) 828-0206
Proprietor: Guy and Tammy Anderson
Open:
> Mon – Fri: 5:30 am to 2:30 pm
> Sat: 7:00 am to 2:00 pm
> Sun: 8:00 am - 2:00 pm

Restaurant Website: www.wingsairportcafe.com
Restaurant Email: info@wingsairportcafe.com
PIREP:
Taxi to the terminal building where you'll find the FBO and Wings
Café. They offer stuffed hamburgers which are quite good. I
particularly enjoy the blue cheese burger.

🍴 **DULUTH, MN (DULUTH INTL - DLH)**
Aprt Mgr: BRIAN D RYKS **PH:** 218-727-2968
Field Elevation: 1428 **CTAF:** 0.000 **FUEL:** 100LLA
Runway: 03/21 **Length:** 5718 **Width:** 150 **Surface:** ASPH-G
Runway: 09/27 **Length:** 10162 **Width:** 150 **Surface:** CONC-F

★ ★ ★ The Afterburner Cafe - (218) 727-1152
Proprietor: Clint Deraas
Open:
> Mon - Sun: 11 am - 9 pm

Restaurant Website: www.duluthairport.com/airport-food.php
PIREP:
Park at the North Country Aviation, they'll give you a lift to the
passenger terminal where the restaurant is located. Lunch and dinner
are standard passenger terminal food. Not good enough to be good and
not bad enough to be bad. This certainly isn't a flyin destination.

★ ★ ★ The Coffee Shop - (218) 727-1152
Proprietor: Clint Deraas
Open:
> Mon - Sun: 6 am - 5 pm

Restaurant Website: www.duluthairport.com/airport-food.php
PIREP:
Park at the North Country Aviation, they'll give you a lift to the passenger terminal where the restaurant is located. Come here for breakfast which is OK but not more than that. This is flight food in an airline passenger terminal is offered more as a diversion for stranded passengers than anything else.

⦿ ORTONVILLE, MN (ORTONVILLE MUNI - VVV)
Aprt Mgr: CHARLEEN GROSSMAN **PH:** 320-839-3846
Field Elevation: 1101 **CTAF:** 122.800 **FUEL:** 100LL
Runway: 16/34 **Length:** 3417 **Width:** 75 **Surface:** ASPH-G
Runway: 04/22 **Length:** 2175 **Width:** 300 **Surface:** TURF-F

★ ★ ★ ★ **Matador Supper Club and Lounge – (320) 839-9981**
Proprietor: Ryan Kehnle
Open:
　　　　Tues - Sun: 4:00 pm - Midnight
Restaurant Website: www.facebook.com
Restaurant Email: thematadorsupperclub@gmail.com
PIREP:
You can park by the FBO or at the west end of the grass runway and walk less than 50 yards. Ortonville airport also offers self-service fuel at a comparatively reasonable price. **The Matador** is in the big brown building. I go strictly for the salad bar. They also offer a full salad bar with daily soups, steaks and a variety of seafood.

$100 Hamburger 2014/15

FlyIn Mississippi

🍽 **GRENADA, MS (GRENADA MUNI - GNF)**
    Aprt Mgr: CHARLES WEATHERS **PH:** 662-227-3440
    Field Elevation: 208 **CTAF:** 122.800 **FUEL:** 100LLA
    Runway: 13/31 **Length:** 7000 **Width:** 150 **Surface:** ASPH-E
    Runway: 04/22 **Length:** 4998 **Width:** 99 **Surface:** ASPH-F

    ★ ★ ★ ★ Williams Aviation, Inc - (662) 227-8402
Proprietor: Guy and Tammy Anderson
Open:
        Mon - Sun: Lunch
Restaurant Website: www.grenadaairport.net/services.htm
Restaurant Email: foxtrot@willerwireless.com
PIREP:
The operator at Grenada Muni is a supper nice guy. He serves Hot Dogs and the all the fixings every day for **FREE**. He enjoys your company.

🍽 **TUNICA, MS (TUNICA MUNI - UTA)**
    Aprt Mgr: "CLIFF NASH, C.M." **PH:** 662-357-7320
    Field Elevation: 194 **CTAF:** 123.000 **FUEL:** 100LLA
    Runway: 17/35 **Length:** 8500 **Width:** 150 **Surface:** ASPH-G

    ★ ★ ★ Cruisers Delta Deli – (662) 357-7370
Proprietor: Terry Lancaster
Open:
        Mon - Sun: 9am – 9pm
PIREP:
The deli is right inside the terminal. Not the greatest little restaurant, but very convenient.
The menu has deli sandwiches, burgers, and barbecue. I had a corn beef and potato salad. The potato salad was really good.

$100 Hamburger 2014/15

FlyIn Missouri

🍽 **CAPE GIRARDEAU, MO (CAPE GIRARDEAU RGNL - CGI)**
 Aprt Mgr: MR BRUCE W LOY **PH:** 573-334-6230
 Field Elevation: 342 **CTAF:** 125.525 **FUEL:** 100LLA
 Runway: 02/20 **Length:** 3996 **Width:** 100 **Surface:** ASPH-CONC-F
 Runway: 10/28 **Length:** 6499 **Width:** 150 **Surface:** CONC-G

 ★★★ **Sandy's Place Restaurant and Bar - (573) 334-0800**
Proprietor: John Canavan
Open:
   Mon - Thurs: 7:30am- 3pm
   Fri: 7:30am- 9pm
   Sat: Closed
   Sun:10:30am - 3:00pm
Restaurant Website: www.facebook.com
PIREP:
Sandy's Place is located in the Cape Girardeau Regional Airport terminal and has become widely recognized for outstanding food and a great atmosphere. Daily specials include Fish Fry Fridays and **all you can eat** Fried Chicken Buffet Sundays. The local's show up on Sunday so you may have to stand in line.

🍽 **COLUMBIA, MO (COLUMBIA RGNL - COU)**
 Aprt Mgr: MR. DON ELLIOTT **PH:** 573-817-5061
 Field Elevation: 889 **CTAF:** 119.300 **FUEL:** 100LLA
 Runway: 13/31 **Length:** 4401 **Width:** 75 **Surface:** ASPH-F
 Runway: 02/20 **Length:** 6501 **Width:** 150 **Surface:** CONC-F

 ★★★ **Skyline Cafe - (573) 442-6774**
Proprietor: Brenda Ravenscraft
Open:
   Mon - Fri: 4:30am - 2:30pm
Restaurant Website: www.flymidmo.com/restaurant.php
PIREP:
The Skyline Cafe is located in the terminal building a short walk away from the FBO. I stopped by for a quick lunch and had a pork burger because I had never had a pork burger before. I will again. Very, very good.

🍽 **DEXTER, MO (DEXTER MUNI - DXE)**
 Aprt Mgr: MIKE WILLIAMS **PH:** 573-624-5959

Field Elevation: 304 **CTAF:** 122.800 **FUEL:** 100LLA
Runway: 18/36 **Length:** 5000 **Width:** 100 **Surface:** ASPH-G

★ ★ ★ **Airways Cafe - (573) 624-4377**
Proprietor: Kathy Cato
Open:
> Mon - Fri: 6:00 am - 2:00 pm
> Sat: 6:00 am - 1:00 pm

Restaurant Website: www.facebook.com
PIREP:
This excellent airport based hometown café may well be on its last legs, at least under current ownership. Currently the airport board is looking for the next operator while the current operator continues. We'll see.

🍴 **JEFFERSON CITY, MO (JEFFERSON CITY MEMORIAL - JEF)**
Aprt Mgr: RON CRAFT **PH:** 573-634-6469
Field Elevation: 549 **CTAF:** 125.600 **FUEL:** 100LLA
Runway: 12/30 **Length:** 6001 **Width:** 100 **Surface:** ASPH-G
Runway: 09/27 **Length:** 3401 **Width:** 75 **Surface:** CONC-G

★ ★ ★ ★ **Nick's Family Restaurant - (573) 634-7050**
Proprietor: Scott Raithel
Open:
> Mon – Thurs: 7:00am - 2:00pm
> Friday: 7:00 m - 9:00pm
> Sun: 10:00am - 7:0 pm

Restaurant Website: www.nicksfamrestaurant.com
Restaurant Email: info@nicksfamrestaurant.com
PIREP:
Nick's Family Restaurant is a family owned and operated restaurant that delivers home cooking at its very best. Go with the pork tenderloins. I have had them twice and they are really good.

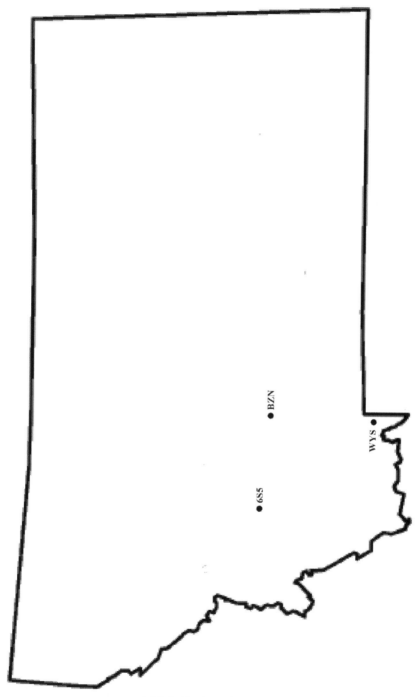

FlyIn Montana

🍽 **BOZEMAN, MT (BOZEMAN YELLOWSTONE INTL - BZN)**
Aprt Mgr: BRIAN SPRENGER **PH:** 406-388-6632
Field Elevation: 4473 **CTAF:** 118.200 **FUEL:** 100 100LLA
Runway: 03/21 **Length:** 2650 **Width:** 75 **Surface:** ASPH-G
Runway: 12/30 **Length:** 8994 **Width:** 150 **Surface:** ASPH-G
Runway: 11/29 **Length:** 3197 **Width:** 80 **Surface:** TURF-G

★ ★ ★ **The Copper Horse Restaurant - (406) 388-6168**
Open:

Mon - Sun: 5am – 11pm
Restaurant Website: www.thecopperhorserestaurant.com
PIREP:
The restaurant is located in the terminal. This is a really good restaurant with really good food and service. I have been here for lunch and had the chicken fried steak sandwich which was better than I hoped.

🍽 **HAMILTON, MT (RAVALLI COUNTY - 6S5)**
Aprt Mgr: PAGE GOUGH **PH:** 406-375-9149
Field Elevation: 3642 **CTAF:** 122.800 **FUEL:** 100LLA
Runway: 16/34 **Length:** 4200 **Width:** 75 **Surface:** ASPH-F

★ ★ ★ **Hangar Cafe - (406) 363-4478**
Proprietor: Max Martz
Open:

Mon - Sun: 11:30am – 8pm
PIREP:
The Hanger Cafe is located on the west side of runway 16/34, at the mid-field intersection taxiway. You can park in front or to the south side in a large parking area. They even offer free chocks to use. The food is the standard airport café variety.

🍽 **WEST YELLOWSTONE, MT** (YELLOWSTONE - WYS)
Aprt Mgr: DON DEGRAW **PH:** 406-646-7631
Field Elevation: 6649 **CTAF:** 123.000 **FUEL:** 100LLA1+
Runway: 01/19 **Length:** 8400 **Width:** 150 **Surface:** ASPH-G

★ ★ ★ ★ **The Smokejumper Café - 406-646-9060**
Proprietor: James Killinger
Open:

Mon - Sun: 8:00 am - 7:00 pm
Restaurant Website: www.facebook.com

$100 Hamburger 2014/15

Restaurant Email: info@glutenfreewestyellowstone.com
PIREP:
Don't go if you're in a hurry or if you don't like refilling your own coffee, it's a one man operation but the food you eventually get is good. They have wonderful mountain view seating, inside and outside. Breakfast is the best time to come. This airport is the gateway to Yellowstone National Park. It is also one of the principle basis from which battles against forest fires that ravage the west in the summer are waged. You'll see some interesting aircraft here during those times.

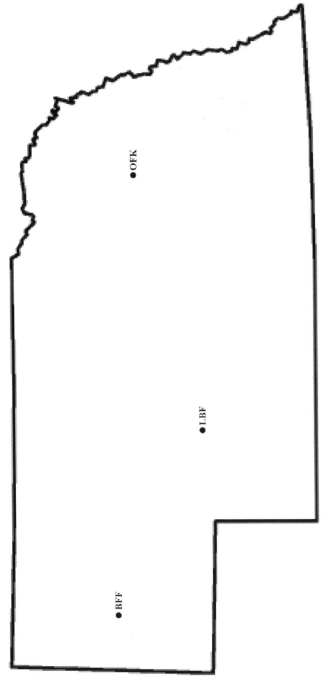

$100 Hamburger 2014/15

FlyIn Nebraska

🍽 NORFOLK, NE (NORFOLK RGNL - OFK)
Aprt Mgr: MS TERRI WACHTER **PH:** 402-371-7210
Field Elevation: 1573 **CTAF:** 122.700 **FUEL:** 100LLA
Runway: 01/19 **Length:** 5800 **Width:** 100 **Surface:** ASPH-G
Runway: 14/32 **Length:** 5800 **Width:** 100 **Surface:** ASPH-G

★★★ Barnstormers of Nebraska - 402-371-8050
Proprietor: Dave Fauss
Open:
> Tue - Thu: 11:00 am - 9:00 pm
> Fri - Sat: 11:00 am - 10:30 pm
> Sun: 10:00 am - 9:00 pm

Restaurant Website: www.facebook.com/pages/Barnstormers-of-Nebraska/143892478954711
PIREP:
The restaurant is in the old terminal building. The menu has a variety of food from prime rib to seafood to one of a kind burgers. The food and the service are both good.

🍽 NORTH PLATTE, NE (NORTH PLATTE RGNL - LBF)
Aprt Mgr: MR. MIKE SHARKEY **PH:** 308-532-1900
Field Elevation: 2777 **CTAF:** 123.000 **FUEL:** 100LLA
Runway: 17/35 **Length:** 4436 **Width:** 100 **Surface:** ASPH-G
Runway: 12/30 **Length:** 8001 **Width:** 150 **Surface:** CONC-E

★★★ Lincoln Highway Diner & Catering Services - 308-534-4340
Open:
> Mon - Sun: 7:00 am - 8:00 pm

Restaurant Website:
northplatteairport.com/airport_inn_restaurant_and_catering.php
Restaurant Email: info@lincolnhighwaydiner.com
PIREP:
If you like people come here on Sunday there'll be a crowd. This is a great Midwestern restaurant with good honest food and courteous service. I have eaten here only twice and have been pleased both times. It doesn't matter much what you eat it's all good but remember don't miss the Blueberry pie. As a matter of fact buy a whole one to take home with you.

🍽 SCOTTSBLUFF, NE (WESTERN NEB. RGNL - BFF)

www.100dollarhamburger.com

Aprt Mgr: DARWIN SKELTON **PH:** 308-635-4941
Field Elevation: 3967 **CTAF:** 123.000 **FUEL:** 100LLA
Runway: 05/23 **Length:** 8002 **Width:** 150 **Surface:** ASPH-G
Runway: 12/30 **Length:** 8279 **Width:** 150 **Surface:** ASPH-G

★ ★ ★ **Skyport Cafe & Lounge - (308) 632-3673**
Proprietor: Scott and Linda Harris, Cherie Olsen
Open:

Sun: 7:00 am - 2:00 pm
Mon –Wed: 7:00 am - 4:00 pm
Thurs: 7:00 am - 8:00 pm
Fri: 7:00 am - 9:00 pm

Restaurant Website: www.flyscottsbluff.com/skyport.html
PIREP:
The facility is modern and first class. It appears the terminal restaurant is not only a favorite for the aircraft folks, but for the local community. Service was friendly. Nothing fancy but really good food. Worth making the trip. I had a BLT and apple pie.

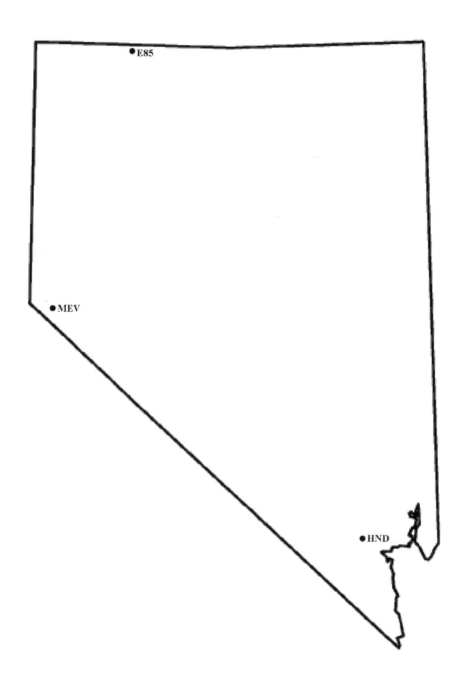

FlyIn Nevada

🍽 **DENIO, NV (DENIO JUNCTION - E85)**
    Aprt Mgr: JOHN RUSSUM **PH:** 775-623-6416
    Field Elevation: 4202 **CTAF:** 122.900 **FUEL:** MOGAS
    Runway: 07/25 **Length:** 3100 **Width:** 100 **Surface:** DIRT-F
    Runway: 02/20 **Length:** 3320 **Width:** 42 **Surface:** DIRT-F
    Runway: 13/31 **Length:** 3430 **Width:** 90 **Surface:** DIRT-F

★ ★ ★ Denio Junction Cafe - (775) 941-0171
Proprietor: Bobby Putney
Open:
        Mon - Sun: Breakfast, Lunch and Dinner
Restaurant Website: www.deniojunctionmotel.com
Restaurant Email: info@deniojunctionmotel.com
PIREP:
This stop is a long way from anywhere but very friendly. It is a dirt strip in really good shape. There is no avgas but you can taxi up to the gas station pumps and fuel up there. The premium blend didn't have any ethanol in it when I was there. The restaurant is friendly and has decent food. This isn't so much a destination as it is a stop along the way.

🍽 **LAS VEGAS, NV (HENDERSON EXECUTIVE - HND)**
    Aprt Mgr: DENNIS ANDERSON **PH:** 702-261-4802
    Field Elevation: 2492 **CTAF:** 125.100 **FUEL:** 100LLA
    Runway: 17L/35R **Length:** 5001 **Width:** 75 **Surface:** ASPH-E
    Runway: 17R/35L **Length:** 6501 **Width:** 100 **Surface:** ASPH-E

★ ★ ★ The Landings HND – (702) 616-3337
Proprietor: Marie
Open:
        Mon – Sun : 7:00 am – 4:00 pm
Restaurant Website: www.thelandingshnd.com/
Restaurant Email: marie@thelandingsHND.com
PIREP:
I have never been here so I am including a **PIREP** from one of the subscribers to the $100 Hamburger website. Here it is:
"The restaurant has a more upscale look than your typical airport restaurant. You enter the restaurant through a small and intimate bar. The bar has a casino Sports Book look to it with signed Muhammad Ali boxing gloves and three TV's tuned to different sports channels behind the bar that seats eight people. The restaurant seating area is open and

inviting. The second story location of the restaurant allows for a great view of the runways and ramp area with window seat tables running along the entire length of the restaurant. Tie-down areas are generally pretty boring with your weathered 172's but this tarmac is a who's who of shiny corporate jets. At the back end of the restaurant there is a small outdoor seating area with both views of the runways and the lights of the Las Vegas Strip in the distance. I was there for breakfast and my omelet was adequate. But it did have the unusual ingredient of cactus which I have never seen offered before."

○ MINDEN, NV (MINDEN-TAHOE - MEV)
Aprt Mgr: BOBBI THOMPSON **PH:** 775-782-9871
Field Elevation: 4722 **CTAF:** 123.050 **FUEL:** 100LLA
Runway: 16/34 **Length:** 7400 **Width:** 100 **Surface:** ASPH-E
Runway: 12/30 **Length:** 5300 **Width:** 75 **Surface:** ASPH-G
Runway: 12G/30G **Length:** 2200 **Width:** 60 **Surface:** DIRT-G

★ ★ ★ The Taildragger Café - (775) 782-9500
Proprietor: Mary Getty
Open:

> Mon – Sun: 6:00 am – 8:00 pm

Restaurant Website: www.facebook.com
PIREP:

The scenery alone is worth the flight. There are two soaring outfits on the field. People that know about such things support one and throw stones at the other though honest soaring pilots disagree about which is which. They all seem to agree as do I that the food and service at **The Taildragger Café** is awesome. I cannot comment on their breakfast as I've only been here for lunch.

$100 Hamburger 2014/15

FlyIn New Hampshire

iⓞi FRANCONIA, NH (FRANCONIA - 1B5)
   Aprt Mgr: JOSEPH M. KWASNIK **PH:** 603-730-7148
   Field Elevation: 978 **CTAF:** 122.800 **FUEL:**
   Runway: 18/36 **Length:** 2305 **Width:** 150 **Surface:** TURF-G

★ ★ ★ ★ **The Franconia Inn - 1-800-473-5299**
Proprietor: Richard and Alec Morris
Open:
   Breakfast: 7:30am -9:30am
   Dinner: 6:00am -8:30pm
Restaurant Website: www.franconiainn.com
Restaurant Email: reservations@franconiainn.com
PIREP:
The Franconia Inn is an upscale and historic resort with its own turf strip. They actually have one package which includes a stay at the resort and a glider ride for each guest. Come up for breakfast once and you'll be hooked. That's what happened to me. Be sure to make reservation for breakfast or dinner. The food and service are amazing and you don't want to be disappointed.

iⓞi HAMPTON, NH (HAMPTON AIRFIELD - 7B3)
   Aprt Mgr: GEORGE FORREST **PH:** 603-964-6749
   Field Elevation: 93 **CTAF:** 122.800 **FUEL:** 100LLMOGAS
   Runway: 02/20 **Length:** 2100 **Width:** 170 **Surface:** TURF-G

★ ★ ★ **Airfield Cafe - (603) 964-1654**
Proprietor: The Aversano Family
Open:
   Mon - Sun: 7am – 2pm
Restaurant Website: www.theairfieldcafe.com
Restaurant Email: theairfieldcafe@comcast.net
PIREP:
Plan on a wait but plan to come. This is a wonderful New England flyin. Breakfast is really good and is served all day. I love their pancakes and always spring for the Maple Syrup. It cost extra and is well worth it.

iⓞi NASHUA, NH (BOIRE FIELD - ASH)
   Aprt Mgr: ROY RANKIN **PH:** 603-882-0661
   Field Elevation: 199 **CTAF:** 133.200 **FUEL:** 100LLA1+
   Runway: 14/32 **Length:** 5501 **Width:** 100 **Surface:** ASPH-F

★ ★ ★ **The Midfield Cafe - (603) 594-0930**
Proprietor: Fred Manhack
Open:

      Mon - Sun: 7am – 2pm
Restaurant Website: www.facebook.com
Restaurant Email: midfieldcafe@yahoo.com
PIREP:
Breakfast. I have been here for breakfast and it was good. It has all of the standard things you expect from an airport café. You can taxi up and park on their ramp. Check! They have a good view of the runway. Check! They have an outdoor deck. Check! They have a a normal American breakfast and lunch menu. Check!

🍽 **NEWPORT, NH (PARLIN FIELD - 2B3)**
      Aprt Mgr: RUSSELL KELSEA **PH:** 603-863-1220
      Field Elevation: 784 **CTAF:** 122.800 **FUEL:** 100LL
      Runway: 18/36 **Length:** 3450 **Width:** 50 **Surface:** ASPH-E
      Runway: 12/30 **Length:** 1950 **Width:** 80 **Surface:** TURF-G

★ ★ ★ **Lil' Red Baron – (603) 863-TACO (8226)**
Proprietor: Matt Maki
Open:

      Tues - Thurs: 4:00 pm - 9:00 pm
      Fri - Sat: 11:00 am - 10:00 pm
      Sun: 11:00 am - 9:00 pm
Restaurant Website: www.lilredbaron.com
Restaurant Email: matt@lilredbaron.com
PIREP:
Taxi to the end of 30, park and tie down on the restaurant's ramp. They also have a picnic/camping area with a covered bridge. It's a Mexican restaurant/bar. I love Mexican food but was a little skittish about buying it in New England. Clams they understand up here but Mexican food? I had my doubts. I ordered up a beef burrito. Heaven! I don't know how good Mexican food found its way to Newport, NH but it did.

FlyIn New Jersey

🍽 BLAIRSTOWN, NJ (BLAIRSTOWN - 1N7)
Aprt Mgr: DENNIS KIERNAN **PH:** 908-362-8965
Field Elevation: 372 **CTAF:** 123.000 **FUEL:** 100LL
Runway: 07/25 **Length:** 3088 **Width:** 70 **Surface:** ASPH-G

★★★ Runway Cafe - (908) 362-9170
Proprietor: Jeanne Anderson
Open:
> Mon - Sun: Breakfast and Lunch

Restaurant Website: www.blairstownairport.com/restaurant.htm
PIREP:
Excellent parking spaces by the office and café. We're talking the "pull-through" variety with chocks just sitting there waiting for you. Very nice! The airport has a lot of gliding activity but it is manageable. This is a good place to interact with other pilots and see the gliders land and take-off. The food is worth the trip and made better by the attentive service.

🍽 LINCOLN PARK, NJ (LINCOLN PARK - N07)
Aprt Mgr: PETER DEROSA **PH:** 973-628-7166
Field Elevation: 182 **CTAF:** 122.800 **FUEL:** 100LL
Runway: 01/19 **Length:** 2942 **Width:** 40 **Surface:** ASPH-G

★★★ Sunset Pub and Grill - 973 694 8700
Proprietor: Frank Skrek
Open:
> Mon –Wed: 11:30 am - 12:00pm
> Thurs: 11:30 am - 1:00 pm
> Fri: 11:30 am - 2:00 am
> Sat: 11:00 am -2:00 am
> Sun: 11:00 am -12:00 am

Restaurant Website: www.sunsetpubandgrill.com
Restaurant Email: info@sunsetpubandgrill.com
PIREP:
N07 is under the NYC class B, Teterboro and Morristown airports. Lots of traffic so be careful. The approach to runway 1 is sloping ground with high trees at the end of runway. If you are looking for a $100 Hamburger but want more of a regular, nice sit down restaurant feel I recommend **Sunset Pub and Grill**. This is a full bar and restaurant with a large patio on the apron so you watch airplanes. Think **Friday's** or **Hoolihan's**

150

● **LUMBERTON, NJ (FLYING W - N14)**
    Aprt Mgr: MINDY REDNER **PH:** 609-267-7673
    Field Elevation: 49 **CTAF:** 122.800 **FUEL:** 100LLA
    Runway: 01/19 **Length:** 3496 **Width:** 75 **Surface:** ASPH-G

    ★ ★ ★ Flying W - **(609) 267-7673**
    Proprietor: Heather Cave
    Open:
        Mon – Sun: 8 am - 2pm
    Restaurant Website: www.flyingwairport.com
    Restaurant Email: info@flyingwairport.com
    PIREP:
    This is the cafe in the operations building, not the old **Avion** restaurant.
    You can taxi right up to the restaurant. It is a burger and breakfast
    kinda' place in a unique location.

● **MILLVILLE, NJ (MILLVILLE MUNI - MIV)**
    Aprt Mgr: MINDY REDNER **PH:** 609-267-7673
    Field Elevation: 49 **CTAF:** 122.800 **FUEL:** 100LLA
    Runway: 01/19 **Length:** 3496 **Width:** 75 **Surface:** ASPH-G

    ★ ★ ★ Verna's Flight Line Restaurant – **(856) 825-3200**
    Proprietor: Verna Herman
    Open:
        Mon - Sun: 6:00 am - 2:00 pm
    Restaurant Website: www.facebook.com
    Restaurant Email: vernasflightline@aol.com
    PIREP:
    In a word – tablecloths. That let's you know that this is a restaurant that
    sets high standards. The food is wonderful and the service impeccable.
    They have chalkboard breakfast and lunch specials every day. I once
    lucked into a COLD meatloaf sandwich – fabulous!

● **MOUNT HOLLY, NJ (SOUTH JERSEY RGNL - VAY)**
    Aprt Mgr: MINDY REDNER **PH:** 609-267-3131
    Field Elevation: 53 **CTAF:** 122.800 **FUEL:** 100LLA
    Runway: 08/26 **Length:** 3881 **Width:** 50 **Surface:** ASPH-G

    ★ ★ ★ Runway Cafe - **(609) 518-0400**
    Proprietor: Vinci Lunt
    Open:
        Mon - Sun: 8:00 am - 4:00 pm
    PIREP:

This is your average $100 Hamburger stop. It's on the ramp and the food and service are adequate.

📷 OCEAN CITY, NJ (OCEAN CITY MUNI - 26N)
Aprt Mgr: WILLIAM R COLANGELO **PH:** 609-525-9223
Field Elevation: 5 **CTAF:** 122.700 **FUEL:** 100LL
Runway: 06/24 **Length:** 2973 **Width:** 60 **Surface:** ASPH-G

★ ★ ★ **Airport Diner - (609) 399-3663**
Proprietor: Lori Pilgrim
Open:

Mon - Sun: 7:00 am - 3:00 pm

PIREP:
The Airport Diner DOES NOT TAKE CREDIT CARDS OR DEBIT CARDS. There is also no ATM in the office at the airport. So have some cash with you. The food and service are good and access is easy.

📷 PITTSTOWN, NJ (SKY MANOR - N40)
Aprt Mgr: SKY MANOR AIRPORT PARTNERS **PH:** 908-996-4200
Field Elevation: 560 **CTAF:** 122.975 **FUEL:** 100LL
Runway: 07/25 **Length:** 2900 **Width:** 50 **Surface:** ASPH-G

★ ★ ★ ★ **Sky Manor - (908) 996-3442**
Proprietor: Marty Lane
Open:

Mon & Thu – 9:00am to 5:00pm
Tue & Wed – Closed
Fri – 9:00am to 5:00pm
Dinner Buffet – 5:00pm to 9:00pm
Sat & Sun – 8:00am to 6:00pm
Sunday Breakfast Buffet – 8:00am to 12:00pm

Restaurant Website: www.skymanorairport.com/restaurant.htm
Restaurant Email: vlane0976@verizon.net
PIREP:
I like it here but I always have to remind myself to be patient. Turns out they make everything to order and everything is fresh, no frozen French fries in this kitchen. I always go with the onion rings (large order) and a BLT. Works for me!

📷 ✈ ROBBINSVILLE, NJ (TRENTON-ROBBINSVILLE - N87)
Aprt Mgr: WILLIAM DEY **PH:** 609-259-1059
Field Elevation: 118 **CTAF:** 123.000 **FUEL:** 100LL
Runway: 11/29 **Length:** 4275 **Width:** 75 **Surface:** ASPH-F

★ ★ ★ ★ **Divots at Miry Run Golf Course - (609) 259-1010**

Proprietor: Heidi Matisa
Open:

Mon - Sun: Lunch

Restaurant Website: www.miryruncc.com
Restaurant Email: miryruncc@optonline.net
PIREP:

Runway 29 leads straight to a beautiful golf course, Miry Run Golf Course. Call from the Kenmarson AeroClub, and they will even send a golf cart down to the airport to pick you up, although it is an easy walk. The best deal is to fly in and play a round. They provide greens fee, a cart and lunch for $35.00. I like the course. Lunch the day I went was a hotdog and the stuff that goes with it. I love hotdogs so it worked for me.

ⓘⓘ SUSSEX, NJ (SUSSEX - FWN)

Aprt Mgr: PAUL STYGER **PH:** 973-875-7337
Field Elevation: 421 **CTAF:** 122.700 **FUEL:** A
Runway: 03/21 **Length:** 3499 **Width:** 75 **Surface:** ASPH-F

★ ★ ★ Airport Diner - (973) 702-7324
Proprietor: Laura Marran
Open:

Mon - Sun: Breakfast and Lunch

PIREP:

A standard place with no surprise and one really good thing. The Chicken Caesar is really worth the stop. They have a self-serve pump so you can save a couple of bucks on fuel.

ⓘⓘ WEST MILFORD, NJ (GREENWOOD LAKE - 4N1)

Aprt Mgr: TIM WAGNER **PH:** 973-728-7721
Field Elevation: 790 **CTAF:** 122.900 **FUEL:** 100LLA
Runway: 06/24 **Length:** 3471 **Width:** 60 **Surface:** ASPH-G

★ ★ ★ Passport Café – (973) 506-7315
Open:

Tue - Sun: 8am -3pm

Restaurant Website: www.greenwoodlakeairport.com/id17.html
PIREP:

The field is hard to see because of the hills around it. There are ridges and trees at both ends of the runway with right traffic on RW 06. This is a great trip for the food but to also to see the spectacular scenery around this part of the country, many beautiful lakes, homes, hills and much more. **The Passport Café** has 5 booths, 4 or 5 tables and a great diner like counter with 8 or 9 stools overlooking the action on the grill. If you prefer they have a wonderful patio with umbrella tables. The food? It is well worth the trip and the service is friendly. I like this place.

◉ WILDWOOD, NJ (CAPE MAY COUNTY - WWD)

Aprt Mgr: THOMAS BERRY **PH:** 609-886-8652
Field Elevation: 23 **CTAF:** 122.700 **FUEL:** 100LLA
Runway: 01/19 **Length:** 4998 **Width:** 150 **Surface:** ASPH-G
Runway: 10/28 **Length:** 4998 **Width:** 150 **Surface:** ASPH-G

★ ★ ★ The Flight Deck Dinner - 609-886-1105

Proprietor: Sean P. McMullan
Chef: DeJohin Nelson
Open:

Mon - Sun: 7:00 am - 2:00 pm
Restaurant Website: www.facebook.com/flightdeckdiner
Restaurant Email: flightdeckdiner@comcast.net
PIREP:

It is located in the terminal and seats about 40 folks total with 10 at a counter and 30 or so at various tables. They serve breakfast all day. The staff is friendly and the food is great and inexpensive. They are doing a great job. You will need to ask for the code to the gate to get back on the airfield.

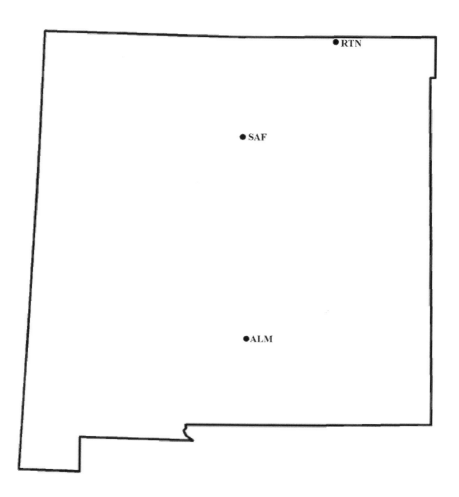

FlyIn New Mexico

📷 **ALAMOGORDO, NM (WHITE SANDS RGNL - ALM)**
Aprt Mgr: MATT MCNEILE **PH:** 575-439-4200
Field Elevation: 4200 **CTAF:** 122.800 **FUEL:** 100LLA A1+
Runway: 03/21 **Length:** 7006 **Width:** 150 **Surface:** ASPH-G
Runway: 16/34 **Length:** 3512 **Width:** 200 **Surface:** DIRT-F

★ ★ ★ ★ **Airport Grille - (505) 439-1093**
Proprietor: Linda Madron
Open:
> Mon - Sat: 8:00am - 2:00pm

Restaurant Website: www.facebook.com
PIREP:
Homemade pies, I picked up a Lemon Meringue to take along with me.
This is a small well cared for diner with good food and happy servers.

📷 **RATON, NM (RATON MUNI/CREWS FIELD - RTN)**
Aprt Mgr: KEITH MANGELSDORF **PH:** 575-445-3076
Field Elevation: 6352 **CTAF:** 122.800 **FUEL:** 100LLA1+
Runway: 07/25 **Length:** 4404 **Width:** 75 **Surface:** ASPH-F
Runway: 02/20 **Length:** 6328 **Width:** 75 **Surface:** ASPH-G

★ ★ ★ **Pegasus Aviation - (505) 445-3076**
Proprietor: Keith and Fern Manglesdorf
Open:
> Daily: Lunch

Restaurant Website: www.pegasusflightservices.com
Restaurant Email: info@pegasusflightservices.com
PIREP:
Pegasus continues to provide their famous green chili and cheese
hamburgers 7 days a week. Just call in your order when you are
inbound and they will have it waiting upon your arrival.

📷 **SANTA FE, NM (SANTA FE MUNI - SAF)**
Aprt Mgr: JAMES H. MONTMAN **PH:** 505-955-2900
Field Elevation: 6348 **CTAF:** 119.500 **FUEL:** 100LLA1 A1+
Runway: 15/33 **Length:** 6307 **Width:** 100 **Surface:** ASPH-E
Runway: 10/28 **Length:** 6300 **Width:** 75 **Surface:** ASPH-G
Runway: 02/20 **Length:** 8342 **Width:** 150 **Surface:** ASPH-G

★ **Santa FE Airport Grill - (505) 471-5227**
Proprietor: Lisa Vanallen

$100 Hamburger 2014/15

Open:

Mon - Sun: 7:00 am - 3:00 pm

PIREP:

Santa Fe is a great place to stop. The Grill in the terminal has semi-good food for a commercial airport diner. I usually park at the Santa Fe Jet Center and walk to the terminal building. Remember you have to enter through the front door. They have airline traffic so they have TSA so it's a hassle. That's the new normal. Be certain to call first on this one as there is a rumor that it may be closing soon.

$100 Hamburger 2014/15

FlyIn New York

***

☺ FULTON, NY (OSWEGO COUNTY - FZY)
    Aprt Mgr: MR BRUCE BISBO **PH:** 315-591-9130
    Field Elevation: 475 **CTAF:** 123.000 **FUEL:** 100LLA
    Runway: 06/24 **Length:** 3996 **Width:** 100 **Surface:** ASPH-G
    Runway: 15/33 **Length:** 5196 **Width:** 100 **Surface:** ASPH-G

***

    ★ ★ Puddle Jumpers - (315) 558-8723
Proprietor: Susan Skinner
Open:
        Seasonal
        Mon - Sun: 7am – 2pm
Restaurant Website: www.facebook.com/PuddleJumpersRestaurant
Restaurant Email: puddle.jumpers.restaurant@gmail.com
PIREP:
Don't expect much. It is a very basic place with very good food.

☺ ₮ GANSEVOORT, NY (HEBER AIRPARK - K30)
    Aprt Mgr: JAMES HEBER **PH:** 518-793-8983
    Field Elevation: 230 **CTAF:** 122.900 **FUEL:**
    Runway: 06/24 **Length:** 2200 **Width:** 24 **Surface:** ASPH-G

***

    ★ ★ ★ The Clubhouse Tavern – (518)792-4144
Proprietor: James and Joan Heber
Open:
        Seasonal
        Mon - Sun: 11am – 2pm
Restaurant Website: www.airwaymeadowsgolf.com
Restaurant Email: golfing@airwaymeadowsgolf.com
PIREP:
The runway is between the 2nd and 8th fairways which makes a tricky landing over trees onto runway 6. If you're playing the course they'll leave a golf-cart at the tie-down for you. The 18-hole course is challenging and worth the flight. The green fee with a cart is less than $50. It's a short walk across 9th fairway to the clubhouse and restaurant. They offer good food in a nice atmosphere.

☺ GLENS FALLS, NY (FLOYD BENNETT MEMORIAL - GFL)
    Aprt Mgr: DONALD DEGRAW **PH:** 518-792-5995
    Field Elevation: 328 **CTAF:** 123.000 **FUEL:** 100LLA
    Runway: 12/30 **Length:** 3999 **Width:** 100 **Surface:** ASPH-E
    Runway: 01/19 **Length:** 5000 **Width:** 150 **Surface:** ASPH-G

★★★★ Carol's Airport Cafe - (518) 761 4043
Proprietor:
Open:

      Seasonal:

      8am to 2pm (October - April)

      8am to 3pm (May - Sep)

Restaurant Website: www.carolsairportcafe.com
PIREP:
The décor is clean and modern. The food is good but what makes this stop a pleasure is the kindness of the owner and staff. They like people and it shows.

🍴 MIDDLESEX, NY (MIDDLESEX VALLEY - 4N2)

Aprt Mgr: ROBERT MINCER **PH:** 585-554-4024
Field Elevation: 770 **CTAF:** 122.700 **FUEL:**
Runway: 03/21 **Length:** 2130 **Width:** 175 **Surface:** TURF-G

★★★Pilot's Lounge Cafe – (585) 554-4024
Proprietor: Robert Mincer
Open:

      Seasonal: May - October

      Sat and Sun: 6:00am - 12:00pm

Restaurant Website:
www.middlesexvalleyairport.com/images/MVA0001.pdf
Pirep:
Take this trip back to the 1930's. You'll be rewarded with a good breakfast and wonderful company. Be warned this is a short (2,200') turf strip and the only fuel on the field is 80 octane MOGAS.

🍴 MILLBROOK, NY (SKY ACRES - 44N)

Aprt Mgr: GINNIE STYLES **PH:** 845-677-5010
Field Elevation: 698 **CTAF:** 122.800 **FUEL:** 100LL
Runway: 17/35 **Length:** 3830 **Width:** 60 **Surface:** ASPH-G

★★★ The Tail Wind Cafe - 845-663-3190
Proprietor: Hope Lucas
Open:

      Thurs – Sun: 7:00am - 3:00pm

Restaurant Website: www.skyacresairport.com/cafe.html
Restaurant Email: 726mick@gmail.com
PIREP:
Its right next door to HerGin Aviation's pilot shop. I like SkyAcres. I like to hang around the place and visit with local pilot crowd. The Café is a diner at a fun airport with standard food.

●| MONTAUK, NY (MONTAUK - MTP)

Aprt Mgr: HELEN GILL **PH:** 631-668-3738
Field Elevation: 7 **CTAF:** 122.700 **FUEL:**
Runway: 06/24 **Length:** 3246 **Width:** 75 **Surface:** ASPH-G

★ ★ ★ ★ ★ **Rick's Crabby Cowboy** - **(631) 668-3200**
Proprietor: Rick Gibbs
Open:
> Mon - Sun: Lunch and Dinner

Restaurant Website: www.crabbycowboy.com
Restaurant Email: crabbycowboy@optonline.net
PIREP:
My favorite stop in New England maybe the whole earth. Nice location, at the end of runway 24, across the road and on Montauk sound. Outside seating is available. Nice airy atmosphere, great food, great service. Rick has great seafood and live music in the evening. I've had the lobster roll and the steamers. Both are awesome.

●| MONTGOMERY, NY (ORANGE COUNTY - MGJ)

Aprt Mgr: GRANT W. SUSSEY **PH:** 845-457-4925
Field Elevation: 364 **CTAF:** 122.725 **FUEL:** 100LLA1
Runway: 08/26 **Length:** 3664 **Width:** 100 **Surface:** ASPH-G
Runway: 03/21 **Length:** 5002 **Width:** 100 **Surface:** ASPH-G

★ ★ ★ ★ ★ **Culinary Creations** – **(845) 457 9328**
Proprietor: Phil, Faith and Michelle
Open:
> Sunday Brunch: 9:00am-2:00pm
> Tue – Wed – Thurs: 11:00am-3:00pm
> Fri - Sat: 11:00am-8:30pm

Restaurant Website: www.culinarycreationscafe.com
PIREP:
This is an excellent stop. The food is really worthwhile. Please call to confirm hours. From time -to-time they have private events in dining room.

●| SARANAC LAKE, NY (ADIRONDACK RGNL - SLK)

Aprt Mgr: ROSS DUBARRY **PH:** 518-891-4600
Field Elevation: 1663 **CTAF:** 123.000 **FUEL:** 100LLA
Runway: 09/27 **Length:** 3998 **Width:** 100 **Surface:** ASPH-G
Runway: 05/23 **Length:** 6573 **Width:** 150 **Surface:** ASPH-G

★ ★ ★ **The Airport Café** – **(518) 354-8063**
Proprietor: Paula Palmer

Open:

Mon - Sun: 7:00am - 3:00pm

PIREP:

This is a glorious part of the world to fly over. I enjoy sitting down here to have a bite before heading out with my load of fall leaf watchers. The food is ordinary and the service acceptable.

🍽 WALLKILL, NY (KOBELT - N45)

Aprt Mgr: WILLIAM RICHARDS **PH:** 845-255-1087
Field Elevation: 420 **CTAF:** 122.800 **FUEL:** 100LL
Runway: 03/21 **Length:** 2864 **Width:** 50 **Surface:** ASPH-G

★ ★ ★ NU-CAVU - (845) 895-9000

Proprietor:
Open:

Wednesday to Sunday: 11:30am -10pm.

Restaurant Website: www.nu-cavu.com
Restaurant Email: nucavu@aol.com
PIREP:

Chicken Saltimbocca is my favorite here. I have dropped in for dinner which is better than lunch though lunch is pretty darn good. This is a slightly upscale place made better for the live entertainment they bring in. I'll be back!!!

🍽 WESTHAMPTON BEACH, NY (FRANCIS S GABRESKI - FOK)

Aprt Mgr: ANTHONY CEGLIO **PH:** 631-852-8095
Field Elevation: 66 **CTAF:** 125.300 **FUEL:** 100LLA
Runway: 01/19 **Length:** 5001 **Width:** 150 **Surface:** ASPH-CONC-G
Runway: 06/24 **Length:** 9001 **Width:** 150 **Surface:** ASPH-CONC-G
Runway: 15/33 **Length:** 5003 **Width:** 150 **Surface:** ASPH-F

★ ★ ★ Cafe at Malloy Air East - (631) 288-2919

Proprietor: Patrick E Malloy
Open:

Mon - Sun: 8:00am - 4:00pm

Restaurant Website: www.malloyaireast.com/cafe.html
Restaurant Email:

The cafe is located inside the Terminal Building of Gabreski Airport. It is easy to find. I like coming to the Hamptons and I like flying over the Hamptons. I prefer paying the $5 landing fee here rather than the $30 landing fee at East Hampton. I come here for lunch and always enjoy the crab cakes.

🍽 WHITE PLAINS, NY (WESTCHESTER COUNTY - HPN)

Aprt Mgr: PETER SCHERRER **PH:** 914-995-4850

$100 Hamburger 2014/15

Field Elevation: 439 **CTAF:** 118.575 **FUEL:** 100LLA
Runway: 11/29 **Length:** 4451 **Width:** 150 **Surface:** ASPH-F
Runway: 16/34 **Length:** 6549 **Width:** 150 **Surface:** ASPH-G

★ ★ **The Traveler's Club Restaurant - (914) 428-0251**
Proprietor: Armand Vartabedian
Open:
> Mon - Sun: Noon - 9:00pm

Restaurant Website:
www.whiteplainsairport.com/pages/concessions.shtml
PIREP:
Busy, very busy, you must pay attention when you head this way. The restaurant is in the passenger terminal. That means you have to park at one of the FBOs. They'll shuttle you to the terminal where you must walk through the front door and deal with TSA. The restaurant is clean and modern and serves exactly what you'd expect at a commercial airline terminal spot. I don't think of this as a Burger destination. That's just me.

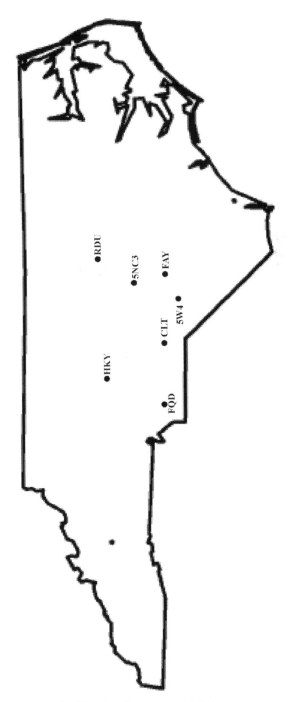

$100 Hamburger 2014/15

FlyIn North Carolina

🍴 **CARTHAGE, NC (GILLIAM - MC CONNELL AIRFIELD - 5NC3)**
Aprt Mgr: S. ROLAND GILLIAM **PH:** 910-947-3599
Field Elevation: 445 **CTAF:** 0.000 **FUEL:** 100LL
Runway: 13/31 **Length:** 2538 **Width:** 36 **Surface:** ASPH-G

★ ★ ★ ★ ★ Pik N Pig BBQ - 910-947-7591
Proprietor: Janie Shepperd
Open:
> Tuesday thru Saturday: 11am - 8pm
> Sunday: Noon to 3pm

Restaurant Website: www.pik-n-pig.com
PIREP:
The airport is listed as Private so prior permission to land is required. The airport's phone number is (910) 947-3599. **Pik N Pig BBQ** is a family run restaurant right on the field, where planes line up on the grass. The BBQ stacks up with some of the best I've ever had.

🍴 **CHARLOTTE, NC (CHARLOTTE/DOUGLAS INTL - CLT)**
Aprt Mgr: JERRY ORR **PH:** 704-359-4000
Field Elevation: 748 **CTAF:** 0.000 **FUEL:** 100LLA
Runway: 05/23 **Length:** 7502 **Width:** 150 **Surface:** ASPH-CONC-G
Runway: 18L/36R **Length:** 8676 **Width:** 150 **Surface:** ASPH-CONC-G
Runway: 18R/36L **Length:** 9000 **Width:** 150 **Surface:** CONC-E
Runway: 18C/36C **Length:** 10000 **Width:** 150 **Surface:** CONC-F

★ ★ ★ Mr. G's - (704) 399-2542
Proprietor: George Stamoulis
Open:
> Mon - Fri: 7:00 am - 3:30 pm
> Sat: 9:00 am - 3:00 pm

Restaurant Website: www.facebook.com
PIREP:
Don't expect much from the décor – this is a true greasy spoon restaurant. Ceiling is yellow with grease and Jerry Springer is on the TV in the dining room. But you get a ton of good comfort food for your money. If you're at the main terminal you'll probably need a ride, it's a bit of a walk. It's over by the GA hangars, near the Museum, just outside the airport fence next to the National Guard facility. This is a popular spot with airport employees.

FAYETTEVILLE, NC (FAYETTEVILLE RGNL - FAY)
Aprt Mgr: BRADLEY S. WHITED **PH:** 910-433-1160
Field Elevation: 189 **CTAF:** 0.000 **FUEL:** 100LLA
Runway: 10/28 **Length:** 4801 **Width:** 150 **Surface:** ASPH-F
Runway: 04/22 **Length:** 7709 **Width:** 150 **Surface:** ASPH-G

★ ★ **Airport Restaurant - (910) 484-2846**
Open:
      Daily: Breakfast, lunch
Restaurant Website: www.flyfay.com/Files/Tenants2.pdf
PIREP:
This is definitely no more than a 2 burger rating, standard airport terminal fare. it's a very short walk from the FBO to the terminal.

HICKORY, NC (HICKORY RGNL - HKY)
Aprt Mgr: TERRY CLARK **PH:** 828-323-7408
Field Elevation: 1190 **CTAF:** 128.150 **FUEL:** 100LLA
Runway: 01/19 **Length:** 4400 **Width:** 150 **Surface:** ASPH-G
Runway: 06/24 **Length:** 6400 **Width:** 150 **Surface:** ASPH-G

★ ★ ★ **Crosswind Cafe - 828-324-7800**
Proprietor: Teresa Rozzelle
Open:
      Monday - Friday: 8am – 3pm
      Saturday: 8am – 2pm
Restaurant Website: www.crosswindcafe.com
Restaurant Email: Teresa@CrosswindCafe.com or
twrozz@charter,net

PIREP:
It has a real chef and a nice menu. Friendly folks, reasonable prices.

RAEFORD, NC (P K AIRPARK - 5W4)
Aprt Mgr: GENE THACKER **PH:** 910-875-3261
Field Elevation: 304 **CTAF:** 123.000 **FUEL:** 100LLA+
Runway: 04/22 **Length:** 3402 **Width:** 60 **Surface:** ASPH-F

★ ★ ★ **PK's Aviator's Pub and Grill - (910) 904-6761**
Proprietor: Thomas Wolfe
Open:
      Mon - Sun: Breakfast, Lunch, Dinner
Restaurant Website: www.facebook.com
Restaurant Email: galco2010@gmail.com
PIREP:

Super Hamburgers! Outstanding BBQ! They serve breakfast, lunch and dinner along with a great bar, pool tables and skydiving. The best part is, they are dirt cheap.

Be careful of MOA's and restricted airspace around Ft. Bragg and Pope AFB on the way in. We asked Fayette ATC to vector us in. They were tremendous. Call before you go to make sure the credit card machine for gas is working.

⧀ RALEIGH/DURHAM, NC (RALEIGH-DURHAM INTL - RDU)
Aprt Mgr: MICHAEL LANDGUTH **PH:** 919-840-7702
Field Elevation: 435 **CTAF:** 0.000 **FUEL:** 100LLA
Runway: 14/32 **Length:** 3570 **Width:** 100 **Surface:** ASPH-G
Runway: 05R/23L **Length:** 7500 **Width:** 150 **Surface:** ASPH-G
Runway: 05L/23R **Length:** 10000 **Width:** 150 **Surface:** CONC-G

★ ★ ★ Crosswinds Cafe - (919) 840-7625
Open:
>   Monday – Friday: 8:00 am - 2:00 pm

Restaurant Website: www.crosswindscafe.com
Restaurant Email: catering@crosswindscafe.com
PIREP:
Located in the airport's general aviation terminal. Crosswinds Cafe features a variety of breakfast selections, innovative lunch and dinner entrees, signature sandwiches, as well as specialty desserts. With health-conscious customers in mind, Crosswinds Cafe offers healthy alternatives such as crisp, fresh salads and sandwich wraps. As for the customer "on the fly", Crosswinds Cafe serves Grab & Go items as well as Fast and Fresh favorites. The Cafe also has a selective menu for children as well.

⧀ RUTHERFORDTON, NC (RUTHERFORD CO - FQD)
Aprt Mgr: AMY THOMAS **PH:** 828-287-0800
Field Elevation: 1077 **CTAF:** 122.800 **FUEL:** 100LLA1+
Runway: 01/19 **Length:** 5000 **Width:** 100 **Surface:** ASPH-G

★ ★ ★ ★ 57 Alpha Cafe - (828) 286-1677
Proprietor: Ron Mc Kinney
Open:
>   Tuesday – Sunday: 1:00 am - 3:00 pm

Restaurant Website: www.57alpha.com
PIREP:
Live Music On The Patio on Saturdays, April thru October. The food is fresh, and the surroundings are friendly and uplifting. Try this if you enjoy a day away from the rat race. This is a small place with very

limited seating indoors but has picnic tables outside. Its banana pudding is legendary in the area.

FlyIn North Dakota

🍴 FARGO, ND (HECTOR INTL - FAR)
> **Aprt Mgr:** SHAWN DOBBERSTEIN **PH:** 701-241-1501
> **Field Elevation:** 901 **CTAF:** 0.000 **FUEL:** 100LLA
> **Runway:** 13/31 **Length:** 3801 **Width:** 150 **Surface:** ASPH-CONC-G
> **Runway:** 09/27 **Length:** 6302 **Width:** 100 **Surface:** CONC-G
> **Runway:** 18/36 **Length:** 9001 **Width:** 150 **Surface:** CONC-G

> ★ ★ **Skydine Restaurant - (701) 356-2124**
> **Proprietor:** Candie Valadez
> **Open:**
>> Mon-Fri : 5:00am to Last Departure
>> Sat-Sun: 6:00am to Last Departure
>
> **Restaurant Website**: www.fargoairport.com/tenants.html
> **Restaurant Email:** fargoairport@marlinsfamilyrestaurant.com
> **PIREP**:
> This restaurant is located in the scheduled service passenger service. It is what you would expect it to be; a place to hang out during a flight delay and a place to pick-up "grab and go food". The best that can be said is the ambiance and the food are serviceable.

🍴 GRAND FORKS, ND (GRAND FORKS INTL - GFK)
> **Aprt Mgr:** PATRICK DAME **PH:** 701-795-6981
> **Field Elevation:** 845 **CTAF:** 118.400 **FUEL:** 100LLA
> **Runway:** 17R/35L **Length:** 7351 **Width:** 150 **Surface:** ASPH-F
> **Runway:** 09R/27L **Length:** 3300 **Width:** 60 **Surface:** CONC
> **Runway:** 17L/35R **Length:** 3901 **Width:** 75 **Surface:** CONC-F
> **Runway:** 09L/27R **Length:** 4206 **Width:** 100 **Surface:** CONC-G

> ★ ★ **Red River Valley Grill and Market - (701)738-4630**
> **Proprietor:** Oakwells Stores
> **Open:**
>> Mon - Sun: 5:00 am - 6:00 pm
>
> **Restaurant Website**: www.gfkairport.com/terminal-services/
> **PIREP**:
> If you're stuck at the airport and you're hungry, as in starving, this place will suffice. It is in the main passenger terminal and will require a trip through security.

FlyIn Ohio

🍴 **CARROLLTON, OH (CARROLL COUNTY-TOLSON - TSO)**
   Aprt Mgr: ALAN MILLER **PH:** 330-627-5501
   Field Elevation: 1163 **CTAF:** 122.700 **FUEL:** 100LLA
   Runway: 07/25 **Length:** 4297 **Width:** 75 **Surface:** ASPH-G

   ★★★ **Carroll County Airport Restaurant - (330) 627-5250**
   Proprietor: Lisa McCord
   Manager: Rhonda Vincent
   Open:
         Mon - Sun: 7:00am - 7:00pm
   Restaurant Website: www.carrollcountyairportrestaurant.webs.com
   Restaurant Email: am332904@gmail.com
   PIREP:
   Great home cooked food, nice folks, and a good view of airplanes. Lisa
   McCord does everything from scratch. The food is **WONDERFUL**.
   Her specialty is a wide variety of homemade pies (try the mint Oreo).

🍴 **CINCINNATI, OH (LUNKEN FIELD - LUK)**
   Aprt Mgr: FRED ANDERTON **PH:** 513-352-6340
   Field Elevation: 483 **CTAF:** 118.700 **FUEL:** 100LLA+
   Runway: 03L/21R **Length:** 3802 **Width:** 100 **Surface:** ASPH-F
   Runway: 07/25 **Length:** 5128 **Width:** 100 **Surface:** ASPH-F
   Runway: 03R/21L **Length:** 6101 **Width:** 150 **Surface:** ASPH-F

   ★★★★★ **Sky Galley Inn - (513) 871-7400**
   Proprietor: Kirby Brakvill
   Open:
         Mon – Thu: 11:00am - 9:00pm
         Fri – Sat: 11:00am - 10:00pm
         Sun: 11:00am - 9:00pm
   Restaurant Website: www.skygalley.net
   Restaurant Email: info@ skygalley.net
   PIREP:
   From the art deco building to the amazing food to the uninterrupted
   airport view The Sky Galley is a **MUST** stop. It has long been one of
   my favorites.

🍴 **CLEVELAND, OH (CUYAHOGA COUNTY - CGF)**
   Aprt Mgr: KEVIN M. DELANEY **PH:** 216-289-4111
   Field Elevation: 879 **CTAF:** 118.500 **FUEL:** 100LLA A1+
   Runway: 06/24 **Length:** 5102 **Width:** 100 **Surface:** ASPH-F

$100 Hamburger 2014/15

★ ★ **J.B. Milano's - (216) 289-4000**
Proprietor: Eva Fani
Open:

> Monday - Thursday: 11am to 9 pm
> Friday: 11am to 10pm
> Saturday: 5pm to 10pm

Restaurant Website: www.sites.google.com/site/jbmilanos/home
PIREP:

It's an okay Italian restaurant, located right on the field with reasonable prices. That's the bad news. The good news is that Italian food is a welcome change from the normal airport restaurant "burger and French fries" fare. It's a short walk from the FBO.

⦿ COLUMBUS, OH (BOLTON FIELD - TZR)

Aprt Mgr: CHARLIE GOODWIN **PH:** 614-851-9900
Field Elevation: 905 **CTAF:** 128.100 **FUEL:** 100LLA1+
Runway: 04/22 **Length:** 5500 **Width:** 100 **Surface:** ASPH-F

★ ★ ★ **JP's Ribs - 614-878-7422**
Proprietor: The Makar Family
Open:

> Mon: 11:00am - 3:00pm
> Tues-Fri: 11:00am - 8:00pm
> Sat-Sun: 12:00am - 8:00pm

Restaurant Website: www.jpsbbq.com/home.asp
PIREP:

Come for the Ribs, you'll be glad you did. Stay for the fun. This is the only place I've found that has horse shoes, volley ball and putt-putt plus a HUGE outdoor patio.

⦿ COLUMBUS, OH (PORT COLUMBUS INTL - CMH)

Aprt Mgr: "ELAINE ROBERTS, A.A.E." **PH:** 614-239-4000
Field Elevation: 815 **CTAF:** 0.000 **FUEL:** 100 A1+
Runway: 10L/28R **Length:** 8000 **Width:** 150 **Surface:** ASPH-G
Runway: 10R/28L **Length:** 10125 **Width:** 150 **Surface:** ASPH-G

★ ★ ★ ★ **94th Aero Squadron - 614-237-8887**
Proprietor: Chad Pew
Manager: Tom Kanbybowicz
Open:

> Monday - Thursday: 4:00pm -9:00pm
> Friday - Saturday: 4:00pm - 10:00pm
> Sunday Brunch: 10:00am - 2:30pm
> Sunday Dinner: 3:00pm - 8:00pm

Restaurant Website: www.the94thaero.com/default.aspx
Restaurant Email: chadpew@94thaero.com
Restaurant Email: tomkandybowicz@94thaero.com
PIREP:
The **94th Aero Squadron** has been a tradition in central Ohio for nearly 30 years. It is a great place to enjoy a sizzling steak dinner while watching the arriving and departing traffic just outside the huge windows of this 1914 French farmhouse replica. It sits immediately off of runway 10R/28L Either FBO will be pleased to give you a ride over and pick you up when you're ready.

๏ COSHOCTON, OH (RICHARD DOWNING - I40)
Aprt Mgr: BETHEL R. TOLER **PH:** 740-622-2252
Field Elevation: 979 **CTAF:** 123.000 **FUEL:** 100LLA
Runway: 04/22 **Length:** 5000 **Width:** 75 **Surface:** ASPH-G

★ ★ ★The Fly In Patio Grill - (740) 829-2421
Proprietor: Rick and Sherry Spragg
Open:
> Fri: 5:00 - 8:00 pm
> Sat: 11:00 am - 7:00 pm
> Sun: 11:00 am - 6:00 pm

Restaurant Website: www.coshoctoncounty.net/agency/airport/
PIREP:
The restaurant is located o the ramp. It features Pulled Pork and Baby Back Ribs and many other favorites. The restaurant may not be the best reason to come here. This is stop is about a small airport with a BIG vision. They even have an Airport Amphitheater where you can catch some pretty good concerts. Once a year they host a very nice airshow – **Wings over Coshocto.**

๏ MANSFIELD, OH (MANSFIELD LAHM RGNL - MFD)
Aprt Mgr: MARK T. DAUGHERTY **PH:** 419-522-2191
Field Elevation: 1297 **CTAF:** 119.800 **FUEL:** 100LLA
Runway: 05/23 **Length:** 6800 **Width:** 150 **Surface:** ASPH-F
Runway: 14/32 **Length:** 9001 **Width:** 150 **Surface:** ASPH-G

★ ★ ★ Subway - (419) 524-0700
Proprietor: Rick and Sherry Spragg
Open:
> Monday - Sunday: 5:00am to 7:00 pm

Restaurant Website: www.subway.com
PIREP:
It's a Subway like any other Subway EXCEPT it's at a great airport and access is really easy with convenient parking right out front. Grab your

sandwich and pick out a chair anywhere in the passenger lounge area. This airport has NO commercial flights so there is no security issue.

🍽 MOUNT VICTORY, OH (ELLIOTTS LANDING - O74)
Aprt Mgr: EDWARD ELLIOTT II **PH:** 937-354-2851
Field Elevation: 1045 **CTAF:** 122.900 **FUEL:**
Runway: 15/33 **Length:** 2750 **Width:** 110 **Surface:** TURF-F

★ ★ ★ ★ Plaza Inn - (937) 354-2851
Proprietor: Joan Wagner and Ed Elliot
Open:
Monday - Sunday: Breakfast, Lunch & Dinner
Restaurant Website: www.plazainn.net
Restaurant Email: plazainn@plazainn.net
PIREP:
The strip is 2,800 feet of turf. It can be bumpy but its usually mowed. Tie-down areas are avialble on the ramp BUT you must bring your own tie downs. There is no fuel at this airport which is good and bad. Good because you don't have to buy any and bad because you're in a pickle if you need fuel.

The restaurant is a treat. Get your mouth set for home cooking. The Plaza Inn has been in business since 1959 and has grown from 42 to 250 seats so they must be doing something right. I like this spot a bunch because I like family restaurants and this is a great example. They offer a menu and a buffet.

🍽🏛 PORT CLINTON, OH (CARL R KELLER FIELD - PCW)
Aprt Mgr: JACK STABLES **PH:** 419-734-6297
Field Elevation: 590 **CTAF:** 122.800 **FUEL:** 100LLA
Runway: 09/27 **Length:** 5646 **Width:** 100 **Surface:** ASPH-E
Runway: 18/36 **Length:** 4001 **Width:** 75 **Surface:** ASPH-F

★ ★ ★ ★ ★ Tin Goose Diner - (419) 732-0236
Proprietor: Joan Wagner and Ed Elliot
Open:
Monday - Sunday: 7am – 7pm
Restaurant Website: www.tingoosediner.com
Restaurant Email: plazainn@plazainn.net
PIREP:
This diner is authentic, built by the Jerry O'Mahony Diner Company of Elizabeth, New Jersey, in the 1950's. It was originally operated as the Sunrise Diner in Jim Thorpe, Pennsylvania. The food is wonderful diner food straight out of the '50s. Want a malt? This is the place to get it.

★★Liberty Aviation Museum - (419) 732-0234
Open:

       Sun. - Thu.: 10:00am - 4:00pm
       Friday: 10:00am - 5:00pm
       Saturday: 10:00am - 5:00pm

Restaurant Website: www.libertyaviationmuseum.org
Restaurant Email: info@libertyaviationmuseum.org
PIREP:

One reason to come to the **Tin Goose Diner** is its connection with the **Liberty Aviation Museum**. Here you'll find a few (very few) examples from *The Golden Age of Aviation* and they are all wonderfully presented. They also have a PT Boat and some other WWII gear.

🍽 **PORTSMOUTH, OH (GREATER PORTSMOUTH RGNL - PMH)**
    Aprt Mgr: PAUL BROGDON **PH:** 740-820-2700
    Field Elevation: 663 **CTAF:** 122.800 **FUEL:** 100LLA1+
    Runway: 18/36 **Length:** 5001 **Width:** 100 **Surface:** ASPH-G

★★★Skyline Family Restaurant – (740) 820-2203
Proprietor: Robert Montgomery
Manager: Beverly
Open:

       Monday - Sunday: 7am – 8pm

Restaurant Website: www.facebook.com/pages/Skyline-Family-Restaurant-Inc/346305094264
PIREP:

The restaurant is in the terminal with parking right out front. Home Style Cooking, Breakfast served all day.

🍽 **SALEM, OH (SALEM AIRPARK INC - 38D)**
    Aprt Mgr: MICHAEL PIDGEON **PH:** 330-332-4400
    Field Elevation: 1162 **CTAF:** 122.700 **FUEL:** 100LL
    Runway: 10L/28R **Length:** 3404 **Width:** 50 **Surface:** ASPH-G
    Runway: 10R/28L **Length:** 2593 **Width:** 85 **Surface:** TURF-G

★★★★ Skyline Diner - 330-332-4400
Proprietor: The Pidgeon Family
Open:

       Mon: 7am – 2pm
       Tue: Closed
       Wed. – Fri: 7am – 2pm
       Sat. & Sun: 7am -3pm

Restaurant Website: www.salemairpark.com/#skyline-diner

PIREP:

The airport has long parallel runways; one is turf the other asphalt and both are in great shape. The Skyline is on the main ramp. I like it for the freshness of their meats. The beef comes from the Pidgeon family's farm. The pork is also raised and butchered locally. They offer the only real 100 Hamburger I have ever heard of. The burger comes with an airplane ride. Great idea!

⏐●⏐ 🏛 URBANA, OH (GRIMES FIELD - I74)
Aprt Mgr: CAROL HALL **PH:** 937-652-4319
Field Elevation: 1068 **CTAF:** 122.700 **FUEL:** 100LLA
Runway: 02/20 **Length:** 4400 **Width:** 100 **Surface:** ASPH-G

★ ★ ★ Airport Cafe - 937-484-2010
Open:
> Tue - Sun: 7am - 8pm

Restaurant Website: www.airportcafeurbana.com/
PIREP:

This is another example of a Midwestern on-airport family restaurant. They are all good and this one certainly measures up with some of the best. While here you'll want to visit the museum and see the B-17 they are restoring. They claim to have the "Best Pies and the Skies". I can't argue with that assessment.

★ ★ Champaign Aviation Museum - (937) 652-4710
Open:
> Tue- Sat:10am to 4pm

Restaurant Website: www.champaignaviationmuseum.org
PIREP:

Open to the public with FREE admission. They have a B-17 which is undergoing restoration and a few very nice WWII era Warbirds.

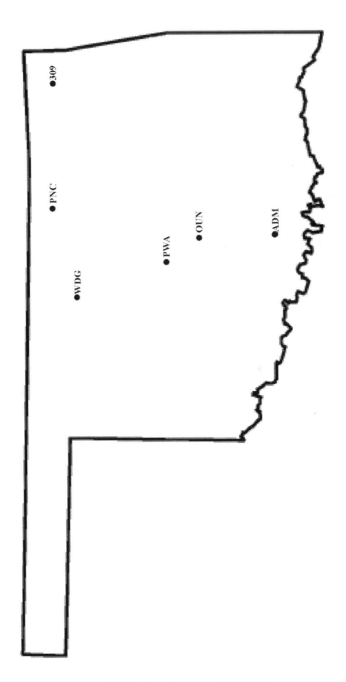

$100 Hamburger 2014/15

FlyIn Oklahoma

▣ AFTON, OK (GRAND LAKE RGNL - 3O9)
Aprt Mgr: DUANE MAYNARD **PH:** 918-257-2400
Field Elevation: 792 **CTAF:** 122.700 **FUEL:** 100LLA
Runway: 17/35 **Length:** 3925 **Width:** 60 **Surface:** CONC-G

★★★★Aqua Bar & Grill – (918) 257-4440
Proprietor: Paul Staten
Open:
> Tuesday: 11am to 8pm
> Friday: 11am to 9pm
> Saturday: 11am to 9pm
> Sunday: 11am to 6pm

Restaurant Website:
www.thelandingsgrandlake.com/aquabar_grill.htm
Restaurant Email: pstaten@grandlakeregionalairport.com
PIREP:
The Aqua Bar is located on the southeast edge of the Grand Lake Regional Airport just as runway 17 meets the water. It is a floating restaurant offering upscale food and views at fair prices. The flight over Grand Lake is beautiful; day or night over.

★★★ The Landing Market & Grill – (918) 257-8602
Proprietor: Paul Staten
Open:
> Mon-Thur: 6am-9pm
> Fri-Sun: 6am-9pm

Restaurant Website:
www.thelandingsgrandlake.com/market_and_grill.htm
Restaurant Email: pstaten@grandlakeregionalairport.com
PIREP:
The Landings Market and Grill located on the edge of Grand Lake, is a fully stocked convenience store/gas station that serves pretty good food. Actually, the burgers & fries are great!

The airport office is in this building. Very nice takeoff and landing over the lake.

▣ ARDMORE, OK (ARDMORE MUNI - ADM)
Aprt Mgr: CHRIS BRYANT **PH:** 580-389-5238

Field Elevation: 777 **CTAF:** 118.500 **FUEL:** 100LLA
Runway: 17/35 **Length:** 5350 **Width:** 100 **Surface:** ASPH-G
Runway: 13/31 **Length:** 9001 **Width:** 150 **Surface:** CONC-E

★ ★ ★ ★ ★ **Jake's Joint** – (580) 389-5040
Proprietor: Jerry Allan King-Echevarria - JAKE
Open:

> Mon – Fri: 11am to 2pm

Restaurant Website: www.jakesjointrestaurant.com
PIREP:
This place is perfect with one BIG exception.

First for the good news, all food is prepared by a chef who is a graduate of the Culinary Institute of America. All desserts are home made, and many are **JAKE's** favorite recipes from his home and ranch. When you order an "alcoholic drink" at **JAKE'S JOINT** it is going to be **JAKE's** very own Puerto Rican Bacardi Superior Rum in a tall glass with two limes and diet coke. The best thing on the menu changes every day. It's **JAKE'S Blue Plate Special** which comes with your choice of two sides, yeast rolls and dessert and a drink for ten bucks. **JAKE** hopes that you enjoy your meal but it's to his standards and no one else's! Needless to say that is why the place is called **JAKE'S JOINT** where the food is truly **"Food Fit for a King!"**

So what's the problem? Easy, it is not open on the weekends. If it were, **Jake's Joint** would have been awarded the **$100 Hamburger Best of the Best Award** every year. That's too bad for this is one of the best fly-in restaurants in America.

🍴 **ENID, OK (ENID WOODRING RGNL - WDG)**
Aprt Mgr: DAN OHNESORGE **PH:** 580-234-5476
Field Elevation: 1167 **CTAF:** 118.900 **FUEL:** 100LLA
Runway: 13/31 **Length:** 3149 **Width:** 108 **Surface:** ASPH-G
Runway: 17/35 **Length:** 6249 **Width:** 100 **Surface:** CONC-G

★ ★ ★ **The Barnstormer** - (580) 234-9913
Open:

> Mon – Fri: 8am- 2pm

Restaurant Website: www.enid.org/index.aspx?page=445
PIREP:
The Barnstormer has an expansive circular floor to ceiling glass window that overlooks the airport. Through it you'll see young Air Force pilots in training doing touch and goes as you eat some of the best and most artery clogging food you've ever had. Even the club

sandwich is grilled! I love this place. It is covered with model airplanes and populated by hangar flying pilots.

NORMAN, OK (UNIVERSITY OF OKLAHOMA - OUN)
Aprt Mgr: WALT STRONG **PH:** 405-325-7233
Field Elevation: 1182 **CTAF:** 118.000 **FUEL:** 100LLA
Runway: 03/21 **Length:** 4748 **Width:** 100 **Surface:** ASPH-G
Runway: 17/35 **Length:** 5199 **Width:** 100 **Surface:** ASPH-G

★★ Ozzie's - (405) 364-9835
Proprietor: Martin Van
Open:
> Mon – Sat: 6:00am - 9:00pm
> Sunday: 6:00am - 3:00pm

PIREP:
Bring a BIG appetite and cash. Breakfast is an all you can eat deal. They don't do plastic. The atmosphere is strictly small-town diner. It's a good stop.

OKLAHOMA CITY, OK (WILEY POST - PWA)
Aprt Mgr: TIM WHITMAN **PH:** 405-789-4061
Field Elevation: 1300 **CTAF:** 126.900 **FUEL:** 100LLA
Runway: 17R/35L **Length:** 5002 **Width:** 75 **Surface:** ASPH-CONC-G
Runway: 13/31 **Length:** 4214 **Width:** 100 **Surface:** CONC-G
Runway: 17L/35R **Length:** 7199 **Width:** 150 **Surface:** CONC-G

★★★★ Annie Okie's Runway Cafe - (405) 737-7732
Open:
> Mon – Sat: 7am-3pm.
> Sun: 8am-3pm.

Restaurant Website:
www.wileypostairport.com/Page/AirportDirectory#
PIREP:
You can keep an eye on your airplane from the restaurant atrium. The food is excellent especially the omelets and the burgers. This place really fills up on the weekends.

PONCA CITY, OK (PONCA CITY RGNL - PNC)
Aprt Mgr: DON NUZUM **PH:** 580-767-0470
Field Elevation: 1008 **CTAF:** 123.000 **FUEL:** 100LLA
Runway: 17/35 **Length:** 7201 **Width:** 150 **Surface:** CONC-F

★★★★★ Enrique's Mexican Restaurant - (580) 762-5507
Proprietor: Michael Avila

Open:

Mon – Fri: 11am- 2pm
Mon – Fri: 4:30pm-9pm
Sat: 11am – 9 pm
Sun: CLOSED

Restaurant Website: www.enriquesmexicanrestaurant.com/
Restaurant Email: michael.avila@yahoo.com
PIREP:
I love Mexican food and I love flying put the two together and I'm good to go. Enrique's has been serving some of the best Mexican food I have ever eaten since 1982 and doing from the present runway location. No wonder that Enrique's has been a three-peat on the **$100 Hamburger Best of the Best** list.

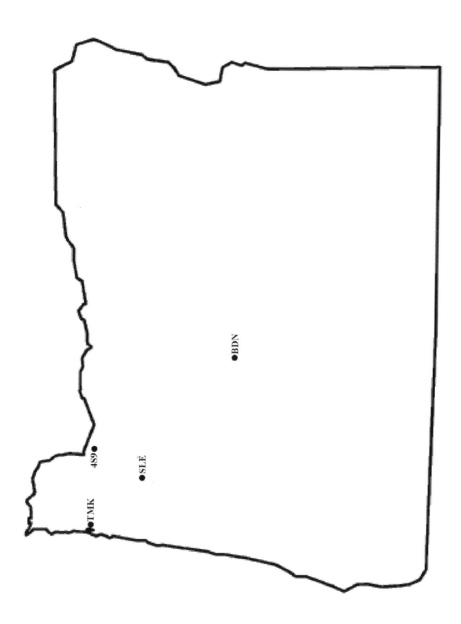

FlyIn Oregon

🍽 **BEND, OR (BEND MUNI - BDN)**
  Aprt Mgr: GARY JUDD **PH:** 541-389-0258
  Field Elevation: 3460 **CTAF:** 123.000 **FUEL:** 100LLA
  Runway: 16/34 **Length:** 5200 **Width:** 75 **Surface:** ASPH-E

  ★ ★ ★ Bend Airport Cafe - 541-318-8989
  Open:
      Mon - Sun: 7:30 am - 8:00 pm
  Restaurant Website:
  www.ci.bend.or.us/Modules/ShowDocument.aspx?documentID=6811
  PIREP:
  This is no greasy spoon. The chef is right there in an open to the dining
  room kitchen. The food is really very good. There's a nice FBO
  downstairs. The broad windows provide the added benefit of watching
  a number of impressive airplanes flying to and from the airport. This is
  a great place to stop, with nearby tower-controlled Redmond just to the
  north and the smaller Sunriver just a 10-minute hop to the southwest.

🍽 **PORTLAND-MULINO, OR (MULINO STATE - 4S9)**
  Aprt Mgr: OREGON DEPT OF AVIATION **PH:** 503-378-4880
  Field Elevation: 260 **CTAF:** 123.050 **FUEL:**
  Runway: 14/32 **Length:** 3425 **Width:** 100 **Surface:** ASPH-G

  ★ ★ ★ Mulino Hangar Cafe & Roadhouse - (503) 829-7555
  Proprietor: Stephanie and Ed Huff
  Open:
      Mon - Thu: 6:00 am - 9:00 pm
      Fri - Sat: 6:00 am - 10:00 pm
      Sun: 7:00 am - 9:00 pm
  Restaurant Website: www.mulinocafe.com
  Restaurant Email: mulinocafe@gmail.com
  PIREP:
  Nice family owned and operated restaurant with local ambiance. They
  use locally grown food and you can really tell the difference. In dry
  weather you can taxi on the grass from the midfield parking lot to
  within 75 feet of the cafe. **Mulino Hangar Cafe & Roadhouse** has
  worthwhile specials every day of the week. They range from Pizza to
  Prime Rib.

🍽 **SALEM, OR (MCNARY FLD - SLE)**
  Aprt Mgr: JOHN PASKELL **PH:** 503-588-6314

Field Elevation: 214 CTAF: 119.100 FUEL: 100LLA
Runway: 16/34 Length: 5145 Width: 100 Surface: ASPH-G
Runway: 13/31 Length: 5811 Width: 150 Surface: ASPH-G

★ ★ ★ ★ Flight Deck Restaurant and Lounge - (503) 581-5721
Proprietor: Natalie Frajola and Barry Bowers
Open:
>   Mon - Fri: 11:00 am - 9:00 pm
>   Sat - Sun: 8:00 am - 9:00 pm
Restaurant Website: www. flightdeckrestaurant.com
Restaurant Email: dine@flightdeckrestaurant.com
PIREP:
The Flight Deck Restaurant offers a spectacular view of the Cascade
Mountains as well as landing and departing aircraft. The food is
extraordinary; you'll certainly not be disappointed whether you order a
steak, a burger or anything in between. Their clam chowder has won
statewide awards (there is a large plaque on the wall by the cash
register.) It is much better than any of the "famous" chowder places you
find along the coast. The Willamette Valley of Oregon is known for
flavorful berries. The Flight Deck chef makes good use of them in a
triple berry cobbler that must not be missed.

⁌ 🏛 TILLAMOOK, OR (TILLAMOOK - TMK)
Aprt Mgr: COLBY LOVITT PH: 503-842-2413
Field Elevation: 36 CTAF: 122.800 FUEL: 100LLA
Runway: 01/19 Length: 2910 Width: 75 Surface: ASPH-G
Runway: 13/31 Length: 5001 Width: 100 Surface: ASPH-G

★ ★ ★ Air Base Cafe - (503) 842-1130
Open:
>   Seasonal: Closes November 1 for the winter
>   Mon - Sun: 9:00 am - 4:00 pm
Restaurant Website: www.tillamookair.com/air-base-cafeacute.html
Restaurant Email: info@tillamookair.com
PIREP:
The Air Base Café is inside the Tillamook Air Museum. The good
news is that you can taxi to the museum's ramp. The Air Base Café
offers pleasant dining in 40's/50's style café decor. They offer a lunch
menu of burgers, fries, fish & chips, hot dogs and chili along with hot
and cold drinks. The food is good and the service friendly.

★ ★ ★ ★ Tillamook Air Museum - (503) 842-1130
Museum Curator: Christian Gurling
Open:
>   Mon - Sun: 9:00 am - 5:00 pm

www.100dollarhamburger.com

Restaurant Website: www.tillamookair.com
Restaurant Email: info@tillamookair.com
PIREP:
The Tillamook Air Museum is one of the world's premiere air museums. Its collection is displayed inside the largest wooden structure in the world. Many of its airplanes are flyable and rides can be purchased in them. As you would imagine the collection includes many WWII era warbirds including a B-17. What is unusual is the mix of modern era fighters including an F-14. The hangar that houses the collection was built in WWII as a home for eight K Class blimps.

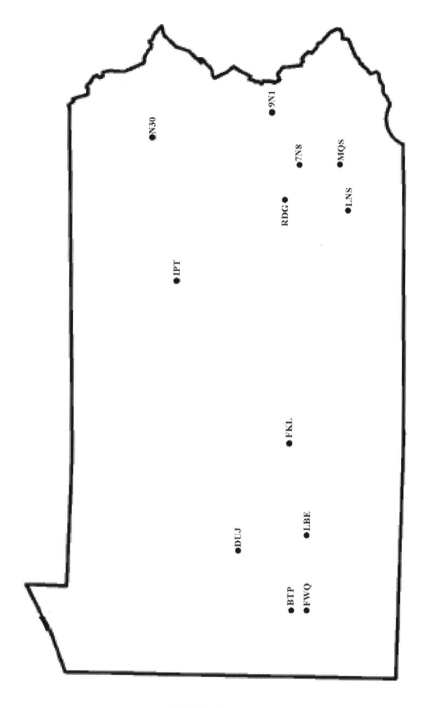

FlyIn Pennsylvania

━━━━━━━━━━━━━━━━━━━━━━━━━━━━━━━

🍴 ✈ **BALLY, PA (BUTLER VALLEY GOLF PORT - 7N8)**
Aprt Mgr: JOHN L. GEHMAN **PH:** 610-845-2491
Field Elevation: 500 **CTAF:** 122.800 **FUEL:**
Runway: 16/34 **Length:** 2420 **Width:** 85 **Surface:** ASPH-TURF-G

━━━━━━━━━━━━━━━━━━━━━━━━━━
★★ **Runway Grill - 610-845-2491**
Grill Manager: Connie Babb
Open:

> Seasonal Closed: November 1 thru April 1
> Tuesday – Saturday: 11:00 am – 10:00 pm
> Sunday: 10:00 am – 9:00 pm

Restaurant Website: www.buttervalley.com
Restaurant Email: connie@buttervalley.com
PIREP:
Located in the club house of the Butter Valley Golfport. The Runway is a fun destination. You can watch planes land and golfers finish their round from behind the massive windows. It's a breakfast and burger kinda' place that offers tasty food and friendly service for golfers and pilots.

━━━━━━━━━━━━━━━━━━━━━━━━━━
★★★★ **Butter Valley Golf Club- 610-845-2491**
Proprietor: John Gehman
Open:

> Seasonal
> Daily

Restaurant Website: www.buttervalley.com
Restaurant Email: connie@buttervalley.com
PIREP: I love golf and I love airplanes but I hate pretension. This place was built for me. It's beautiful rolling terrain, without condos or other nearby buildings, provides the same natural feeling that you experienced on golf courses decades ago. It's the perfect place to "Renew the Spirit" with family and friends. That experience begins when you line up for landing. The strip is in the center of the golf course. It is rolling and short at just 2,500 feet. Half is asphalt and half is turf. When you tiedown, a golf cart will appear to drive you to the club house.

🍴 **BUTLER, PA (BUTLER COUNTY/K W SCHOLTER FIELD - BTP)**
Aprt Mgr: JOHN L. GEHMAN **PH:** 610-845-2491
Field Elevation: 500 **CTAF:** 122.800 **FUEL:**
Runway: 16/34 **Length:** 2420 **Width:** 85 **Surface:** ASPH-TURF-G

★ ★ ★ **Runway Sports Bar & Grill - 724-586-6599**
Proprietor: Dena Hochbein
Open:

Tuesday – Saturday: 11:00 am – 10:00 pm
Sunday: 10:00 am – 9:00 pm

Restaurant Website: www.runwaygrille.com
Restaurant Email: info@runwaygrille.com
PIREP:

The Runway Sports Bar & Grill is a fun destination because it's a sports bar in an airport setting. Does it get any better than that? You can watch planes land and takeoff out the expansive windows while cheering on your favorite team. They have the best crabcakes I've ever eaten. Everyone agrees that the Prime Rib is the best for miles around. It is a Friday evening special that you shouldn't miss. Everything on the menu (I've sampled much of it) is very, very good.

|◉| **COATESVILLE, PA (CHESTER COUNTY G O CARLSON - MQS)**
Aprt Mgr: GARY L HUDSON **PH:** 610-383-6057
Field Elevation: 660 **CTAF:** 122.700 **FUEL:** 100LLA
Runway: 11/29 **Length:** 5400 **Width:** 100 **Surface:** ASPH-G

★ ★ ★ **The Flying Machine - (610) 380-7977**
Open:

Mon - Fri: 11:00 am - 10:00 pm
Sat: 8:00 am - 10:00 pm
Sun: 8:00 am - 9:00 pm

Restaurant Website: www.flyingmachinecafe.com/
Restaurant Email: contact@flyingmachinecafe.com
PIREP:

Applying the phrase "it has stood the test of time" isn't a bad idea for **The Flying Machine**. It opened in 1994. Clearly, they're doing something right. They check all of my boxes. It is spotlessly clean with great food, friendly service and an impressive view of an active airport. Every Wednesday is Wild Wings Special Night. Get an order of 10 chicken wings, any way you want, for only $5! My personal favorite is "Jet Engine Style" but I like a lot of heat! Dessert? Easy! Go with the triple chocolate cake.

|◉| **DUBOIS, PA (DUBOIS RGNL - DUJ)**
Aprt Mgr: ROBERT W. SHAFFER **PH:** 814-328-5311
Field Elevation: 1817 **CTAF:** 123.000 **FUEL:** 100LLA
Runway: 07/25 **Length:** 5503 **Width:** 100 **Surface:** ASPH-TRTD-G

★ ★ ★ **The Flight Deck Restaurant & Lounge - (814) 328-5281**

Proprietor: Patrick Doksa
Open:

Mon - Wed: 8:00 am - 8:00 pm
Thu - Sat: 8:00 am - 9:00 pm
Sun: 9:00 am - 8:00 pm

Restaurant Email: theflightdeck@windstream.net
PIREP:

You know an airport restaurant has good food when there are more than pilots. **The Flight Deck Restaurant & Lounge** is such a place. Thursday is Steak Night. You can grab any steak you like at a price you won't believe. My personal favorite is the 16 oz. NY Strip for less than 10 bucks. That's hard to beat.

🍽 🏛 **ERWINNA, PA (VANSANT - 9N1)**

Aprt Mgr: GEORGE TAYLOR **PH:** 610-847-8494
Field Elevation: 390 **CTAF:** 122.800 **FUEL:** 100LL
Runway: 05G/23G **Length:** 1340 **Width:** 200 **Surface:** TURF-G
Runway: 07/25 **Length:** 3058 **Width:** 120 **Surface:** TURF-G

★ ★ **Airport Grille** – (610) 847-1119
Proprietor: Bar and Dannie
Open:

Seasonal:
Sat & Sun: Lunch

Restaurant Website: www.vansantairport.com
Restaurant Email: BarAndDannie@866mustfly.com
PIREP:

On weekends during the flying season Linda is there with her grill serving up hot dogs, hamburgers and veggie burgers. She usually has chips, cookies, fruit and an assortment of drinks available. Don't come here for the food. This stop is all about the planes and the airport. They offer hotdogs and burgers and chips and drinks. Don't expect much and you won't be disappointed.

★ ★ ★ ★ ★ **Van Sant Historic Airfield** – (610) 847-1119
Proprietor: Bar and Dannie
Open:

Summer: Wednesday thru Sunday 9:00 to 6:00.
Winter: Wednesday thru Sunday 8:30 to 4:00

Website: www.vansantairport.com
Email: BarAndDannie@866mustfly.com
PIREP:

This is what an aviation museum is supposed to be. There are plenty of old airplanes to see and even touch and plenty of folks who love them around to tell you about each of them. That gets you to first base.

Seeing them all fly from this gorgeous turf strip is clearly a triple. Here's the home run. You can buy a ride in any or all of them and if you really catch the bug you can be instructed in how to fly them. Can you imagine landing a Stearman or a J3 Cub? How about going for a sightseeing tour over historic and beautiful Bucks County in a 1928 Travel Air? That's what this place is all about. It's a time machine that you get to step into not merely peer through the looking glass.

⭐ FRANKLIN, PA (VENANGO RGNL - FKL)
Aprt Mgr: GEORGE TAYLOR **PH:** 610-847-8494
Field Elevation: 390 **CTAF:** 122.800 **FUEL:** 100LL
Runway: 05G/23G **Length:** 1340 **Width:** 200 **Surface:** TURF-G
Runway: 07/25 **Length:** 3058 **Width:** 120 **Surface:** TURF-G

★ ★ ★ ★ ★ Primo Barone's Restaurant - (814) 432-2588
Proprietor: Giuseppe Barone
Open:

> Mon - Thu: 11:00 am - 9:00 pm
> Fri - Sat: 11:00 am - 11:00 pm
> Sun: 11:00 am - 9:00 pm

Restaurant Website: www.flyfranklin.org/restaurant.asp
PIREP:
Primo Barone's Restaurant & Lounge consistently delivers gourmet food expertly prepared. They have a lively piano bar nightly and a jazz combo on Friday nights. Can you think of another airport restaurant that offers Baked Alaska? I use one word to define **Primo's** – OUTSTANDING!

⭐ HONESDALE, PA (CHERRY RIDGE - N30)
Aprt Mgr: BILL MOTT **PH:** 570-253-5181
Field Elevation: 1357 **CTAF:** 122.800 **FUEL:** 100LL
Runway: 18/36 **Length:** 2986 **Width:** 50 **Surface:** ASPH-F

★ ★ ★ Cherry Ridge Airport Café - (570) 253-5517
Proprietor: Mike Lovelace
Open:

> Sat & Sunday: 7 a.m. until 3 p.m.

Restaurant Website: www.cherry-ridge-airport.com/restaurant
PIREP:
The cafe features a deck on the side for patrons to sit during the summer months, and a spot for pilots to park their planes in front of the café. The view of the runway and pond is unobstructed. The food is OK. I enjoy coming here for breakfast more than lunch.

⭐ LANCASTER, PA (LANCASTER - LNS)

www.100dollarhamburger.com

Aprt Mgr: DAVID F EBERLY **PH:** 717-569-1221
Field Elevation: 403 **CTAF:** 120.900 **FUEL:** 100LLA
Runway: 13/31 **Length:** 4101 **Width:** 100 **Surface:** ASPH-G
Runway: 08/26 **Length:** 6934 **Width:** 150 **Surface:** ASPH-G

★ ★ ★ ★ **Fiorentino's Bar and Grill - (717) 569-6732**
Proprietor: Robert and Rose Billas
Open:

Mon - Thurs: 11 am to 10 pm
Fri - Sat: 11 am to 11 pm
Sun: 11 am to 10 pm

Restaurant Website: www.fiorentinos.com/
Restaurant Email: rob@fiorentinos.com
PIREP:
Fiorentino's Bar and Grill is a pleasant break from the normal airport burger joints. It is a nice Italian restaurant which happens to be located on an airport. Hence you can get a really good lunch or dinner with a runway view. Off airport it would be worth three stars because its on the runway, it deserves four.

⦿ LATROBE, PA (ARNOLD PALMER RGNL - LBE)

Aprt Mgr: GABE MONZO **PH:** 724-539-8100
Field Elevation: 1199 **CTAF:** 125.000 **FUEL:** 100LLA
Runway: 03/21 **Length:** 3609 **Width:** 75 **Surface:** ASPH-G
Runway: 05/23 **Length:** 8222 **Width:** 100 **Surface:** ASPH-G

★ ★ ★ ★ ★ **DeNunzio's Italian Chophouse and Sinatra Bar - (724) 539-3980**
Proprietor: Amy Templeton
Open:

Sunday: 10:30am - 9pm
Monday: 11am - 9pm
Tues. – Thurs: 11am - 10pm
Fri & Sat: 11am - 11pm

Restaurant Website:
www.denunziosrestaurant.com/DeNunzios_Latrobe.html
Restaurant Email: denunzio@wpa.net
PIREP:
I love coming to Latrobe. It is Arnold Palmer's boyhood home. He is the world's greatest golfer and a darn good pilot. Airplanes and golf are my greatest passions so a trip to Latrobe is way up on my bucket list.

DeNunzio's is in the terminal building and is easily accessed via the FBO next door. The ambiance is impressive while remaining invitingly casual. The food is very, very good and the service stellar. It is a great place to fly your significant other for a birthday dinner. Plan to come on a weekend evening and enjoy the live entertainment.

🍽 MONONGAHELA, PA (ROSTRAVER - FWQ)
Aprt Mgr: GABE MONZO **PH:** 724-379-6980
Field Elevation: 1228 **CTAF:** 122.800 **FUEL:** 100LLA
Runway: 08/26 **Length:** 4002 **Width:** 75 **Surface:** ASPH-G

★ ★ ★ EAGLE'S LANDING - (724) 379-8830
Proprietor: Bobbi Lawson
Open:

>   Tue – Fri: 9:00am - 8:00pm
>   Sat: 8:00am - 8:00pm
>   Sun: 8:00am - 7:00pm

PIREP:
This is good cross country fuel stop. 100LL prices are typically low. The service at the restaurant is fast, the food is good and the runway view is nice. Not bad.

🍽 READING, PA (READING RGNL/CARL A SPAATZ FIELD - RDG)
Aprt Mgr: TERRY P. SROKA **PH:** 610-372-4666
Field Elevation: 344 **CTAF:** 119.900 **FUEL:** 100LLA
Runway: 18/36 **Length:** 5151 **Width:** 150 **Surface:** ASPH-F
Runway: 13/31 **Length:** 6350 **Width:** 150 **Surface:** ASPH-G

★ ★ ★ Malibooz Bar & Grill - 610-898-8490
Open:

>   Mon – Sat: 11am – 9pm
>   Sunday: 12pm – 9pm

Restaurant Website: www.maliboozbarandgrill.biz
Restaurant Email: maliboozbarandgrill@yahoo.com
PIREP:
The restaurant is in the terminal building. You'll have a great view of runway 13/31. Make certain to write down or memorize the door code on the entrance to the terminal. You won't be able to get back out to your airplane if you don't.

The food and service are inconsistent. Sometimes both are good, sometimes not. When everything is working this is a fun stop. It's has a sport's bar feel with planned customer involvement activities.

🍽 WILLIAMSPORT, PA (WILLIAMSPORT RGNL - IPT)
Aprt Mgr: THOMAS J. HART **PH:** 570-368-2444

Field Elevation: 528 **CTAF:** 119.100 **FUEL:** 100LLA
Runway: 12/30 **Length:** 4280 **Width:** 150 **Surface:** ASPH-G
Runway: 09/27 **Length:** 6824 **Width:** 150 **Surface:** ASPH-G

★★★★★ **Cloud 9 Airport Restaurant and Lounge** – (570) 601-4603
Proprietor: The Daniele Family
Open:
　　　　Mon - Sun: 9:00 am - 5:00 pm
Restaurant Website: www.cloudnineairportrestaurant.com
Restaurant Email: cloud.9restaurant@yahoo.com
PIREP:
You're immediately presented with a beautiful view of the mountain range just beyond the runway at this upscale jewel. Yes, there are table clothes. The food is superb and includes Coquille St. Jacques, Broiled Salmon and Slow Roasted Bacon Wrapped Prime Rib. Cloud 9 offers an intimate atmosphere with warm lighting perfect for a romantic evening or a special gathering with family and friends. This is one of my personal favorites.

BID

FlyIn Rhode Island

BLOCK ISLAND, RI (BLOCK ISLAND STATE - BID)
   Aprt Mgr: MARK HELMBOLDT **PH:** 401-466-5511
   Field Elevation: 108 **CTAF:** 123.000 **FUEL:**
   Runway: 10/28 **Length:** 2502 **Width:** 100 **Surface:** ASPH-E

   ★ ★ ★ ★ **Bethany's Airport Diner - (401) 466-3100**
   Proprietor: Bethany Campbell
   Open:
      Mon – Sun: 6:00am - 3:00pm
   Restaurant Website: www.blockislandairport.com
   PIREP:
   A word to the wise; this airport doesn't sell fuel. There is no landing
   fee charged for an up to two hour stop at **Bethany's.** A flight to Block
   Island is a doable adventure. When you get back to your home port
   you'll feel that you have been somewhere special because you have.
   This is my favorite breakfast stop in New England. The food is more
   than good. It's amazing. The ambiance is *"Wings"* which wasn't
   filmed here but it could have been!

FlyIn South Carolina

⦿ GREENVILLE, SC (GREENVILLE DOWNTOWN - GMU)
    Aprt Mgr: JOE FRASHER **PH:** 864-242-4777
    Field Elevation: 1048 **CTAF:** 119.900 **FUEL:** 100LLA
    Runway: 01/19 **Length:** 5393 **Width:** 100 **Surface:** ASPH-E
    Runway: 10/28 **Length:** 3998 **Width:** 80 **Surface:** ASPH-G

    ★★★ Runway Cafe - 864-991-8488
    Open:
        Sun – Tues: 11am - 2:30pm
        Wed –Thu: 11am - 2:30pm ; 5:00pm-8:30pm
        Fri – Sat: 11am - 8:30pm
    Restaurant Website: www.runwaycafegmu.com
    Restaurant Email: Runwaycafegmu@gmail.com
    PIREP:
I am a big fan of the airport and I like the view from the restaurant. The food is a cut above average. I don't come here often but I do feel its worthy of a look if you're in the area.

⦿ GREER, SC (GREENVILLE SPARTANBURG INTL - GSP)
    Aprt Mgr: "DAVID EDWARDS, JR." **PH:** 864-877-7426
    Field Elevation: 964 **CTAF:** 120.100 **FUEL:** 100LLA
    Runway: 04/22 **Length:** 11000 **Width:** 150 **Surface:** ASPH-CONC-G

    ★★ Windows Restaurant and Lounge - (864) 877-7417
    Proprietor: Woody Duernberger
    Open:
        Mon – Sun: 5:00am - 8:00pm
    PIREP:
Windows is located in the main terminal building and has a beautiful view of a fountain garden overlooking the runway. They not only have a good beef hamburger, but also have an ostrich burger on a multi-grain bun for the health conscious. This is an upscale airport restaurant with a wide menu. Here's the problem; it's on the other side of security so you have to deal with the TSA. I am rarely hungry enough to make that trade. It is important that this is a small commercial airport so the security line isn't that long.

⦿ LAKE CITY, SC (LAKE CITY MUNI CJ EVANS FIELD - 51J)
    Aprt Mgr: "DAVID EDWARDS, JR." **PH:** 864-877-7426

Field Elevation: 964 **CTAF:** 120.100 **FUEL:** 100LLA
Runway: 04/22 **Length:** 11000 **Width:** 150 **Surface:** **ASPH**-CONC-G

★★★ The Patio Restaurant – (843) 699-9033
Open:

Mon - Sat: 11:00am - 8:00pm

Restaurant Email: thepatio_restaurant@yahoo.com
PIREP:

The Patio Restaurant is located by the side of the runway. It's easy to find. There is a patio *(hence the name)* which is heated and lighted so you can opt to sit inside or outside. The menu is broad and includes everything from a chicken Caesar wrap to pork schnitzel.

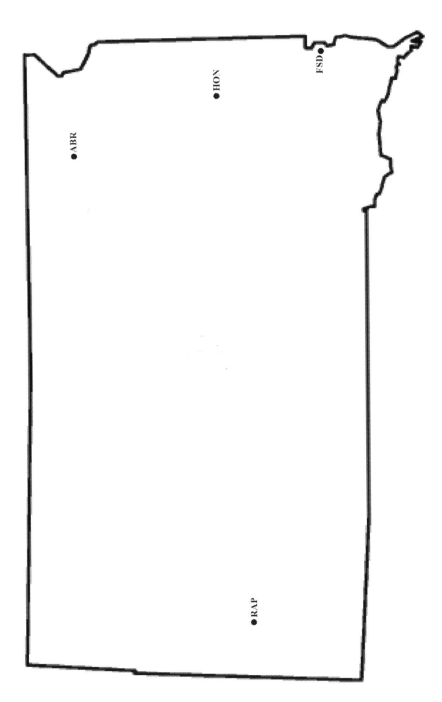

$100 Hamburger 2014/15

FlyIn South Dakota

◉ ABERDEEN, SD (ABERDEEN RGNL - ABR)
Aprt Mgr: MICHAEL WILSON **PH:** 605-626-7020
Field Elevation: 1302 **CTAF:** 122.700 **FUEL:** 100LLA MOGAS
Runway: 17/35 **Length:** 5500 **Width:** 100 **Surface:** ASPH-F
Runway: 13/31 **Length:** 6901 **Width:** 100 **Surface:** CONC-G

★★★ **Airport Cafe and Lounge - (605) 225-7210**
Proprietor: Ron Erickson
Open:
>   Mon - Sat: 5:30am - 1:30pm
>   Sun: 6:30am - 1:30pm

Restaurant Website: www.airporttravelcentersd.com
PIREP:
Aberdeen is home to some of the best pheasant hunting in the US. If you're up this way you'll be pleased with the friendly service. The food is very basic but quite good.

◉ HURON, SD (HURON RGNL - HON)
Aprt Mgr: LARRY COOPER **PH:** 605-353-8516
Field Elevation: 1289 **CTAF:** 123.600 **FUEL:** 100LLA
Runway: 17/35 **Length:** 5000 **Width:** 75 **Surface:** CONC-G
Runway: 12/30 **Length:** 7201 **Width:** 100 **Surface:** CONC-G

★★★★★ **Ryan's Hangar Restaurant & Ace Lounge - (605) 352-1639**
Proprietor: Ryan Hofer
Open:
>   Mon - Sun: 4pm – 10pm

Restaurant Website: www.ryanshangar.com
Restaurant Email: ryan@ryanshangar.com
PIREP:
Ryan's is a **GREAT** find with one huge problem.

First the good news. The food is excellent, the service amazing and the ambiance over-the-top.

The spacious Dining Room provides a panoramic view of the runway. The atmosphere is casual and relaxed, crisp white table clothes and dimmed lighting set the mood for a very enjoyable dinner.

Steaks, ribs and seafood followed by the best three layer carrot cake in the country. All prepared to perfection. I have never had anything but an exceptional meal here.

What's the bad news? They don't offer lunch, only dinner. It is one of the best dinners you'll ever have at an airport restaurant but I really wish they'd do lunch at least one day a week.

⭐ RAPID CITY, SD (RAPID CITY RGNL - RAP)

Aprt Mgr: CAMERON HUMPHRES **PH:** 605-394-4195
Field Elevation: 3204 **CTAF:** 125.850 **FUEL:** 100LLA
Runway: 05/23 **Length:** 3601 **Width:** 75 **Surface:** ASPH-G
Runway: 14/32 **Length:** 8701 **Width:** 150 **Surface:** CONC-G

★★★ **Airport Restaurant – (605) 393-8000**
Proprietor: Airhost, Inc.
Open:
        Mon - Sun: 5am –
Restaurant Website:
        www.rcgov.org/Airport/terminal-concessions.html
PIREP:
The FBO will run you over to the terminal or you can walk the short distance. This is standard commercial airport faire. The good news is one of the two restaurants is before security so you can get in and get out with no TSA hassle. **The Airport Restaurant** has two locations on the second level of the terminal building: the first location is across from the gift shop, **just prior to the security concourse** and the second location is beyond the screening checkpoint across from gate 3. The restaurant hours are from 5:00 a.m. until the last flight departs. A complete line of pastries along with breakfast sandwiches will be offered in conjunction with popular salads and a variety of deli sandwich selections, freshly prepared daily. A hot breakfast and daily luncheon feature will be available during the appropriate meal hours at the pre-screening location. breakfast and daily luncheon feature will be available during the appropriate meal hours at the pre-screening location.

⭐ SIOUX FALLS, SD (JOE FOSS FIELD - FSD)

Aprt Mgr: DANIEL J. LETTELLIER **PH:** 605-336-0762
Field Elevation: 1430 **CTAF:** 118.300 **FUEL:** 100LLA
Runway: 09/27 **Length:** 3151 **Width:** 75 **Surface:** CONC-F
Runway: 15/33 **Length:** 8000 **Width:** 150 **Surface:** CONC-F
Runway: 03/21 **Length:** 8999 **Width:** 150 **Surface:** CONC-F

★★★ **Landmark Cafe – (605) 336-7791**

Proprietor: Joel Cherry
Open:
> Daily: 8am – 6pm

Restaurant Website: www.landmarkaviation.com/fbo/fsd
Restaurant Email: fsd@landmarkaviation.com
PIREP:

Inside the Landmark FBO there is a really terrific Café. I was served the biggest and perhaps the best pancakes I have ever seen. I knew that Landmark did a superb job with inflight catering items but had no idea about the Café. I'll be back.

$100 Hamburger 2014/15

FlyIn Tennessee

◉ BRISTOL/JOHNSON, TN (TRI-CITIES RGNL TN/VA - TRI)
Aprt Mgr: MR. PATRICK WILSON **PH:** 423-325-6001
Field Elevation: 1519 **CTAF:** 119.500 **FUEL:** 100LLA
Runway: 09/27 **Length:** 4442 **Width:** 150 **Surface:** ASPH-F
Runway: 05/23 **Length:** 8000 **Width:** 150 **Surface:** ASPH-F

★★ **Tailwind Restaurant and Lounge** - (423) 325-6282
Open:

> Sun - Friday 5am – 7pm
> Sat: 5am – 6pm

PIREP:

Tailwind Restaurant and Lounge and **Tailwind Express** are both in the main terminal. **Tailwind Express** is on the lower concourse level. It serves snacks and coffee from 5:00am until the last flight departs. **Tailwind Restaurant and Lounge** on the other hand is a full service sit down and enjoy yourself restaurant. It includes a full service bar for the road warrior who's been stuck in a center seat for the last two hours to unwind and reconnect with his inner self. The FBO will run you over. The TSA is not much of a hassle in this terminal so you can get in and get out fairly easily. I don't think it's worth the fuel to proclaim this as a destination but if you happen to be here and are hungry……..

FlyIn Texas

🍴 AMARILLO, TX (RICK HUSBAND AMARILLO INTL - AMA)
Aprt Mgr: PATRICK RHODES **PH:** 806-335-1671
Field Elevation: 3607 **CTAF:** 118.300 **FUEL:** 100LLA1+ B
Runway: 13/31 **Length:** 7901 **Width:** 150 **Surface:** CONC-G
Runway: 04/22 **Length:** 13502 **Width:** 200 **Surface:** CONC-G

---

*★★★ English Field House Restaurant - (806) 335-2996
Proprietor: Jose Vasquez
Open:

> Mon – Fri: 8am – 4pm
> Sat – Sun: 8am – 3pm

Restaurant Website: www.facebook.com/pages/English-Field-House/169217716451929

Restaurant Email: pointbeaver@yahoo.com

PIREP:

English Field House Restaurant is immediately adjacent to TAC Air and overlooks runway 4/22. They offer Mexican food and pretty much everything else including spaghetti and ribeye steak and breakfast of course. All served by a friendly staff that seems happy to see you.

🍴 ANGLETON, TX (TEXAS GULF COAST RGNL - LBX)
Aprt Mgr: PATRICK RHODES **PH:** 806-335-1671
Field Elevation: 3607 **CTAF:** 118.300 **FUEL:** 100LLA1+ B
Runway: 13/31 **Length:** 7901 **Width:** 150 **Surface:** CONC-G
Runway: 04/22 **Length:** 13502 **Width:** 200 **Surface:** CONC-G

★★★ Crosswinds Cafe – (979) 849-5995
Proprietor: Mary Parks
Open:

> Mon: 11:00 am - 3:00 pm
> Tue - Thu: 11:00 am - 8:00 pm
> Fri - Sat: 11:00 am - 9:00 pm
> Sun: 11:00 am - 3:00 pm

Restaurant Website: www.facebook.com
PIREP:

I come here for the fried Gulf Shrimp. Many locals come to watch the planes and enjoy their shrimp PoBoys. Who can blame them? This is a comfortable café with food that I really enjoy and a good view of the runway.

🍴 BRENHAM, TX (BRENHAM MUNI - 11R)

www.100dollarhamburger.com

Aprt Mgr: KIM HODDE **PH:** 979-337-7212
Field Elevation: 318 **CTAF:** 123.075 **FUEL:** 100LLA
Runway: 16/34 **Length:** 6003 **Width:** 75 **Surface:** ASPH-G

★★★★★ **Southern Flyer Diner - (979) 836-5462**
Proprietor: Jack and Janet Hess
Open:
> Daily: 11am to 3pm

Restaurant Website: www.southernflyer.com
Restaurant Email: soflyer11r@gmail.com
PIREP:

The Southern Flyer Diner has won the annual **$100 Hamburger Best of the Best** award five times. Most recently for 2013! To say I like this place is a big understatement. The ambiance is perfect and the food is amazing. I come here for the Chicken Fried Steak and yes even the Fried Pickles and I gladly stand in line behind all of the locals and wait my turn for a seat. If you can only make one flight this year make it to **The Southern Flyer Diner.**

✸ DALLAS, TX (DALLAS EXECUTIVE - RBD)
Aprt Mgr: LANA FURRA **PH:** 214-670-7612
Field Elevation: 660 **CTAF:** 127.250 **FUEL:** 100LLA
Runway: 17/35 **Length:** 3800 **Width:** 150 **Surface:** ASPH-CONC-G
Runway: 13/31 **Length:** 6451 **Width:** 150 **Surface:** ASPH-CONC-G

★★★★ **Delta Charlie's - 214-623-9944**
Proprietor: Mark and Dirk Kelcher
Open:
> Tue – Sun: 8:00 am - 10:00 pm

Restaurant Website: www.deltacharlies.com
PIREP:

This is a very nice to upscale restaurant with an excellent mid-field view of the usually active runway. The menu items are impressive but the prices are reasonable. When I am lucky enough to be around for breakfast I jump on the homemade cinnamon rolls; nothing beats fresh from the oven. They combine a wonderful dinner with a sightseeing flight for their non-pilot diners. This is a great place to come on date night. Be sure to check Groupon as Delta Charlie's offers some wonderful deals there.

✸ FORT WORTH, TX (HICKS AIRFIELD - T67)
Aprt Mgr: DON BROWNING **PH:** 817-296-0189
Field Elevation: 855 **CTAF:** 123.050 **FUEL:** 100LL
Runway: 14/32 **Length:** 3740 **Width:** 60 **Surface:** ASPH-G

★ ★ ★ **Beacon Cafe & Country Store - 817-439-1041**
Proprietor: Christie and Gene Bingham
Open:
                Tue – Sun: 7:00 am - 2:00 pm
Restaurant Website: www.thebeaconcafe.com
PIREP:
It's a friendly, unpretentious airport cafe with an unexceptional but well executed regional menu. You can tell the food is good because the place fills up with locals particularly for breakfast when they offer everything from Migas to Blueberry pancakes. For lunch I go with the B.L.T. because it is made with really good tomatoes, a half-pound of bacon and a generous slathering of mayonnaise. When I'm really hungry I add a Greek Salad. I like this place. You will too.

🍽 ⊲**FREDERICKSBURG, TX (GILLESPIE COUNTY - T82)**
Aprt Mgr: DON BROWNING **PH:** 817-296-0189
Field Elevation: 855 **CTAF:** 123.050 **FUEL:** 100LL
Runway: 14/32 **Length:** 3740 **Width:** 60 **Surface:** ASPH-G

───────────────

★ ★ ★ **The Airport Diner (830) 997-4999**
Proprietor: Steven Claypole
Open:
                Wed –Thurs: 11am till 2pm
                Fri: 8am till 2pm
                Sat: 8am till 4pm
                Sun: 8am till 2pm
Restaurant Website: www.hangarhotel.com/diner.htm
Restaurant Email: garrett@hangarhotel.com
PIREP:
The Airport Diner is a classic 1940's diner, located next door to the **Hangar Hotel** and immediately adjacent to the Gillespie County Airport aircraft parking ramp. You get a great view of the airport from the booths. The menu offers the standard airport restaurant selections, the difference is the quality. The malts are prepared with ice-cream that is made especially for **The Airport Diner**. While the malts are good don't pass on the hand battered onion rings. If its breakfast you're after; know that the biscuits are homemade.

───────────────

★ ★ ★ ★ ★ **The Hangar Hotel (830) 997-9990**
Proprietor: Steven Claypole
Open:
                24 hours a day / 7 days a week
Restaurant Website: www.hangarhotel.com
Hotel Email: kelly@hangarhotel.com
PIREP:

Hotels at GA airports are about ass rare as hen's teeth. The $100 Hamburger knows about a few but far too few. What is even rarer is an aviation themed hotel at a GA airport. **The Hangar Hotel** is a trip back in time. It was uniquely designed with an exterior appearance of a WWII hangar. It is a stylish adult environment featuring airplane memorabilia and the romance of the 1940's all wrapped in a blanket of luxury. While all of that is good, the geography makes it even better. This is the Texas Hill Country. There is no better place to be on earth. Don't miss this experience.

l●l ↝ 🏛 ⅃ GALVESTON, TX (SCHOLES INTL AT GALVESTON - GLS)
Aprt Mgr: HUD HOPKINS **PH:** 409-741-4609
Field Elevation: 6 **CTAF:** 120.575 **FUEL:** 100LLA
Runway: 13/31 **Length:** 6000 **Width:** 150 **Surface:** ASPH-CONC-G
Runway: 17/35 **Length:** 6001 **Width:** 150 **Surface:** CONC-G

★ ★ ★ ★ ★ Shearn's Seafood and Prime Steaks - (409) 683-4554
Chef: Urs Schmid
Open:
> Tues – Sat: Dinner

Restaurant Website: www.facebook.com/shearnsfinedining
Restaurant Email:
PIREP:
Call the FBO on approach and let them know you'll need the hotel shuttle. It'll be there when you land. There was a time when you could walk to the hotel but the gate has been removed. **Shearn's Seafood and Prime Steaks** is in the Moody Gardens Hotel which is part of the Moody Garden's Complex that abuts the airport. It is one of only 11 Houston/Galveston area restaurants to receive AAA's Four Diamond Award of Excellence and has done so each year since 2004. It is Galveston's finest restaurant unsurpassed in cuisine and service with an upscale ambiance. Dressy Casual attire required. No jeans, shorts, swimwear, cutoffs, tank tops or hats allowed in the dining area. Collared shirts and sandals are acceptable. It's pricey but not atmospheric. I come here for special occasions and have never been disappointed. The views are spectacular. Normally we have dinner, spend the night, take in the museum and play a round of golf. They'll even run you over to the beach which is only three blocks away.

★ ★ ★ The Terrace Restaurant - (979) 233-0205
Open:
> Daily: Breakfast, Lunch and Dinner

PIREP:
Call the FBO on approach and let them know you'll need the hotel shuttle. It'll be there when you land. **The Terrace Restaurant** is

located in the lobby level. It is a casual venue that provides pretty standard hotel coffee shop faire. The food is more than OK but less than wonderful. The service is friendly and the pricing fair.

★★★★ The Moody Gardens Hotel - (409) 683-4000
Open:
> **Daily**

Restaurant Website: www.moodygardenshotel.com

PIREP: It is right on the airport and three blocks away from the beach. If that's not enough it sits in the middle of a 240 acre family entertainment venue which includes a pretty darn good golf course. It is a nice hotel that deserves its superior rating. Rooms go for $150 to $250 a night depending on the season. It is a large hotel with 400 plus rooms but not mammoth. I like the place and have RONed here more than once. They've got a good SPA which I'm not much into but my wife is. While she SPAs I golf. Life is filled with trade-offs.

★★ Moody Gardens (800) 582-4673
Open:
> 10:00am - 6:00pm

Restaurant Website: www.moodygardens.com
PIREP:

Moody Gardens is one of the top 10 attractions in the state of Texas. It bills itself as an educational destination utilizing nature in the advancement of rehabilitation, conservation, recreation, and research. That means that have a lot of animals for you in see in habitants that are hopefully more upscale than your local zoon. With that the combine guest experiences that include a lazy river and an 1800 replica paddle wheel steam boat. The focal point of the 240 acre park is a glass pyramid that contains many creatures and much plant and aquatic life. To my taste the whole place other the hotel and the golf course is thread bear. It was once nice but they simply are doing the maintenance. Have a look at the website and form your own opinion. Here's the good news. It is an airport located animal based theme park similar to Seaword. It is a good trip!

★★★★ The Moody Gardens Golf Course - (409) 683-4000
Open:
> 7 Days a Week

Restaurant Website: www.moodygardensgolf.com
PIREP: This is a Jacobsen Hardy designed links golf course which says it's challenging but not enough to leave you in tears. The Houston Chronicle rates it as the most scenic course in the Houston Metro area. A round will set you back about $65. I should point out that this is a public course. Originally it was the Galveston Municipal Golf Course.

It needed work, a lot of work. So the Moody's stepped in with $16,000,000 to take care of it. The deal resulted in a name change but it is still a public course. I've played it a few times in the winter but never in August. It gets really hot on the Texas Coast in late summer and the mosquitoes are the size of Cessna 150s.

⦿ GRAND PRAIRIE, TX (GRAND PRAIRIE MUNI - GPM)
Aprt Mgr: RANDY BYERS **PH:** 972-237-7591
Field Elevation: 588 **CTAF:** 128.550 **FUEL:** 100LLA
Runway: 17/35 **Length:** 4001 **Width:** 75 **Surface:** CONC-G

★★★ Mixed-Up Burgers - (972) 595-5420
Proprietor: Jay Ellis
Open:
> Mon-Fri: 10:30am - 9pm
> Sat: 11am - 9pm
> Sun: 11am - 6pm

Restaurant Website: www.mixedupburgers.com
Restaurant Email: mixedupburgers@gmail.com
PIREP:
Unique is the word that best describes **Mixed-Up Burgers.** It's a cool burger joint not a run of the mill airport café. The long ball though is all in the name. If you order a bacon mushroom burger anyplace else you get bacon and mushrooms placed on top of your burger. Great! That's not what happens here. The bacon and mushrooms are inside the burger. That's a big deal. They can't cook it until you order it so your burger is fresh. If you come here once you're likely to come back. The food is really good and the atmosphere is fun. $1 beer, how fun is that?

⦿ HOUSTON, TX (LONE STAR EXECUTIVE - CXO)
Aprt Mgr: SCOTT SMITH **PH:** 936-788-8311
Field Elevation: 245 **CTAF:** 124.125 **FUEL:** 100LLA
Runway: 01/19 **Length:** 5000 **Width:** 100 **Surface:** CONC-G
Runway: 14/32 **Length:** 6000 **Width:** 150 **Surface:** CONC-G

★★★ Black Walnut Café - (936) 202-2824
Proprietor: George Pallottas
Open:
> Mon - Sun: 7am to 3pm

Restaurant Website: blackwalnutcafe.com
PIREP:
The Black Walnut Café is located inside Galaxy FBO (www.galaxyfbo.com). It is on the third floor and provides an amazing airport view from its expansive floor to ceiling windows and the comfortable deck. The ambiance is contemporary casual. The food is

expertly prepared from premium ingredients enthusiastically presented by a professional wait staff. I ordered the Pot Roast Grilled Cheese sandwich for its uniqueness and was rewarded by its quality.

❖ HOUSTON, TX (DAVID WAYNE HOOKS MEMORIAL - DWH)
Aprt Mgr: ROGER SCHMIDT **PH:** 281-376-5436
Field Elevation: 152 **CTAF:** 118.400 **FUEL:** 100LLA
Runway: 17R/35L **Length:** 7009 **Width:** 100 **Surface:** ASPH-F
Runway: 17L/35R **Length:** 3987 **Width:** 35 **Surface:** ASPH-P

★★★★ The Aviator's Grille - (281) 370-6279
Proprietor: Jim and Rory Duffy
Open:
>   Tues - Friday: 7am - 2:30pm
>   Sat, Sun, and Mon: 11am - 2:30pm

Restaurant Website: www.aviatorsgrill.com
Restaurant Email:
PIREP:

Hooks is a little towered airport with a high speed cut-off from the main runway (17R – 35L). I like that. It is also interesting that they have the only man made water landing runway I have ever seen or heard of. **The Aviator's Grille** has been a Houston flying community fixture since 1995. I have eaten here more times than I can count on all my fingers and toes and have always looked forward to my next visit. It is a supper Texas friendly place.

❖ LANCASTER, TX (LANCASTER RGNL - LNC)
Aprt Mgr: MARK DIVITA **PH:** 972-227-5721
Field Elevation: 501 **CTAF:** 122.700 **FUEL:** 100LLA
Runway: 13/31 **Length:** 6502 **Width:** 100 **Surface:** ASPH-G

★★ Taxiway Café - (972) 227-2233
Open: 7-3 Tuesday - Sunday
PIREP:

Lancaster has had bad luck with their on airport café's. The current edition is called the **Taxiway Café**. I'm not a great fan at this point. They do an OK job of breakfast and lunch. Breakfast is definitely better. Call first to make certain they are still open and to verify hours.

❖ ROANOKE, TX (NORTHWEST RGNL - 52F)
Aprt Mgr: GLEN HYDE **PH:** 817-430-1905
Field Elevation: 643 **CTAF:** 122.900 **FUEL:** 100LL
Runway: 17/35 **Length:** 3500 **Width:** 40 **Surface:** ASPH-F

★★★ Blue Hangar Cafe - (817)491-8283

Proprietor: Brian and Tavia Ovens
Open:
>Mon – Fri: 10:30am – 2:00 pm
>Sat: 7:00am – 2:00 pm

Restaurant Website: www.thebluehangar.com
Restaurant Email: eat@TheBlueHangar.com
PIREP:
This is more than the normal airport café that slides burgers and pancakes across the counter. Chef Brian grinds all of his meats nothing is frozen. That makes a huge difference. I come here for lunch though breakfast is mighty tasty as well. Normally I go with the Bacon Bleu Cheese Burger and a half Greek Salad. I've been coming to Northwest Regional for many years. It puts the friendly back into the Metroplex.

๏ SAN ANGELO, TX (SAN ANGELO RGNL/MATHIS FIELD - SJT)
Aprt Mgr: LUIS E. ELGUEZABAL **PH:** 325-659-6409
Field Elevation: 1919 **CTAF:** 118.300 **FUEL:** 100LLA B+
Runway: 09/27 **Length:** 4402 **Width:** 75 **Surface:** ASPH-G
Runway: 03/21 **Length:** 5939 **Width:** 150 **Surface:** ASPH-G
Runway: 18/36 **Length:** 8049 **Width:** 150 **Surface:** ASPH-G

★★★ **Mathis Field Cafe - (325) 942-1172**
Proprietor: Rose and Sam Ng
Open:
>Mon - Thu: 11:00am - 8:00pm
>Fri - Sat: 11:00am - 9:00pm

Restaurant Website: www.facebook.com/MathisFieldCafe
PIREP:
This is a highly improbable find for an airport in West Texas. It is a small café located inside the terminal serving Chinese cuisine. Yes they have some American dishes as well but you should come here for the Chinese. It's a welcome break from burgers and chicken fried steak. The food is good. Last time I was through here I ate light and just had a couple of egg rolls (homemade) and the Spicy Chicken Noodle Soup. They don't do breakfast. Maybe the Chinese don't eat breakfast.

๏ SAN MARCOS, TX (SAN MARCOS MUNI - HYI)
Aprt Mgr: TEXAS AVIATION PARTNERS **PH:** 512-216-6039
Field Elevation: 597 **CTAF:** 126.825 **FUEL:** 100LLA
Runway: 17/35 **Length:** 5213 **Width:** 100 **Surface:** ASPH-G
Runway: 13/31 **Length:** 5603 **Width:** 150 **Surface:** ASPH-G
Runway: 08/26 **Length:** 6330 **Width:** 100 **Surface:** ASPH-G

★★ **Redbird Skyport - (512) 878-6670**
Open:

Mon – Sun: 6am-10 pm
Restaurant Website: www.redbirdskyport.com/fbo/
Restaurant Email: skyport@redbirdskyport.com
PIREP:

The food is pre-wrapped sandwiches, chips and a refrigerator of drinks. I grabbed a cheeseburgers that was prepared on the grill outside by the line guys. That doesn't happen all the time. So plan on having a 7-11 style sandwich and be happy if you score an open air grilled cheese burger. OK, not the best lunch I have ever had, HOWEVER Redbird sims headquarters here. They produce fully functional FAA sims on the opposite side of the building. Smile and ask about them and you just may get to play for a while. That is worth the trip.

STEPHENVILLE, TX (CLARK FIELD MUNI - SEP)
Aprt Mgr: BILL SMITH **PH:** 254-965-2795
Field Elevation: 1321 **CTAF:** 122.800 **FUEL:** 100LLA
Runway: 14/32 **Length:** 4209 **Width:** 75 **Surface:** ASPH-G

★★★★★ **The Hard Eight - 254 968 5552**
Proprietor: Chad Decker
Open:

Mon - Thur: 10:30am – 9 pm
Fri - Sat: 10:30am – 10 pm
Sun: 10:30am – 8 pm
Restaurant Website: www.hardeightbbq.com/
PIREP:

I'm strictly a brisket guy. **The Hard Eight** does brisket right. Maybe that's why they've been on the annual **$100 Hamburger Best of the Best** list more than once. I also love flying into Stephenville and spending a good part of the day there. On the ramp you'll find a flock of golf carts. Take one for the short trip to the **Hard Eight**. Order whatever food you like but don't forget the pecan pie. Drink only Dr. Pepper as they get the good stuff from the original Dr. Pepper Bottling Company in nearby Dublin.

TYLER, TX (TYLER POUNDS RGNL - TYR)
Aprt Mgr: DAVIS DICKSON **PH:** 903-531-2343
Field Elevation: 544 **CTAF:** 120.100 **FUEL:** 100LLA
Runway: 17/35 **Length:** 4850 **Width:** 150 **Surface:** ASPH-G
Runway: 13/31 **Length:** 5200 **Width:** 150 **Surface:** ASPH-G
Runway: 04/22 **Length:** 7200 **Width:** 150 **Surface:** ASPH-G

★★★ **SkyLine Cafe - 903-593-7455**
Open:

Mon – Fri: 8am – 2pm

Sat: 8am – 2pm
Sun: 11am – 2pm

Restaurant Website: www.skylinecafe.org
Restaurant Email: skylinecafe@rocketmail.com
PIREP:

Park at the Jet Center and walk into the **Skyline's** front door. They are located right inside the terminal building. The menu item I like the best is the 8oz **SkyLine** burger. It is made from Angus beef and comes out juicy and flavorful. This is a very good breakfast or lunch stop whenever you're in east Texas.

🍽 VICTORIA, TX (VICTORIA RGNL - VCT)
Aprt Mgr: JASON MILEWSKI **PH:** 361-578-2704
Field Elevation: 115 **CTAF:** 126.075 **FUEL:** 100LLA
Runway: 06/24 **Length:** 4200 **Width:** 75 **Surface:** ASPH-F
Runway: 17/35 **Length:** 4908 **Width:** 75 **Surface:** ASPH-G
Runway: 12L/30R **Length:** 9111 **Width:** 150 **Surface:** ASPH-G
Runway: 12R/30L **Length:** 4643 **Width:** 150 **Surface:** CONC-P

★★★ The Sky Restaurant – (361) 576-5335
Proprietor: Loc Phan
Open:

Mon – Fri: 11am – 10pm
Sat: 4pm – 10pm

Restaurant Website: www.theskygrill.com
Restaurant Email: locphan@theskygrill.com
PIREP:

Sky serves wonderful seafood and steaks for lunch and dinner every day of the week except Sunday. Like so many airports in this part of Texas, VCT was a military airfield dedicated to pilot training during WWII. That means more than one runaway. In this case, there is also an ILS approach. Airlines come here but only twice a day so commercial traffic isn't a problem. **Sky** is located in what was once the Officer's Club. It is roomy and nicely decorated. I come here for the fried oyster. They are freshly shucked and perfectly prepared. You'll find many choices on the menu to make you smile whether you're here for lunch or dinner. The prices are moderate.

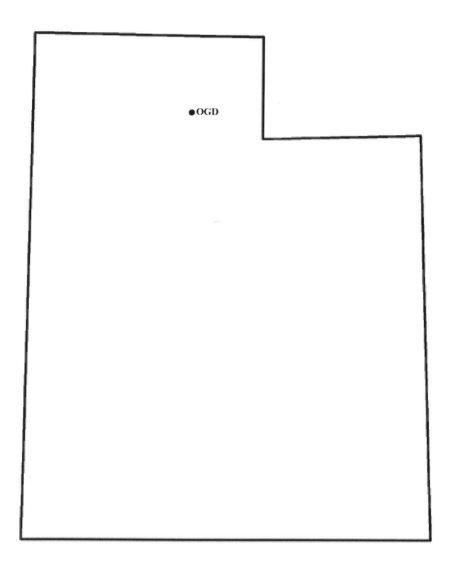

FlyIn Utah

● OGDEN, UT (OGDEN-HINCKLEY - OGD)
Aprt Mgr: ROYAL ECCLES **PH:** 801-629-8251
Field Elevation: 4473 **CTAF:** 118.700 **FUEL:** 100 A1+
Runway: 03/21 **Length:** 8103 **Width:** 150 **Surface:** ASPH-E
Runway: 16/34 **Length:** 5195 **Width:** 100 **Surface:** ASPH-F
Runway: 07/25 **Length:** 3618 **Width:** 150 **Surface:** ASPH-P

★★★ The Auger Inn - 801-334-9790
Proprietor: Paul Cornwell
Open:
> Mon- Sat: 7am – 7pm
> Sun: 7am – 5pm

Restaurant Website: www.flyogden.com/food/auger-inn/
Restaurant Email: auger.inn.rest@gmail.com
PIREP:
This is the grandfather of all airport restaurants. **The Auger Inn** has been located in the original terminal building for fifty years. It offers a very casual, friendly environment and homemade breakfast, lunch, or dinner at affordable prices. I'm hooked on the cinnamon rolls which they bake fresh daily. Ogden is an interesting stop. Three ski resorts are within 30 minutes of the airport. The Dinosaur Park is about 8 miles away. The Hill AFB Aerospace Museum is just 3 miles. My favorite is the Union Station Museum which is loaded with trains, Browning firearms and automobiles. It too is within 5 miles.

★★★ Doolittle's Deli – (801) 627-3200
Proprietor: Makinzee Kemp
Open:
> Mon – Sat: Lunch

Restaurant Website: www.flyogden.com/food/doolittles-deli/
Restaurant Email: doolittlesdeli@live.com
PIREP:
Doolittle's Deli serves Soups, Salads, Sandwiches, Pizzas, Pastas and Calzones. It is a deli-styled restaurant located in the building which houses Kemp Jet Services, at the end of runway 16. Everything on the menu is made fresh daily including the potato chips and NOTHING comes out of a box. They are mostly known for their fried pizza and calzones. You read correctly - fried pizza! **Rickenbacker's Bistro** is right upstairs.

★★★★★ Rickenbacker's Bistro – (801) 627-4100

$100 Hamburger 2014/15

Proprietor: Kris Lundeen
Open:
>Mon –Thu: 11am–9pm
>Fri – Sat: 11am–10pm

Restaurant Website: www.rickenbackersbistro.com
PIREP:

"Come for the food and stay for the view." **Rickenbacker's** is one of the ten best airport located steakhouses in the USA. Here's what surprised me. They use grilling methods perfected in the Texas Hill country all the way up here in Utah and they do a better job of it than most places in Texas. The secret to their success is simple. Captain Eddie Rickenbacker's **Bear Creek Ranch** was located in the Texas Hill country. Captain Eddie knew how to cook and serve a steak. If you are in Utah **DO NOT** miss having a meal here. It's that good.

$100 Hamburger 2014/15

FlyIn Vermont

🍴 BURLINGTON, VT (BURLINGTON INTL - BTV)
Aprt Mgr: ROBERT MCEWING **PH:** 802-863-2874
Field Elevation: 335 **CTAF:** 118.300 **FUEL:** 100LLA
Runway: 15/33 **Length:** 8320 **Width:** 150 **Surface:** ASPH-CONC-G
Runway: 01/19 **Length:** 3611 **Width:** 75 **Surface:** ASPH-G

★★★ Skinny Pancake – (802) 497-0675
Proprietor: Jonny and Benjy Adler
Open:
        Mon- Sun: 4:30am – 7pm
Restaurant Website:
www.skinnypancake.com/locations/burlington-international-airport
PIREP:
Out with the old in with the new. In 2013 **FOUR** new restaurants opened in the terminals of the Burlington International Airport. Skinny Pancake is a crepe restaurant. It serves a **WIDE** variety of sweet and savory crepes. All of them made from locally grown ingredients. There are more items on the menu including a really good burger. There is a Skinny Pancake in the North Terminal and another in the South terminal. Each are on the wrong side of the security gate. If you are willing to deal with the TSA you'll be well pleased with the Skinny Pancake experience. If not you can enjoy a stop at their sister shop, **The Chubby Muffin** which is outside security just across from the ticket counters in both terminals. Don't expect much, it is merely a kiosk.

★ The Chubby Muffin – (802) 497-0653
Proprietor: Jonny and Benjy Adler
Open:
        Mon- Sun: 4:30am – 7pm
Restaurant Website:
www.skinnypancake.com/locations/burlington-international-airport
PIREP:
The Chubby Muffin is a sister-company to the **Skinny Pancake**, the 'Robin' to the Skinny Pancake's 'Batman' and is located on BTV's first level, across from the United and US Airways ticket counters. Don't expect much, it is merely a kiosk.

🍴 🏛 VERGENNES, VT (BASIN HARBOR - B06)
Aprt Mgr: "ROBERT BEACH, JR." **PH:** 802-475-2311
Field Elevation: 132 **CTAF:** 122.800 **FUEL:**
Runway: 02/20 **Length:** 3000 **Width:** 90 **Surface:** TURF-G

★ ★ ★ ★ The Red Mill Restaurant – (802) 475-2317
Open:

> Mon - Fri: 11:30am – 9pm
> Sat – Sun: 11:30am – 10pm

Restaurant Website: www.basinharbor.com
Restaurant Email: info@basinharbor.com
PIREP:

The Basin Harbor Resort on the shores of Lake Champlain is a gorgeous stop whether you're coming for lunch or longer. The 3,200-foot grass airstrip is one of the best I've seen in New England, but it has no landing lights or avgas and you must bring your own tie-downs. **The Red Mill Restaurant** renovated 1940 sawmill sits right on the resorts runway. Everything on the Lunch and dinner menu looks good. I've been here only twice for lunch and opted for the Fried Chicken & Waffles both times. It comes with a Cherry Compote and real Vermont Maple syrup (no surprise there). It is a very nice dish.

★ ★ ★ ★ ★ The Basin Harbor Resort – (802) 475.2311
Open:

> Daily

Restaurant Website: www.basinharbor.com
Restaurant Email: info@basinharbor.com
PIREP:

The Basin Harbor Resort on the shores of Lake Champlain is a gorgeous. The 3,200-foot grass airstrip is one of the best I've seen in New England, but it has no landing lights or avgas and you must bring your own tie-downs. It is an old time New England resort. The accommodations are superb, the staff is friendly and well trained, the food is fabulous and the wine list is first rate. You can golf, swim, boat, hike or just relax. A weekend here is expensive and worth it.

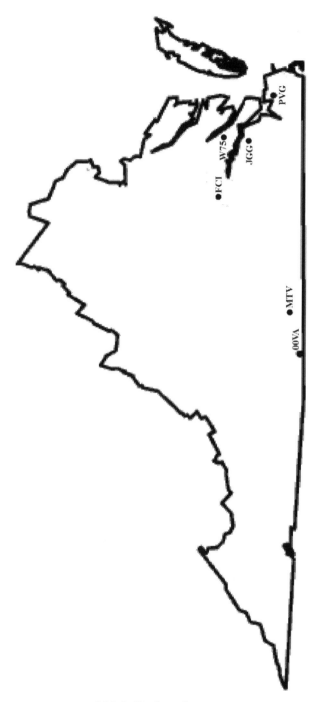

FlyIn Virginia

|●| Ɪ ALTON, VA (VAUGHAN - 00VA)
  Aprt Mgr: RONNIE D. VAUGHAN **PH:** 434-753-1260
  Field Elevation: 551 **CTAF:** 0.000 **FUEL:**
  Runway: 01/19 **Length:** 1300 **Width:** 100 **Surface:** TURF

★★★ Fireside Express Grill - 540-856-2121 x 259
Proprietor: Rob Schwartz
Open:

  Seasonal:
  Closes for winter: October 27
  April 27 re-opens:
  Sat – Sun: 8am – 5pm

Restaurant Website: www.bryceresort.com
PIREP:
The Bryce Resort operates year round. It is wise to call first to check on runway conditions, especially in the winter. The pilots' lounge at the airport has been renovated and pilots are welcome to use it. Please enter the VFR Xpdr code to open the door. The adjacent library has a Wi-Fi connection. **The Fireside Express Grill** of the Bryce Resort is a short distance (200 yards?) from the airstrip and overlooks the golf course's 1st and 10th tees. It offers pizza, burgers, specialty sandwiches, coffee, soda and beer.

★★★ Restaurant @ Bryce Resort- 540-856-2121 x 245
Proprietor: Rob Schwartz
Open:

  Fri - Sat: 5pm – 9pm
  Sun: 9am -12pm (Brunch)

Restaurant Website:

  www.bryceresort.com/Dining/Restaurant-Bar.aspx

PIREP:
The Bryce Resort operates year round. It is wise to call first to check on runway conditions, especially in the winter. The pilots' lounge at the airport has been renovated and pilots are welcome to use it. Please enter the VFR Xpdr code to open the door. The adjacent library has a Wi-Fi connection. **The Restaurant @ Bryce Resort** is more upscale than **The Fireside Express Grill** and is open year round for dinner. Count on good steaks and god wine with decent service.

★★★★ The Bryce Resort- 540-856-2121
Proprietor: Rob Schwartz

Open:

Daily

Resort Website: www.bryceresort.com

PIREP:

The Bryce Resort operates year round and is all about activities. You don't come to sit around. Here's a partial list of what you can **DO**:

Golf
Ski
Mountain Bike
Hike
Zip Line

In the summer they have grass skiing, which I have never done and summer tubing which is very, very fun. Oddly, they do not have a lodge or any housing on the resort property there are nearby hotels, RV parks and camping facilities. With a little luck you can rent a house on the property.

❶ MARTINSVILLE, VA (BLUE RIDGE - MTV)

Aprt Mgr: JASON DAVIS **PH:** 276-957-2291

Field Elevation: 941 **CTAF:** 122.700 **FUEL:** 100LLA

Runway: 12/30 **Length:** 5002 **Width:** 100 **Surface:** ASPH-G

★★ The Blue Ridge Café – (276) 957-1985

Open:

Mon - Sat: 11:00 am - 2:30 pm

Restaurant Website: www.flyblueridge.com/fboservices.htm

Restaurant Email: blueskiesgrille@yahoo.com

PIREP:

The Blue Ridge Café offers breakfast, lunch and dinner. It has an outside patio available where you can eat and watch arriving and departing aircrafts. The dining room has large windows if you prefer to eat inside and still enjoy the view. This is not one of my favorite stops but it is an OK place with decent food and a friendly environment.

❶ NORFOLK, VA (HAMPTON ROADS EXECUTIVE - PVG)

Aprt Mgr: ANDY GIBBS **PH:** 757-465-0260

Field Elevation: 23 **CTAF:** 123.000 **FUEL:** 100LLA

Runway: 02/20 **Length:** 3525 **Width:** 70 **Surface:** ASPH-G

Runway: 10/28 **Length:** 4057 **Width:** 70 **Surface:** ASPH-G

★★★ Blue Skies Grille – (757) 405-3313

Proprietor: Karen

Open:

Mon - Sat: 11:00 am - 2:30 pm
Restaurant Website: www.facebook.com
Restaurant Email: blueskiesgrille@yahoo.com
PIREP:

It's packed at lunchtime every day, mostly by locals. I suppose that says something about the quality of the food and the service. They offer the normal things like tasty burgers plus a daily special. I've been here just to have a cup of coffee and do some hangar flying. Prices are reasonable.

◉ RICHMOND, VA (CHESTERFIELD COUNTY - FCI)
   Aprt Mgr: TOM TRUDEAU **PH:** 804-743-0771
   Field Elevation: 236 **CTAF:** 123.050 **FUEL:** 100LLA
   Runway: 15/33 **Length:** 5500 **Width:** 100 **Surface:** ASPH-G

   ★★★★ King's Korner Restaruant – (804) 743-9333
   Proprietor: Debbie Cromie
   Open:
      Mon -Fri: 11am – 2pm
      Fri & Sat: 5pm – 9pm
      Sunday Brunch: 10:30am – 2:30pm
   Restaurant Website: www.kingskornercatering.com
   Restaurant Email: debbiec@kingskornercatering.com
   PIREP:
The food isn't just good, its great and the view is wonderful. The service is buffet style. I try to get here on Monday when they have Country Fried Steak on the buffet. I love this place and you will too. The King family understands food and service. An adult trip through the buffet line goes for $7.50 plus $1.99 for your drink. It is an amazing value.

◉ SALUDA, VA (HUMMEL FIELD - W75)
   Aprt Mgr: MARCIA JONES **PH:** 804-758-4330
   Field Elevation: 30 **CTAF:** 123.000 **FUEL:** 100LL
   Runway: 01/19 **Length:** 2270 **Width:** 45 **Surface:** ASPH-G

   ★★★★ Eckhard's – (804) 758.4060
   Open:
      Wed – Sat: 4:30pm - 9:00pm
      Sun: 3:30pm - 8:00pm
   Restaurant Website: www.eckhards.com/
   PIREP:
An unexpectedly good discovery in an unlikely location! Excellent German and Italian food, with an amazing selection of German beers. Reservations strongly suggested. I really like the Wiener Schnitzel. For

dessert try the Bread Pudding. This is one of few places that can actually deliver it with a decent hot Bourbon sauce.

Taxi into the grass parking area at the approach end of Runway 1, and you're a 30 yard walk from the front door. Tie down points, but no ropes, on the small concrete pads. W75 also has self-service 24 hour fuel and pilot-controlled runway lighting, a great small airport. Watch out for the trees on approach and departure.

♨ WILLIAMSBURG, VA (WILLIAMSBURG-JAMESTOWN - JGG)
Aprt Mgr: "DON W. BROADY, JR." **PH:** 757-229-9256
Field Elevation: 49 **CTAF:** 122.800 **FUEL:** 100LLA
Runway: 13/31 **Length:** 3204 **Width:** 60 **Surface:** ASPH-G

★★★ **Charly's Airport Restaurant - (757) 258-0034**
Proprietor: Jean Waltrip
Open:
            Daily: 11:00am - 3:00pm
Restaurant Website: www.facebook.com/charlys.jgg
PIREP:

Charly's was once really great and actually made it to the annual **$100 Hamburger Best of the Best** list. It has slipped in both service and food. Hence the three star rating rather the five of better times. That said, they still have a wonderful deck just off the runway. It is a great place to come and "hangar fly" if only over a coke or a cup of coffee. Don't expect perfection and you'll enjoy your visit.

$100 Hamburger 2014/15

FlyIn Washington

---

101 ARLINGTON, WA (ARLINGTON MUNI - AWO)
Aprt Mgr: ROBERT PUTNAM **PH:** 360-403-3470
Field Elevation: 142 **CTAF:** 122.700 **FUEL:** 100LLA
Runway: 11/29 **Length:** 3498 **Width:** 75 **Surface:** ASPH-G
Runway: 16/34 **Length:** 5332 **Width:** 100 **Surface:** ASPH-G

★★ Restaurant NASA - (360) 403-3345
Proprietor: Hans von der Hofen
Manager: Staci Clifford
Open:
> Tue – Thur: 8am - 4pm
> Fri – Sun: 6am - 4pm

Restaurant Website: www.facebook.com
Restaurant Email: restaurantnasa@gmail.com
PIREP:
The restaurant's name is tied to the airfield's historic past. **NASA** stands for **Naval Air Station Arlington**, a historic reference to the 1940s when the airport was built as a U.S. Navy training base in World War II. It is right on the ramp and has a good view of the runway. The service is slow and the food is best described as average.

101 BREMERTON, WA (BREMERTON NATIONAL - PWT)
Aprt Mgr: FRED SALISBURY **PH:** 360-674-2381
Field Elevation: 444 **CTAF:** 123.050 **FUEL:** 100LLA
Runway: 01/19 **Length:** 6000 **Width:** 150 **Surface:** ASPH-G

★★★★ Airport Diner - (360) 674-3720
Proprietor: Tom and Kathy Dacy
Open:
> Sun –Thur: 7am - 8pm
> Fri –Sat: 7am - 9pm

Restaurant Website: www.bremertonairportdiner.com
Restaurant Email: bremertonairportdiner@hotmail.com
PIREP:
Bremerton can get a little crowded on busy days, and the non-towered field can quickly turn into an "uncontrolled" field. It features a long (6,000') and wide (150') runway. There is ample transient parking right in front of the **Airport Diner**. Service is wonderful, fast and friendly and the food is even better. I always order the fish and chips. They are excellent and can be crafted from either cod or halibut; your call. **The Airport Diner** is a wonderful stop. Don'

🍽 🏛 BURLINGTON/MOUNT VERNON, WA (SKAGIT RGNL - BVS)
   Aprt Mgr: SARA K. YOUNG PH: 360-757-0011
   Field Elevation: 144 CTAF: 123.075 FUEL: 100LLA
   Runway: 04/22 Length: 3000 Width: 60 Surface: ASPH-G
   Runway: 10/28 Length: 5477 Width: 100 Surface: ASPH-G

★★★ Kitty Hawk Cafe – (360) 707-0348
Proprietor: Melissa & Jonathan Quast
Open:

> Mon - Wed: 8:00am - 3:00pm\
> Thur - Sat: 8:00am - 8:00pm
> Sunday: 8:00am - 3:00pm

Restaurant Website: www.kittyhawkcafe.net
Restaurant Email: melissa@melissaquast.com
PIREP: Breakfast, lunch and dinner at an on ramp restaurant with an aviation museum just steps away is a good place to start. The restaurant is small and though it does have ramp facing windows the opportunity to sit behind them is limited so get there early. The food is good and the service friendly and crisp. I normally order the Chicken and Biscuits from the breakfast menu which is served all day. It's delicious!!!!

★★★ Heritage Flight Museum – (360) 733-4422
Proprietor: Maj. Gen. William A. Anders
Open:

> **Grand Opening:** Saturday, 26 April 2014
> **Hours:** TBD
> **Fly Days:** 12pm - 4pm the third Saturday of the month.
> Weather permitting

Museum Website: www.heritageflight.org
Museum Email: admin@heritageflight.org
PIREP:
The Heritage Flight Museum is dedicated to the preservation and flying of historic military aircraft. The collection includes a selection of flying World War II, Korean and Vietnam era aircraft and memorabilia and artifacts from the same periods. Many of the aircraft are flyable and are demonstrated in flight on the third Saturday of each month. Admission to the museum is 'by donation' – $8/adult, $5/child over 5 years.

🍽 🏛 EVERETT, WA (SNOHOMISH COUNTY (PAINE FLD) - PAE)
   Aprt Mgr: DAVID T WAGGONER **PH:** 425-388-5125
   Field Elevation: 606 **CTAF:** 132.950 **FUEL:** 100LLA
   Runway: 16R/34L **Length:** 9010 **Width:** 150 **Surface:** ASPH-CONC-G

Runway: 16L/34R **Length:** 3000 **Width:** 75 **Surface:** ASPH-F
Runway: 11/29 **Length:** 4514 **Width:** 75 **Surface:** ASPH-G

★★ **Café at the Future of Flight - (360) 756-0086**
Proprietor: Future of Flight
Open:
        Seasonal:
        Memorial Day – Labor Day: 9am - 5pm
        Labor Day – Memorial Day: 9am - 2:30pm
Museum Website: www.futureofflight.org
Museum Email: info@futureofflight.org
PIREP:
No tickets for the museum are required to dine in the Café. **The Café at the Future of Flight** offers a wide range of tasty and healthy menu items, including snacks, beverages, sandwiches, soups and salads. However; coming here for the food which is mediocre at best and not visiting the museum or touring the Boeing factory is a huge mistake.

★★★★★ **Future of Flight & Boeing Tour - (360) 756-0086**
Proprietor: Boeing Aircraft Company
Open:
        Seven days a week: 8:30 am - 5 pm
Museum Website:
www.boeing.com/boeing/commercial/tours/index.page
Museum Website: www.futureofflight.org
Museum Email: info@futureofflight.org
PIREP:
Either FBO at Paine Field can provide ground transportation to get you over to Future Flight. There is no longer an entrance into the facility from the ramp. **The Future of Flight Aviation Center** is a unique learning and interpretive facility. The 73,000-square-foot facility includes an Aviation Gallery with interactive exhibits and displays, 9,000-square-foot rooftop observation deck overlooking Paine Field, Boeing Tour Center and a125-seat café. One of Seattle's favorite aviation attractions and is where the Boeing Factory Tour begins. The center offers the only opportunity to tour a commercial jet assembly plant in North America. The Future of Flight & Boeing Tour are made possible through the collaboration of the Boeing Company, Future of Flight Foundation. You will go behind the scenes at Boeing—in the world's largest building to watch the very same commercial jets you are often a passenger on being assembled.

🍴 HOQUIAM, WA (BOWERMAN - HQM)
    Aprt Mgr: SHANNON ANDERSON **PH:** 360-533-9528

Field Elevation: 18 **CTAF:** 122.700 **FUEL:** 100LLA
Runway: 06/24 **Length:** 5000 **Width:** 150 **Surface:** ASPH-G

★ ★ ★ **Lana's Hangar Cafe - 360-533-8907**
Proprietor: Shelly Dixon
Open:

        Mon – Thurs: 6am - 7pm
        Fri: 6am - 8pm
        Sat: 8am - 8pm
        Sun: 8am - 7pm

Restaurant Website: www.lanashangarcafe.blogspot.com
PIREP:
Come here for breakfast. I usually go for the pancakes. If you happen by later in the day order a milk shake. They are made with a good quality hand dipped ice cream and worth the calorie excursion. Here's a plus, the entrance to the **Grays Harbor National Wildlife Refuge** is at the west end of the airport's north access road that passes in front of **Lana's Hangar Cafe.** You can walk off lunch by taking a 2-mile stroll that includes a boardwalk that passes through some of **Grays Harbor** marshlands and mud flats that are adjacent to HQM. You'll encounter a large variety of local shorebirds and raptors.

🍴 **PORT TOWNSEND, WA (JEFFERSON COUNTY INTL - 0S9)**
Aprt Mgr: LARRY CROCKETT **PH:** 360-385-2323
Field Elevation: 108 **CTAF:** 123.000 **FUEL:** 100LL
Runway: 09/27 **Length:** 3000 **Width:** 75 **Surface:** ASPH-G

★ ★ ★ **Spruce Goose Cafe - (360) 385-3185**
Proprietor: Christine Pray
Open:

        Mon – Sun: 7am to 4pm

Restaurant Website: www.sprucegoosecafe.com
PIREP:
I like this place. It is best for two things: pies, which are homemade and daily lunch special which are awesome. You park on the ramp right by the front door.

🍴 **PUYALLUP, WA (PIERCE COUNTY - THUN FIELD - PLU)**
Aprt Mgr: BRUCE THUN **PH:** 253-841-3779
Field Elevation: 538 **CTAF:** 122.700 **FUEL:** 100LL
Runway: 16/34 **Length:** 3650 **Width:** 60 **Surface:** ASPH-F

★ ★ ★ **Hangar Inn - (253) 848-7516**
Proprietor: Craig Rosenthal
Open:

Mon – Thurs: 7am – 8pm
Fri – Sat: 6am – 9pm
Sun: 6am – 8pm
Restaurant Website: www.thehangarinn.com
PIREP:
You come here for the majestic view of Mt. Ranier. Sit on the deck.
The view is really amazing. The food is someplace between OK and
acceptable at lunch and dinner. Breakfast is pretty darn good.

RICHLAND, WA (RICHLAND - RLD)
Aprt Mgr: JOHN HAAKENSON **PH:** 509-375-3060
Field Elevation: 394 **CTAF:** 122.700 **FUEL:** 100LLA
Runway: 08/26 **Length:** 3995 **Width:** 100 **Surface:** ASPH-G
Runway: 01/19 **Length:** 4009 **Width:** 75 **Surface:** ASPH-G

★★★ **Almost Gourmet at the Port - (509) 943-7604**
Open:
Sat – Sat: 7:30am – 2pm
Restaurant Website: www.facebook.com/AlmostGourmetPort
Restaurant Email: AlmostGourmetAtThePort@gmail.com
PIREP:
Almost Gourmet At the Port is right by the gas pumps. It has been
here for several years and has a good local reputation. The food is good
and the prices are fair. This is a basic sandwich and soup kinda' place
at lunch. Breakfast is similar; good but nothing to write home about.

SEATTLE, WA (BOEING FIELD/KING COUNTY INTL - BFI)
Aprt Mgr: ROBERT I. BURKE AAE **PH:** 206-296-7380
Field Elevation: 21 **CTAF:** 0.000 **FUEL:** 100LLA
Runway: 13L/31R **Length:** 3710 **Width:** 100 **Surface:** ASPH-G
Runway: 13R/31L **Length:** 10000 **Width:** 200 **Surface:** ASPH-G

★★★ **Wings Café at the Museum of Flight - (206) 764-5720**
Proprietor: Museum of Flight
Open:
Mon – Sun: 10am - 5pm
1st Thurs of the Month: 10am - 9pm
Restaurant Website: www.museumofflight.org/wings-cafe
PIREP:
Wings Café is open during Museum hours but does not require
admission. On nice days, you can sit out on the deck and watch the
airshow that is Boeing Field's B taxiway and long runway. First, and
foremost, **Wings Café** does not have burgers....what they do have are
some nice salads, a few hot entrees and usually a tasty soup.

★★★ ★★The Museum of Flight - (206) 764-5720
Proprietor: Museum of Flight
Open:
> Mon – Sun: 10am - 5pm

Restaurant Website: www.museumofflight.org
PIREP:
This is the **largest** and **best** individually funded aviation museum in the world. Its permanent exhibit includes over 150 aircraft. Temporary exhibits are rotated constantly. I was fortunate to catch the late 2013 exhibit titled "In Search of Amelia Earhart". It included a viewing of the museum newly acquired Lockheed Model 10-E Electra which is sister ship of what our girl flew on her fateful circumnavigation attempt. For itinerant parking at the **Museum of Flight**, call 206-764-5710. There is a $5.00 fee for parking 12 hours or less. If you are ever in this part of the world don't miss this.

★★★ CAVU Cafe - (206) 764.4929
Open:
> Mon – Sat: 7am – 6pm
> Sat: 11am – 9pm (April – September)

Restaurant Website: www.cavucafe.com
Restaurant Email: cavucafe@gmail.com
PIREP:
The Cavu Cafe is in the main-terminal building. Great selection of Italian-style sandwiches at reasonable prices. I normally go with the Panini paired with a side Caesar.

⦿ SNOHOMISH, WA (HARVEY FIELD - S43)
> **Aprt Mgr:** K HARVEY **PH:** 360-568-1541
> **Field Elevation:** 22 **CTAF:** 123.000 **FUEL:** 100 A
> **Runway:** 15L/33R **Length:** 2671 **Width:** 36 **Surface:** ASPH-G
> **Runway:** 15R/33L **Length:** 2430 **Width:** 100 **Surface:** TURF-E

★★ The Buzz Inn Steakhouse- (360) 568-3970
Proprietor: Laurie Klick
Open:
> Mon – Sun: 8am – 8pm

Restaurant Website: www.buzzinnsteakhouse.com
Restaurant Email: snohomish@buzzinnsteakhouse.com
PIREP:
The Buzz Inn Steakhouse at Harvey field is part of a steak house chain that has been in this are for thirty years. The food is very good though the service was spotty in the past. On my last visit they were really on top of things. I haven't had breakfast here only lunch. For me, that means the Chicken Fried Steak Burger and a bowl of Billy's Chili.

The view from the outside deck is hard to beat, especially when the drop zone is active.

🍴 SPOKANE, WA (FELTS FIELD - SFF)
Aprt Mgr: RYAN SHEEHAN **PH:** 509-455-6455
Field Elevation: 1957 **CTAF:** 132.500 **FUEL:** 100LLA1+
Runway: 03R/21L **Length:** 2650 **Width:** 75 **Surface:** ASPH-G
Runway: 03L/21R **Length:** 4499 **Width:** 150 **Surface:** CONC-G

★★★★ Skyway Cafe - (509) 534-5986
Proprietor: John & Sandy Melter
Open:
>
> Mon: 6:00am - 3:00pm
> Tue – Sat: 6:00am - 9:00pm
> Sun: 7:00am - 3:00pm

Restaurant Website: www.skywaycafe.com
Restaurant Email: Skywaycafe@windwireless.net
PIREP:

The Skyway Cafe may be the crown jewel for Spokane. Great food, great atmosphere, great service, great folks. It is located on the ramp and has a great view of the runway which is usually very active. Everything is made from scratch. For me, it's the Chicken Fried Steak at lunch and the cinnamon rolls at breakfast. The place is a hangout for EAA and 99 types, so come prepared to hangar fly.

🍴 WESTPORT, WA (WESTPORT - 14S)
Aprt Mgr: RANDY LEWIS **PH:** 360-268-0131
Field Elevation: 14 **CTAF:** 122.900 **FUEL:**
Runway: 12/30 **Length:** 2318 **Width:** 50 **Surface:** ASPH-G

★★★★ Original House of Pizza – (360) 268-0901
Proprietor: Tisha Quinby and Wendy Anderson
Open:
>
> Mon – Thurs: 11am – 7:30pm
> Fri – Sat: 11am – 8:30pm

Restaurant Website:
> www.bryceresort.com/Dining/Fireside-Express-Grills.aspx

Restaurant Email: ohopizza@hotmail.com
PIREP:

Great family pizza place that is just around on the back side of the blue hanger at the SW end of the airport (about 150 feet from transient parking). Make sure you bring your own chocks and tiedowns if you are planning on staying for any length of time as it is not attended and there is nothing there. They have great calzones and pizza. All pizza dough is homemade and hand tossed. Pizza and Planes, what's not to like?

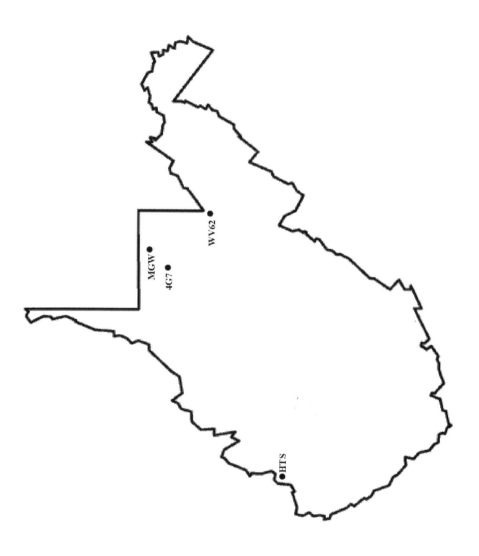

FlyIn West Virginia

⦿↩DAVIS, WV (WINDWOOD FLY-IN RESORT - WV62)
    Aprt Mgr: JOE BEAM **PH:** 888-359-4667
    Field Elevation: 3210 **CTAF:** 0.000 **FUEL:**
    Runway: 06/24 **Length:** 3000 **Width:** 40 **Surface:** ASPH

★★★ Amelia's (888) 359-4667
Proprietor: Joe Beam
Open:
        Wed – Sat: 7:30am - 9pm
        Sunday: 7:30 am - 3pm
Restaurant Website: www.windwoodresort.com/Restaurant.htm
Restaurant Email: amelia@windwoodresort.com
PIREP:
Amelia's has good food and friendly service. The owner of **Amelia's** flies his 310 into this little strip (3,000' x 40'), so it's actually quite possible to land any single or twin. It's on the sectionals. The resort owns the airstrip, and they have a radio...and sometimes they feel like answering it. **Amelia's** is located inside the hotel about 200' from the landing strip.

★★★ Windwood Resort (304) 755-9433
Proprietor: Joe Beam
Open:
        Daily
Restaurant Website: www.windwoodresort.com
Restaurant Email: info@windwoodresort.com
PIREP:
Adjacent to the landing strip is the 17 room lodge. The rooms are clean and nice and very affordable. The setting is amazing. Everything you might care to do, golf in the summer skiing in the winter are close by. The resort keeps a couple of beaters which you can rent to get around the area. This is a fun place to spent one night and go for a hike. Don't expect luxury that it surely can't deliver. It is in a very beautiful are.

⦿↩FAIRMONT, WV (FAIRMONT MUNI-FRANKMAN FIELD - 4G7)
    Aprt Mgr: DONNIE TUCKER **PH:** 304-366-1300
    Field Elevation: 1029 **CTAF:** 122.800 **FUEL:** 100LL
    Runway: 05/23 **Length:** 3194 **Width:** 75 **Surface:** ASPH-G

★★★ DJ's Diner - 304) 366-8110
Proprietor: DJ Rundle

Open:

Mon - Thu: 7:00am - 10:00pm
Fri - Sat: 7:00am - noon
Sun: 7:00am - 10:00pm

Restaurant Website: www.facebook.com/DJsDinerWV
Restaurant Email: jeff@thejinglehouse.com
PIREP:

It is a real diner with a real juke box and a group of servers called the Pink Ladies. I like everything from their slogan "Break the Chain – **EAT LOCAL**" to their meatloaf. I really like this place and so will you. It's the real deal and is located a short *(less than a 100 yards)* walk from the FBO.

★★ **Comfort Inn & Suites - (304) 367-1370**
Open:

Daily

Motel Website:
www.comfortinn.com/hotel-fairmont-west_virginia-WV010#listpos
PIREP:

It is located new to **DJ's Diner**. Arrive late in the day, have dinner at **DJ's**, fill-up at the FBO's 24 hour self-service pump, RON at the **Comfort Inn & Suites,** have breakfast at **DJ's** and you're good to go. You could eat breakfast at the **Comfort Inn** as it's included in the price of your room but it isn't even close when it comes to good. Free Wi-Fi, an exercise room and a pool round out the offering. It's a long way from a bad hotel but it is also a long way from a great hotel.

|●| HUNTINGTON, WV (TRI-STATE - HTS)
Aprt Mgr: JERRY BRIENZA **PH:** 304-453-6165
Field Elevation: 828 **CTAF:** 0.000 **FUEL:** 100LLA
Runway: 12/30 **Length:** 7016 **Width:** 150 **Surface:** ASPH-G

★★★ **Gino's Pizzeria & Pub - (304) 453-2196**
Proprietor: Rick Duncan
Open:

Mon – Sun: 7am - 10pm

Restaurant Website:
www.tristateairport.com/airport-guide/restaurant/
PIREP:

Gino's Pizzeria & Pub is in the main terminal, an easy walk from the FBO. Fortunately it is outside the security zone so no problems with TSA. It is a relaxing and cozy environment to grab drink or a bite to eat. They offer a full bar with an extensive menu of wine and beer selections. Also served is **Gino's** legendary pizza, pub style sandwiches, chicken wings and other appetizers. There is a landing fee, even for small singles, which is waived with a fuel purchase.

★★★ Tudor's Biscuit World - (304) 453-2196
Proprietor: Rick Duncan
Open:
> Mon – Sun: 7am - 10pm

Restaurant Website:
> www.tristateairport.com/airport-guide/restaurant/

PIREP:

Tudor's Biscuit World is in the main terminal, an easy walk from the FBO. Fortunately it is outside the security zone so no problems with TSA. It offers a wide variety of breakfast and lunch selections. Breakfast items include made-from-scratch biscuits with your favorite breakfast meats and toppings such as sliced or melted cheese, egg, fried apples and hash browns just to name a few. For those with a more hearty appetite, breakfast platters are also available including the popular biscuits and gravy and Super Breakfast. **Tudor's** lunch menu features a large selection of made-to-order sandwiches including pulled pork BBQ, 1/3 pound hamburgers and **Tudor's** famous hot dogs. There is a landing fee, even for small singles, which is waived with a fuel purchase.

⭐ MORGANTOWN, WV (MORGANTOWN MUNI - MGW)
Aprt Mgr: "MICHAEL CLOW, A.A.E." **PH:** 304-291-7461
Field Elevation: 1248 **CTAF:** 125.100 **FUEL:** 100LLA
Runway: 18/36 **Length:** 5199 **Width:** 150 **Surface:** ASPH-G

★★★★ Ali Baba - 304.292.4701
Proprietor: Mike & D'zeneta Rothenback
Open:
> Mon - Thu: 11:00 am - 8:00 pm
> Fri - Sat: 11:00 am - 9:00 pm

Restaurant Website: www.alibabaexpress.com
Restaurant Email: alibabaexpress@hotmail.com
PIREP:

I come here for two dishes, Tabbouleh and the Gyro. Imagine for a moment how good a restaurant with a Middle Eastern menu would have to be to succeed in WV. No imagine that the restaurant is at the airport not in the city center. That's a tough fact set. Now imagine that the restaurant has been here for 35 years. This place is as good as you imagine.

FlyIn Wisconsin

✈ CABLE, WI (CABLE UNION - 3CU)
Aprt Mgr: MIKE NICHOLS **PH:** 715-798-3240
Field Elevation: 1360 **CTAF:** 122.800 **FUEL:** 100LL
Runway: 16/34 **Length:** 3709 **Width:** 75 **Surface:** ASPH-E
Runway: 08/26 **Length:** 2828 **Width:** 150 **Surface:** TURF-G

★★★ Telemark Golf Course-(715) 798-3104
Proprietor: Rich and Judy Titus
Open:
> May - October

Restaurant Website: www.telemarkgolfcourse.com/index.html
Restaurant Email: tgc@cheqnet.net
PIREP:

The Telemark Resort is now closed but the golf course is still operating. This is one of the few land, taxi-up and play golf courses in Wisconsin. The setting is unbeatable and the course is really fun. The green fee is low to reasonable. Clubs are rentable if you don't want to schlep yours in the plane. Here's what you get. An18 hole, par 72 golf course that measures 6372 yards from the longest tees and has a slope rating of 121 and a 71.1 USGA rating. The course features 4 sets of tees for different skill levels. I like the course but miss the resort and restaurant.

🍽 EAU CLAIRE, WI (CHIPPEWA VALLEY RGNL - EAU)
Aprt Mgr: CHARITY SPEICH **PH:** 715-839-4900
Field Elevation: 913 **CTAF:** 118.575 **FUEL:** 100LLA
Runway: 14/32 **Length:** 5000 **Width:** 100 **Surface:** ASPH-CONC-G
Runway: 04/22 **Length:** 8101 **Width:** 150 **Surface:** CONC-TRTD-G

★★★ Farm on Starr – (715) 514-5073
Proprietor: Glen & Sarah Hein
Open:
> Mon-Thurs: 11am - 9pm
> Fri: 11am - 10pm
> Sat-Sun: 7:30am - 9pm

Restaurant Website: www.farmonstarr.com
Restaurant Email: owner@farmonstarr.com
PIREP:

Truth be told, I have only been here for breakfast. It was awesome. Someday I hope to get back for dinner. A NY Strip with REAL mashed potatoes could down real easy. It's a short walk from the GA FBO to the terminal where the restaurant is located.

JANESVILLE, WI (SOUTHERN WISCONSIN RGNL - JVL)
Aprt Mgr: RON BURDICK **PH:** 608-757-5768
Field Elevation: 808 **CTAF:** 118.800 **FUEL:** 100LLA
Runway: 18/36 **Length:** 5003 **Width:** 75 **Surface:** ASPH-F
Runway: 04/22 **Length:** 6700 **Width:** 150 **Surface:** ASPH-F
Runway: 14/32 **Length:** 7301 **Width:** 150 **Surface:** CONC-F

★★★ **Kealy's Airport Kafe - (608)754-9039**
Proprietor: Matthew Kealy
Open:
>   Mon - Thu: 6:00 am - 3:00 pm
>   Fri: 6:00 am - 8:00 pm
>   Sat - Sun: 6:00 am - 3:00 pm

Restaurant Website: www.facebook.com
Restaurant Email: kealymatthew@aol.com
PIREP:
When I come up for the Big Show at nearby Oshkosh I always land and tiedown at Janesville, before heading out I grab a meal at Kealy's. Its located right inside the terminal. For me it's, the fried chicken, mashed potatoes and gravy. I have also had the pork chops which are amazing. The view from Kealy's is big and aimed straight at the runway. Kealy's should be on your list.

LAND O' LAKES, WI (KINGS LAND O' LAKES - LNL)
Aprt Mgr: RANDY RUTH **PH:** 715-547-3337
Field Elevation: 1705 **CTAF:** 122.800 **FUEL:** 100LLMOGAS
Runway: 14/32 **Length:** 4001 **Width:** 75 **Surface:** ASPH-G
Runway: 05/23 **Length:** 2577 **Width:** 130 **Surface:** TURF-F

★★★ **Gateway Lodge Restaurant and Lounge - (715) 547-3321**
Proprietor: Christina and Keith Williams
Open:
>   Tue - Sat: 5:00 pm - 9:00 pm

Restaurant Website: www.gateway-lodge.com
Restaurant Email: gateway@gateway-lodge.com
PIREP:
Adjacent to the **Gateway Lodge** is the Land O' Lakes Municipal Airport. **Gateway Lodge Restaurant and Lounge** is located in the lodge. Landing before and departing after dinner is no big deal as the runway is 4,000 feet of lighted asphalt with GPS and NDB approaches for 14/32. Fuel is available 24/7 from the self-service pump. The dinner

menu is varied and worthwhile. I have enjoyed the Great Lakes Perch.

★★★ Gateway Lodge Restaurant - (715) 547-3321
Proprietor: Christina and Keith Williams
Open:
Year Round
Restaurant Website: www.gateway-lodge.com
Restaurant Email: gateway@gateway-lodge.com
PIREP:
The **Gateway Lodge Restaurant** has 72 customized and newly renovated suites and studios, an indoor pool, a steaming hot tub and a redwood sauna. The historic lodge is a convenient gateway to a number of area recreational opportunities, from trap shooting and golfing to waterfall chasing, skiing and shopping, it's all within reach. There is a first rate Gun Club on the property as well as bike, ATV and snowmobile trails.

|●| LONE ROCK, WI (TRI-COUNTY RGNL - LNR)
Aprt Mgr: MARC HIGGS **PH:** 608-583-2600
Field Elevation: 717 **CTAF:** 123.000 **FUEL:** 100LLA
Runway: 18/36 **Length:** 1850 **Width:** 60 **Surface:** ASPH-G
Runway: 09/27 **Length:** 5000 **Width:** 75 **Surface:** ASPH-G

★★★ Piccadilly Lilly Airport Diner - (608) 583-3318
Proprietor: Kathryn Stenulson
Open:
Mon-Sun: 6am - 2pm
Restaurant Website: www.piccadillylillydiner.com
Restaurant Email: info@piccadillylillydiner.com
PIREP:
I like this airport and I like this restaurant. Breakfast is a treat as everything is made from scratch so the food tastes better. It doesn't stop there though; hash browns are made to order. Most places have a huge mound of greasy hash browns sitting in the back that they cooked two hours ago and send out with your egg order. The good left fifteen minutes after they were cooked what is left needs a lot of salt, pepper and ketchup. **Piccadilly Lily** starts cooking 'em after you say you want some. **FRESH!** Here's something else that blows my mind, their pricing. A bowl of oatmeal goes for $3.11, not three bucks or three fifty but three eleven. I thought that was quirky then I noticed that you can add raisins for another fifty-three cents. Go figure.

|●| MADISON, WI (DANE COUNTY RGNL-TRUAX FIELD - MSN)
Aprt Mgr: "BRADLEY S. LIVINGSTON, AAE" **PH:** 608-246-3380

Field Elevation: 887 **CTAF:** 119.300 **FUEL:** 100LLA
Runway: 14/32 **Length:** 5846 **Width:** 150 **Surface:** CONC-G
Runway: 03/21 **Length:** 7200 **Width:** 150 **Surface:** CONC-G
Runway: 18/36 **Length:** 9006 **Width:** 150 **Surface:** CONC-G

★ ★ ★ Pat O'Malley's Jet Room - (608) 268-5010
Proprietor: Pat O'Malley
Open:
Mon - Sat: 6:00 am - 2:00 pm
Sun: 8:00 am - 2:00 pm
Restaurant Website: www. jetroomrestaurant.com
Restaurant Email: info@jetroomrestaurant.com
PIREP:
Located within Wisconsin Aviation's building. They offer great views from floor to ceiling windows that run the length of the restaurant. The coffee is good, the seating is fast and the ambiance is all airport. Pat runs one of only two restaurants' I know of that offers a Burger that costs a hundred bucks. The burger comes with a scenic airplane ride over Madison which is one of America's most beautiful cities.

⭐ MOSINEE, WI (CENTRAL WISCONSIN - CWA)
Aprt Mgr: TONY YARON **PH:** 715-693-2147
Field Elevation: 1277 **CTAF:** 119.750 **FUEL:** 100LLA
Runway: 17/35 **Length:** 6501 **Width:** 150 **Surface:** CONC-F
Runway: 08/26 **Length:** 7648 **Width:** 150 **Surface:** CONC-G

★ ★ Fly Away Cafe – (715) 693-3028
Proprietor: Mary Jo Onopa
Open:
Mon-Sun: 4:45am – 5:45pm
Restaurant Website: www.fly-cwa.org/services/amenities
Restaurant Email: julrick@fly-cwa.org
PIREP:
The **Fly Away Cafe** is located in the concourse area of the terminal just past the security checkpoint. It is about a two minute walk from the FBO to the terminal. You go here if you are hungry, it is not to be confused in anyway with the term "destination restaurant". I once had the three cheese grilled sandwich here. It was actually pretty good.

🏛 OSHKOSH, WI (WITTMAN RGNL - OSH)
Aprt Mgr: PETER MOLL **PH:** 920-236-4930
Field Elevation: 808 **CTAF:** 118.500 **FUEL:** 100LLA+
Runway: 13/31 **Length:** 3061 **Width:** 75 **Surface:** ASPH-F
Runway: 04/22 **Length:** 3697 **Width:** 75 **Surface:** ASPH-F

Runway: 09/27 **Length:** 6179 **Width:** 150 **Surface:** CONC-G
Runway: 18/36 **Length:** 8002 **Width:** 150 **Surface:** CONC-G

★★★★★ **EAA AirVenture Museum - (920) 426-4800**
Proprietor: Ron Twellman
Open:
        Mon-Sun: 10am - 5pm
Restaurant Website: www.airventuremuseum.org
Restaurant Email: museum@eaa.org
PIREP:
The EAA AirVenture Museum, has become one of the world's most extensive aviation attractions, and a year-round family destination. It is located on the site of the world's largest aviation event, EAA AirVenture.

The collection of historic artifacts began in 1962 when Steve Wittman donated his famous air racer "Bonzo". It now comprises more than 20,000 aviation objects of historic importance. Included are 250 historic airplanes, the count grows almost weekly as exhibits are constantly added. Everything from a powered parachute to a B-17 Flying Fortress is maintained in airworthy condition! Some are available to give ordinary people the chance to fly in historic aircraft. Most are used to provide flight demonstrations or support special activities such as the EAA Young Eagles program.

The EAA AirVenture Museum's library contains almost 9,000 volumes. The collection covers a variety of topics including biographies, aerodynamics, history, fiction, aeronautics, air racing and homebuilding.

The library's photographic collection archives more than 100,000 images of aircraft, spacecraft and the people made and flew them. Many photos chronicle the homebuilding movement of the early 1950s. They tell the story of an emerging group of people determined to design, build and fly their own aircraft. Important photo archives donated by private collectors are curated here. Included are:

The Radtke Collection: One thousand negatives of military aircraft, civilian aircraft and famous aviators from the '30s.

The Worthington Collection: 125 plus, glass negatives donated taken by an unknown photographer.

The Zeigler Collection: Over 200 glass negatives of early German aviators of post WWI era.

$100 Hamburger 2014/15

The Norman Collection: Hundreds of eight by ten black and white photographs covering the golden years of aviation.

This is truly one of the great aviation museums. Do not pass up an opportunity to visit. Be warned! Timing your visit to coincide with the EEA's annual airshow is a great mistake. It becomes very crowded and is hardly "user friendly" at those times. Plan you trip for a nice spring or summer weekend. Combine you trip with a visits to The Pioneer Airport, it is right next door. Here you want to spend thoughtful time and soak-up the history that is all around you. Plan to spend time here.

Food? Yes, they have food but that's not the reason to come!

¡●¡ SUPERIOR, WI (RICHARD I BONG - SUW)
Aprt Mgr: WILLIAM AMORDE **PH:** 715-394-6444
Field Elevation: 674 **CTAF:** 122.700 **FUEL:** 100LLA
Runway: 13/31 **Length:** 4001 **Width:** 75 **Surface: ASPH**-G
Runway: 03/21 **Length:** 5100 **Width:** 75 **Surface: ASPH**-G

★★★ The Upper Deck - 715-395-8376
Proprietor: Ronald Goble
Open:
>Tue - Sat: 8:00 am - 9:00 pm
>Sun: 8:00 am - 8:00 pm

Restaurant Website: www.facebook.com
PIREP:
The Upper Deck offers a lunch and dinner buffet Tuesday through Saturday and a Breakfast buffet on Sundays. It is a very typical airport café.

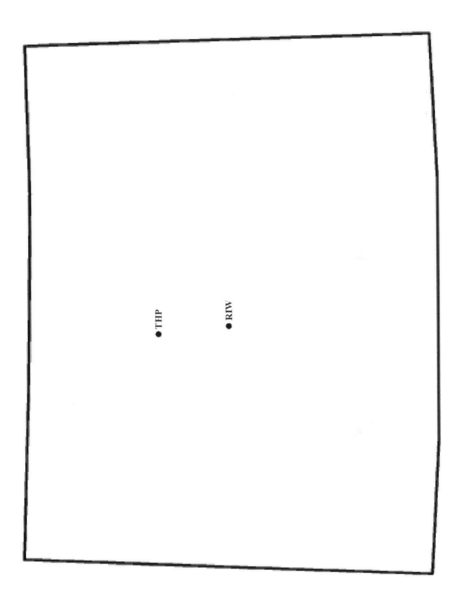

FlyIn Wyoming

🍴 RIVERTON, WY (RIVERTON RGNL - RIW)
Aprt Mgr: WILLIAM A. URBIGKIT **PH:** 307-856-9128
Field Elevation: 5528 **CTAF:** 122.800 **FUEL:** 100LLA
Runway: 10/28 **Length:** 8204 **Width:** 150 **Surface:** ASPH-F
Runway: 01/19 **Length:** 4800 **Width:** 75 **Surface:** ASPH-G

★★★ Airport Café - (307) 856-2838
Proprietor: Cheryl Large
Open:
>   Daily: 7am – 3pm

Restaurant Website: www.flyriverton.com
PIREP:
The Riverton Regional Airport is the year-round gateway to Yellowstone and Grand Teton National. **The Airport Café** is in the terminal building. Since 1995 they've been serving up pretty good food with amazing service. The best deal here is pie. They are all homemade and they are really good. For lunch, go with the meatloaf.

🍴 🍴 THERMOPOLIS, WY (THERMOPOLIS MUNI - THP)
Aprt Mgr: TARA CHESNUT **PH:** 307-864-2488
Field Elevation: 4592 **CTAF:** 122.800 **FUEL:** 100LL
Runway: 01/19 **Length:** 4800 **Width:** 100 **Surface:** ASPH-P

★★★ Stone's Throw - (307) 864-9494
Proprietors: Clyde and Jennifer Fisher and Ethan Brooks
Open:
>   Lunch (Summer Only)
>   Thurs – Fri: 11:30am – 1:30pm
>   Sat – Sun: 11:30am – 3:00pm
>   Dinner (Year Round)
>   Tue – Sat: 5:00pm – 9:00pm

Restaurant Website: www.stonesthrowthermopolis.com
Restaurant Email: jljeffs1@hotmail.com
PIREP:
It's a surprising steakhouse with a surprising wine list. You cannot go wrong with a 16 oz. rib eye in Wyoming but I have ordered the Jägerschnitzel and been very pleased. It's located exactly across the parking lot from the FBO maybe a 50 foot walk from your tiedown. The runway slopes uphill to the south (19), so until winds are greater than 15 knots it's best to land 19 and takeoff 01 according to Walt Urbigkit, the airport manager.

★★ Legion Town and Country Club Golf Course - (307) 864-5294
Proprietors: Mike McManis
Open:

Seasonal

PIREP:

Legion Town and Country Club Golf Course sits right across the parking lot from the FBO. It is a 9 hole public course that's fun to play with just enough terrain roll to make you remember that you are in Wyoming. If you are in the area, be sure to stop by and play this one. It's a great little course with terrific views. The green fee ranges from $18 on the weekend to $16 during the week.

This Page Intentionally Left Blank

FREE

100dollarhamburger.com

SUBSCRIPTION

NAME_____

ADDR_____

ADDR2_____

CITY _____

STATE_____

ZIP   _____

EMAIL_____

Simply fill out and mail this form to:

$100 Hamburger Publishing
PO Box 915441
Longwood, FL 32791-5441

Or scan and email to:
pirep@100dollarhamburger.com

$100 Hamburger 2014/15

Made in the USA
Charleston, SC
14 April 2014